I0309053

C-966 CAREER EXAMINATION SERIES

This is your PASSBOOK for...

Court Officer

Test Preparation Study Guide
Questions & Answers

NLC®

NATIONAL LEARNING CORPORATION®

COPYRIGHT NOTICE

This book is SOLELY intended for, is sold ONLY to, and its use is RESTRICTED to individual, bona fide applicants or candidates who qualify by virtue of having seriously filed applications for appropriate license, certificate, professional and/or promotional advancement, higher school matriculation, scholarship, or other legitimate requirements of education and/or governmental authorities.

This book is NOT intended for use, class instruction, tutoring, training, duplication, copying, reprinting, excerption, or adaptation, etc., by:

1) Other publishers
2) Proprietors and/or Instructors of "Coaching" and/or Preparatory Courses
3) Personnel and/or Training Divisions of commercial, industrial, and governmental organizations
4) Schools, colleges, or universities and/or their departments and staffs, including teachers and other personnel
5) Testing Agencies or Bureaus
6) Study groups which seek by the purchase of a single volume to copy and/or duplicate and/or adapt this material for use by the group as a whole without having purchased individual volumes for each of the members of the group
7) Et al.

Such persons would be in violation of appropriate Federal and State statutes.

PROVISION OF LICENSING AGREEMENTS – Recognized educational, commercial, industrial, and governmental institutions and organizations, and others legitimately engaged in educational pursuits, including training, testing, and measurement activities, may address request for a licensing agreement to the copyright owners, who will determine whether, and under what conditions, including fees and charges, the materials in this book may be used them. In other words, a licensing facility exists for the legitimate use of the material in this book on other than an individual basis. However, it is asseverated and affirmed here that the material in this book CANNOT be used without the receipt of the express permission of such a licensing agreement from the Publishers. Inquiries re licensing should be addressed to the company, attention rights and permissions department.

All rights reserved, including the right of reproduction in whole or in part, in any form or by any means, electronic or mechanical, including photocopying, recording, or by any information storage and retrieval system, without permission in writing from the Publisher.

Copyright © 2024 by

National Learning Corporation

212 Michael Drive, Syosset, NY 11791
(516) 921-8888 • www.passbooks.com
E-mail: info@passbooks.com

PUBLISHED IN THE UNITED STATES OF AMERICA

PASSBOOK® SERIES

THE *PASSBOOK® SERIES* has been created to prepare applicants and candidates for the ultimate academic battlefield – the examination room.

At some time in our lives, each and every one of us may be required to take an examination – for validation, matriculation, admission, qualification, registration, certification, or licensure.

Based on the assumption that every applicant or candidate has met the basic formal educational standards, has taken the required number of courses, and read the necessary texts, the *PASSBOOK® SERIES* furnishes the one special preparation which may assure passing with confidence, instead of failing with insecurity. Examination questions – together with answers – are furnished as the basic vehicle for study so that the mysteries of the examination and its compounding difficulties may be eliminated or diminished by a sure method.

This book is meant to help you pass your examination provided that you qualify and are serious in your objective.

The entire field is reviewed through the huge store of content information which is succinctly presented through a provocative and challenging approach – the question-and-answer method.

A climate of success is established by furnishing the correct answers at the end of each test.

You soon learn to recognize types of questions, forms of questions, and patterns of questioning. You may even begin to anticipate expected outcomes.

You perceive that many questions are repeated or adapted so that you can gain acute insights, which may enable you to score many sure points.

You learn how to confront new questions, or types of questions, and to attack them confidently and work out the correct answers.

You note objectives and emphases, and recognize pitfalls and dangers, so that you may make positive educational adjustments.

Moreover, you are kept fully informed in relation to new concepts, methods, practices, and directions in the field.

You discover that you are actually taking the examination all the time: you are preparing for the examination by "taking" an examination, not by reading extraneous and/or supererogatory textbooks.

In short, this PASSBOOK®, used directedly, should be an important factor in helping you to pass your test.

COURT OFFICER

Under the direct supervision of a Court Officer Sergeant and the general supervision of the court clerk or other security supervisory personnel, Court Officers are responsible for maintaining order and providing security in courtrooms, court buildings, and grounds. Court Officers are assigned to all trial courts and court agencies. Court Officers are peace officers, required to wear uniforms, and maybe authorized to carry firearms, execute warrants, make arrests and may coordinate the activities of other court security personnel.

Providing courthouse and courtroom security is the primary function of Court Officers. They provide a safe and secure environment for the fair and prompt resolution of all matters before the courts.

The job is actually a blend of security work, public relations, law enforcement, prisoner management, and clerical duties. A strong sense of responsibility is necessary, as well as good judgment, patience and impartiality. Court Officers must not favor one party over another in a court proceeding. They protect and enhance the judicial process itself. A Court Officer is usually the first person a visitor to court will approach for information. The officer's tone and demeanor can help put people at ease and establish confidence in the judicial process. In all their actions, Court Officers must reflect the impartiality, fairness and commitment to justice of the court system itself.

Some aspects of the work are similar to those of police officers or corrections officers. However, the Court Officer job differs in significant ways. Court Officers are usually assigned to a security post in a defined, limited area, whereas police officers patrol large territories. Although Court Officers may escort prisoners, they do so in a different setting than correction officers, who work in prisons or jails.

Court Officers are peace officers. They are required to wear uniforms on the job and after appropriate training may be authorized to carry firearms, execute warrants and make arrests. At all times the officer protects the judge, jurors, court employees, witnesses and spectators. This includes escorting the judge to and from chambers. Court Officers may be assigned to operate a magnetometer, guard people accused or convicted of crimes of all kinds, deliver and retrieve court documents, administer first-aid treatment and respond to other emergencies. They may have to control a crowd of people, or take steps to maintain order or to subdue an unruly person.

A large part of the day's work can involve calling the court calendar, providing information to the public and other court users, screening visitors and handling court documents and forms. Court security staff assists in the swearing in of witnesses and jurors, supervise juries, and handle evidence. They also announce recesses, and remain in the part during recess to safeguard equipment, evidence and documents.

TYPICAL DUTIES

Provides security by standing in the courtroom and patrolling the courthouse; guards criminal defendants accused of both misdemeanors and felonies while in the courtroom and may escort them to and from detention pens; assumes a post or patrols the courthouse to maintain order by removing or calming disruptive individuals; bars entry into security areas or courtrooms of people not properly attired or behaved; talks to potentially disruptive prisoners or spectators to calm them; physically restrains unruly individuals; arrests individuals according to established procedures; escorts, guards, and delivers material to sequestered juries; escorts judges, juries, witnesses and prisoners to and from the courtroom; administers first aid and assistance to individuals during emergencies, accidents or illnesses; provides assistance in emergency situations; operates security equipment, including magnetometers, handheld screening devices and package x-ray machines; uses established search procedures to assure that no weapons or electronic or photographic equipment are brought into the courtroom; checks to ensure that all necessary documents are available prior to court sessions; checks bench to ensure that Judge has adequate supplies, proper forms, and other materials; displays and safeguards exhibits in the courtroom; maintains and updates court records; distributes and posts appropriate documents and court materials; checks any emergency or special equipment such as oxygen tanks, walkie-talkies, and other items to ensure that the equipment is in good working order; reports inoperative equipment to supervisor; provides general information to visitors on court premises; and prepares incident reports.

Subject of Written Examination

The examination will consist of multiple-choice questions and will assess the following:

Remembering Facts and Information
Candidates are provided with a written description of an event or incident involving court officers and are given five minutes to read and study the description before it is removed. Shortly thereafter, candidates will be asked questions about the facts involved in the event or incident.

Reading, Understanding and Interpreting Written Material
These questions measure how well candidates can understand what they have read. The written examination will include two types of questions:

Format A - Candidates are provided with brief reading selections followed by questions regarding the selections. All of the information required to answer the questions is provided in the selections. Candidates are not required to have any special knowledge relating to the content area covered in the selections; and,

Format B - Candidates are provided with short written passages from which words have been removed. Candidates are required to select among four alternatives the word that best fits in each of the spaces.

Applying Facts and Information to Given Situations
These questions measure a candidate's ability to take information which the candidate has read and then apply this information to a specific situation defined by a given set of facts. Each question contains a brief paragraph which describes a regulation, policy or procedure which must be applied to a particular situation. All of the information to answer the questions is contained in the paragraph and in the description of the situation.

Clerical Checking
These questions measure a candidate's ability to distinguish between sets of names, numbers, letters and/or codes which are almost exactly alike. Material usually is presented in three columns, and candidates are asked to compare the information in the three sets.

Court Record Keeping
These questions measure a candidate's ability to read, combine, and manipulate written information organized from several sources. Candidates are presented with different types of tables which contain names, numbers, codes and other information, and must combine and reorganize the information to answer specific questions.

HOW TO TAKE A TEST

I. YOU MUST PASS AN EXAMINATION

A. WHAT EVERY CANDIDATE SHOULD KNOW

Examination applicants often ask us for help in preparing for the written test. What can I study in advance? What kinds of questions will be asked? How will the test be given? How will the papers be graded?

As an applicant for a civil service examination, you may be wondering about some of these things. Our purpose here is to suggest effective methods of advance study and to describe civil service examinations.

Your chances for success on this examination can be increased if you know how to prepare. Those "pre-examination jitters" can be reduced if you know what to expect. You can even experience an adventure in good citizenship if you know why civil service exams are given.

B. WHY ARE CIVIL SERVICE EXAMINATIONS GIVEN?

Civil service examinations are important to you in two ways. As a citizen, you want public jobs filled by employees who know how to do their work. As a job seeker, you want a fair chance to compete for that job on an equal footing with other candidates. The best-known means of accomplishing this two-fold goal is the competitive examination.

Exams are widely publicized throughout the nation. They may be administered for jobs in federal, state, city, municipal, town or village governments or agencies.

Any citizen may apply, with some limitations, such as the age or residence of applicants. Your experience and education may be reviewed to see whether you meet the requirements for the particular examination. When these requirements exist, they are reasonable and applied consistently to all applicants. Thus, a competitive examination may cause you some uneasiness now, but it is your privilege and safeguard.

C. HOW ARE CIVIL SERVICE EXAMS DEVELOPED?

Examinations are carefully written by trained technicians who are specialists in the field known as "psychological measurement," in consultation with recognized authorities in the field of work that the test will cover. These experts recommend the subject matter areas or skills to be tested; only those knowledges or skills important to your success on the job are included. The most reliable books and source materials available are used as references. Together, the experts and technicians judge the difficulty level of the questions.

Test technicians know how to phrase questions so that the problem is clearly stated. Their ethics do not permit "trick" or "catch" questions. Questions may have been tried out on sample groups, or subjected to statistical analysis, to determine their usefulness.

Written tests are often used in combination with performance tests, ratings of training and experience, and oral interviews. All of these measures combine to form the best-known means of finding the right person for the right job.

II. HOW TO PASS THE WRITTEN TEST

A. NATURE OF THE EXAMINATION

To prepare intelligently for civil service examinations, you should know how they differ from school examinations you have taken. In school you were assigned certain definite pages to read or subjects to cover. The examination questions were quite detailed and usually emphasized memory. Civil service exams, on the other hand, try to discover your present ability to perform the duties of a position, plus your potentiality to learn these duties. In other words, a civil service exam attempts to predict how successful you will be. Questions cover such a broad area that they cannot be as minute and detailed as school exam questions.

In the public service similar kinds of work, or positions, are grouped together in one "class." This process is known as *position-classification.* All the positions in a class are paid according to the salary range for that class. One class title covers all of these positions, and they are all tested by the same examination.

B. FOUR BASIC STEPS

1) Study the announcement

How, then, can you know what subjects to study? Our best answer is: "Learn as much as possible about the class of positions for which you've applied." The exam will test the knowledge, skills and abilities needed to do the work.

Your most valuable source of information about the position you want is the official exam announcement. This announcement lists the training and experience qualifications. Check these standards and apply only if you come reasonably close to meeting them.

The brief description of the position in the examination announcement offers some clues to the subjects which will be tested. Think about the job itself. Review the duties in your mind. Can you perform them, or are there some in which you are rusty? Fill in the blank spots in your preparation.

Many jurisdictions preview the written test in the exam announcement by including a section called "Knowledge and Abilities Required," "Scope of the Examination," or some similar heading. Here you will find out specifically what fields will be tested.

2) Review your own background

Once you learn in general what the position is all about, and what you need to know to do the work, ask yourself which subjects you already know fairly well and which need improvement. You may wonder whether to concentrate on improving your strong areas or on building some background in your fields of weakness. When the announcement has specified "some knowledge" or "considerable knowledge," or has used adjectives like "beginning principles of..." or "advanced ... methods," you can get a clue as to the number and difficulty of questions to be asked in any given field. More questions, and hence broader coverage, would be included for those subjects which are more important in the work. Now weigh your strengths and weaknesses against the job requirements and prepare accordingly.

3) Determine the level of the position

Another way to tell how intensively you should prepare is to understand the level of the job for which you are applying. Is it the entering level? In other words, is this the position in which beginners in a field of work are hired? Or is it an intermediate or advanced level? Sometimes this is indicated by such words as "Junior" or "Senior" in the class title. Other jurisdictions use Roman numerals to designate the level – Clerk I, Clerk II, for example. The word "Supervisor" sometimes appears in the title. If the level is not indicated by the title, check the description of duties. Will you be working under very close supervision, or will you have responsibility for independent decisions in this work?

4) Choose appropriate study materials

Now that you know the subjects to be examined and the relative amount of each subject to be covered, you can choose suitable study materials. For beginning level jobs, or even advanced ones, if you have a pronounced weakness in some aspect of your training, read a modern, standard textbook in that field. Be sure it is up to date and has general coverage. Such books are normally available at your library, and the librarian will be glad to help you locate one. For entry-level positions, questions of appropriate difficulty are chosen – neither highly advanced questions, nor those too simple. Such questions require careful thought but not advanced training.

If the position for which you are applying is technical or advanced, you will read more advanced, specialized material. If you are already familiar with the basic principles of your field, elementary textbooks would waste your time. Concentrate on advanced textbooks and technical periodicals. Think through the concepts and review difficult problems in your field.

These are all general sources. You can get more ideas on your own initiative, following these leads. For example, training manuals and publications of the government agency which employs workers in your field can be useful, particularly for technical and professional positions. A letter or visit to the government department involved may result in more specific study suggestions, and certainly will provide you with a more definite idea of the exact nature of the position you are seeking.

III. KINDS OF TESTS

Tests are used for purposes other than measuring knowledge and ability to perform specified duties. For some positions, it is equally important to test ability to make adjustments to new situations or to profit from training. In others, basic mental abilities not dependent on information are essential. Questions which test these things may not appear as pertinent to the duties of the position as those which test for knowledge and information. Yet they are often highly important parts of a fair examination. For very general questions, it is almost impossible to help you direct your study efforts. What we can do is to point out some of the more common of these general abilities needed in public service positions and describe some typical questions.

1) General information

Broad, general information has been found useful for predicting job success in some kinds of work. This is tested in a variety of ways, from vocabulary lists to questions about current events. Basic background in some field of work, such as sociology or economics, may be sampled in a group of questions. Often these are principles which have become familiar to most persons through exposure rather than through formal training. It is difficult to advise you how to study for these questions; being alert to the world around you is our best suggestion.

2) Verbal ability

An example of an ability needed in many positions is verbal or language ability. Verbal ability is, in brief, the ability to use and understand words. Vocabulary and grammar tests are typical measures of this ability. Reading comprehension or paragraph interpretation questions are common in many kinds of civil service tests. You are given a paragraph of written material and asked to find its central meaning.

3) Numerical ability

Number skills can be tested by the familiar arithmetic problem, by checking paired lists of numbers to see which are alike and which are different, or by interpreting charts and graphs. In the latter test, a graph may be printed in the test booklet which you are asked to use as the basis for answering questions.

4) Observation

A popular test for law-enforcement positions is the observation test. A picture is shown to you for several minutes, then taken away. Questions about the picture test your ability to observe both details and larger elements.

5) Following directions

In many positions in the public service, the employee must be able to carry out written instructions dependably and accurately. You may be given a chart with several columns, each column listing a variety of information. The questions require you to carry out directions involving the information given in the chart.

6) Skills and aptitudes

Performance tests effectively measure some manual skills and aptitudes. When the skill is one in which you are trained, such as typing or shorthand, you can practice. These tests are often very much like those given in business school or high school courses. For many of the other skills and aptitudes, however, no short-time preparation can be made. Skills and abilities natural to you or that you have developed throughout your lifetime are being tested.

Many of the general questions just described provide all the data needed to answer the questions and ask you to use your reasoning ability to find the answers. Your best preparation for these tests, as well as for tests of facts and ideas, is to be at your physical and mental best. You, no doubt, have your own methods of getting into an exam-taking mood and keeping "in shape." The next section lists some ideas on this subject.

IV. KINDS OF QUESTIONS

Only rarely is the "essay" question, which you answer in narrative form, used in civil service tests. Civil service tests are usually of the short-answer type. Full instructions for answering these questions will be given to you at the examination. But in case this is your first experience with short-answer questions and separate answer sheets, here is what you need to know:

1) Multiple-choice Questions

Most popular of the short-answer questions is the "multiple choice" or "best answer" question. It can be used, for example, to test for factual knowledge, ability to solve problems or judgment in meeting situations found at work.

A multiple-choice question is normally one of three types—

- It can begin with an incomplete statement followed by several possible endings. You are to find the one ending which *best* completes the statement, although some of the others may not be entirely wrong.
- It can also be a complete statement in the form of a question which is answered by choosing one of the statements listed.

- It can be in the form of a problem – again you select the best answer.

Here is an example of a multiple-choice question with a discussion which should give you some clues as to the method for choosing the right answer:

When an employee has a complaint about his assignment, the action which will *best* help him overcome his difficulty is to

A. discuss his difficulty with his coworkers
B. take the problem to the head of the organization
C. take the problem to the person who gave him the assignment
D. say nothing to anyone about his complaint

In answering this question, you should study each of the choices to find which is best. Consider choice "A" – Certainly an employee may discuss his complaint with fellow employees, but no change or improvement can result, and the complaint remains unresolved. Choice "B" is a poor choice since the head of the organization probably does not know what assignment you have been given, and taking your problem to him is known as "going over the head" of the supervisor. The supervisor, or person who made the assignment, is the person who can clarify it or correct any injustice. Choice "C" is, therefore, correct. To say nothing, as in choice "D," is unwise. Supervisors have and interest in knowing the problems employees are facing, and the employee is seeking a solution to his problem.

2) True/False Questions

The "true/false" or "right/wrong" form of question is sometimes used. Here a complete statement is given. Your job is to decide whether the statement is right or wrong.

SAMPLE: A roaming cell-phone call to a nearby city costs less than a non-roaming call to a distant city.

This statement is wrong, or false, since roaming calls are more expensive.

This is not a complete list of all possible question forms, although most of the others are variations of these common types. You will always get complete directions for answering questions. Be sure you understand *how* to mark your answers – ask questions until you do.

V. RECORDING YOUR ANSWERS

Computer terminals are used more and more today for many different kinds of exams.

For an examination with very few applicants, you may be told to record your answers in the test booklet itself. Separate answer sheets are much more common. If this separate answer sheet is to be scored by machine – and this is often the case – it is highly important that you mark your answers correctly in order to get credit.

An electronic scoring machine is often used in civil service offices because of the speed with which papers can be scored. Machine-scored answer sheets must be marked with a pencil, which will be given to you. This pencil has a high graphite content which responds to the electronic scoring machine. As a matter of fact, stray dots may register as answers, so do not let your pencil rest on the answer sheet while you are pondering the correct answer. Also, if your pencil lead breaks or is otherwise defective, ask for another.

Since the answer sheet will be dropped in a slot in the scoring machine, be careful not to bend the corners or get the paper crumpled.

The answer sheet normally has five vertical columns of numbers, with 30 numbers to a column. These numbers correspond to the question numbers in your test booklet. After each number, going across the page are four or five pairs of dotted lines. These short dotted lines have small letters or numbers above them. The first two pairs may also have a "T" or "F" above the letters. This indicates that the first two pairs only are to be used if the questions are of the true-false type. If the questions are multiple choice, disregard the "T" and "F" and pay attention only to the small letters or numbers.

Answer your questions in the manner of the sample that follows:

32. The largest city in the United States is
    A. Washington, D.C.
    B. New York City
    C. Chicago
    D. Detroit
    E. San Francisco

1) Choose the answer you think is best. (New York City is the largest, so "B" is correct.)
2) Find the row of dotted lines numbered the same as the question you are answering. (Find row number 32)
3) Find the pair of dotted lines corresponding to the answer. (Find the pair of lines under the mark "B.")
4) Make a solid black mark between the dotted lines.

VI. BEFORE THE TEST

Common sense will help you find procedures to follow to get ready for an examination. Too many of us, however, overlook these sensible measures. Indeed, nervousness and fatigue have been found to be the most serious reasons why applicants fail to do their best on civil service tests. Here is a list of reminders:

- Begin your preparation early – Don't wait until the last minute to go scurrying around for books and materials or to find out what the position is all about.
- Prepare continuously – An hour a night for a week is better than an all-night cram session. This has been definitely established. What is more, a night a week for a month will return better dividends than crowding your study into a shorter period of time.
- Locate the place of the exam – You have been sent a notice telling you when and where to report for the examination. If the location is in a different town or otherwise unfamiliar to you, it would be well to inquire the best route and learn something about the building.
- Relax the night before the test – Allow your mind to rest. Do not study at all that night. Plan some mild recreation or diversion; then go to bed early and get a good night's sleep.
- Get up early enough to make a leisurely trip to the place for the test – This way unforeseen events, traffic snarls, unfamiliar buildings, etc. will not upset you.
- Dress comfortably – A written test is not a fashion show. You will be known by number and not by name, so wear something comfortable.

- Leave excess paraphernalia at home – Shopping bags and odd bundles will get in your way. You need bring only the items mentioned in the official notice you received; usually everything you need is provided. Do not bring reference books to the exam. They will only confuse those last minutes and be taken away from you when in the test room.
- Arrive somewhat ahead of time – If because of transportation schedules you must get there very early, bring a newspaper or magazine to take your mind off yourself while waiting.
- Locate the examination room – When you have found the proper room, you will be directed to the seat or part of the room where you will sit. Sometimes you are given a sheet of instructions to read while you are waiting. Do not fill out any forms until you are told to do so; just read them and be prepared.
- Relax and prepare to listen to the instructions
- If you have any physical problem that may keep you from doing your best, be sure to tell the test administrator. If you are sick or in poor health, you really cannot do your best on the exam. You can come back and take the test some other time.

VII. AT THE TEST

The day of the test is here and you have the test booklet in your hand. The temptation to get going is very strong. Caution! There is more to success than knowing the right answers. You must know how to identify your papers and understand variations in the type of short-answer question used in this particular examination. Follow these suggestions for maximum results from your efforts:

1) Cooperate with the monitor

The test administrator has a duty to create a situation in which you can be as much at ease as possible. He will give instructions, tell you when to begin, check to see that you are marking your answer sheet correctly, and so on. He is not there to guard you, although he will see that your competitors do not take unfair advantage. He wants to help you do your best.

2) Listen to all instructions

Don't jump the gun! Wait until you understand all directions. In most civil service tests you get more time than you need to answer the questions. So don't be in a hurry. Read each word of instructions until you clearly understand the meaning. Study the examples, listen to all announcements and follow directions. Ask questions if you do not understand what to do.

3) Identify your papers

Civil service exams are usually identified by number only. You will be assigned a number; you must not put your name on your test papers. Be sure to copy your number correctly. Since more than one exam may be given, copy your exact examination title.

4) Plan your time

Unless you are told that a test is a "speed" or "rate of work" test, speed itself is usually not important. Time enough to answer all the questions will be provided, but this does not mean that you have all day. An overall time limit has been set. Divide the total time (in minutes) by the number of questions to determine the approximate time you have for each question.

5) Do not linger over difficult questions

If you come across a difficult question, mark it with a paper clip (useful to have along) and come back to it when you have been through the booklet. One caution if you do this – be sure to skip a number on your answer sheet as well. Check often to be sure that you have not lost your place and that you are marking in the row numbered the same as the question you are answering.

6) Read the questions

Be sure you know what the question asks! Many capable people are unsuccessful because they failed to *read* the questions correctly.

7) Answer all questions

Unless you have been instructed that a penalty will be deducted for incorrect answers, it is better to guess than to omit a question.

8) Speed tests

It is often better NOT to guess on speed tests. It has been found that on timed tests people are tempted to spend the last few seconds before time is called in marking answers at random – without even reading them – in the hope of picking up a few extra points. To discourage this practice, the instructions may warn you that your score will be "corrected" for guessing. That is, a penalty will be applied. The incorrect answers will be deducted from the correct ones, or some other penalty formula will be used.

9) Review your answers

If you finish before time is called, go back to the questions you guessed or omitted to give them further thought. Review other answers if you have time.

10) Return your test materials

If you are ready to leave before others have finished or time is called, take ALL your materials to the monitor and leave quietly. Never take any test material with you. The monitor can discover whose papers are not complete, and taking a test booklet may be grounds for disqualification.

VIII. EXAMINATION TECHNIQUES

1) Read the general instructions carefully. These are usually printed on the first page of the exam booklet. As a rule, these instructions refer to the timing of the examination; the fact that you should not start work until the signal and must stop work at a signal, etc. If there are any *special* instructions, such as a choice of questions to be answered, make sure that you note this instruction carefully.

2) When you are ready to start work on the examination, that is as soon as the signal has been given, read the instructions to each question booklet, underline any key words or phrases, such as *least, best, outline, describe* and the like. In this way you will tend to answer as requested rather than discover on reviewing your paper that you *listed without describing*, that you selected the *worst* choice rather than the *best* choice, etc.

3) If the examination is of the objective or multiple-choice type – that is, each question will also give a series of possible answers: A, B, C or D, and you are called upon to select the best answer and write the letter next to that answer on your answer paper – it is advisable to start answering each question in turn. There may be anywhere from 50 to 100 such questions in the three or four hours allotted and you can see how much time would be taken if you read through all the questions before beginning to answer any. Furthermore, if you come across a question or group of questions which you know would be difficult to answer, it would undoubtedly affect your handling of all the other questions.

4) If the examination is of the essay type and contains but a few questions, it is a moot point as to whether you should read all the questions before starting to answer any one. Of course, if you are given a choice – say five out of seven and the like – then it is essential to read all the questions so you can eliminate the two that are most difficult. If, however, you are asked to answer all the questions, there may be danger in trying to answer the easiest one first because you may find that you will spend too much time on it. The best technique is to answer the first question, then proceed to the second, etc.

5) Time your answers. Before the exam begins, write down the time it started, then add the time allowed for the examination and write down the time it must be completed, then divide the time available somewhat as follows:
   - If 3-1/2 hours are allowed, that would be 210 minutes. If you have 80 objective-type questions, that would be an average of 2-1/2 minutes per question. Allow yourself no more than 2 minutes per question, or a total of 160 minutes, which will permit about 50 minutes to review.
   - If for the time allotment of 210 minutes there are 7 essay questions to answer, that would average about 30 minutes a question. Give yourself only 25 minutes per question so that you have about 35 minutes to review.

6) The most important instruction is to *read each question* and make sure you know what is wanted. The second most important instruction is to *time yourself properly* so that you answer every question. The third most important instruction is to *answer every question*. Guess if you have to but include something for each question. Remember that you will receive no credit for a blank and will probably receive some credit if you write something in answer to an essay question. If you guess a letter – say "B" for a multiple-choice question – you may have guessed right. If you leave a blank as an answer to a multiple-choice question, the examiners may respect your feelings but it will not add a point to your score. Some exams may penalize you for wrong answers, so in such cases *only*, you may not want to guess unless you have some basis for your answer.

7) Suggestions
   a. Objective-type questions
      1. Examine the question booklet for proper sequence of pages and questions
      2. Read all instructions carefully
      3. Skip any question which seems too difficult; return to it after all other questions have been answered
      4. Apportion your time properly; do not spend too much time on any single question or group of questions

5. Note and underline key words – *all, most, fewest, least, best, worst, same, opposite,* etc.
6. Pay particular attention to negatives
7. Note unusual option, e.g., unduly long, short, complex, different or similar in content to the body of the question
8. Observe the use of "hedging" words – *probably, may, most likely,* etc.
9. Make sure that your answer is put next to the same number as the question
10. Do not second-guess unless you have good reason to believe the second answer is definitely more correct
11. Cross out original answer if you decide another answer is more accurate; do not erase until you are ready to hand your paper in
12. Answer all questions; guess unless instructed otherwise
13. Leave time for review

b. Essay questions
   1. Read each question carefully
   2. Determine exactly what is wanted. Underline key words or phrases.
   3. Decide on outline or paragraph answer
   4. Include many different points and elements unless asked to develop any one or two points or elements
   5. Show impartiality by giving pros and cons unless directed to select one side only
   6. Make and write down any assumptions you find necessary to answer the questions
   7. Watch your English, grammar, punctuation and choice of words
   8. Time your answers; don't crowd material

8) Answering the essay question

Most essay questions can be answered by framing the specific response around several key words or ideas. Here are a few such key words or ideas:

M's: manpower, materials, methods, money, management
P's: purpose, program, policy, plan, procedure, practice, problems, pitfalls, personnel, public relations

a. Six basic steps in handling problems:
   1. Preliminary plan and background development
   2. Collect information, data and facts
   3. Analyze and interpret information, data and facts
   4. Analyze and develop solutions as well as make recommendations
   5. Prepare report and sell recommendations
   6. Install recommendations and follow up effectiveness

b. Pitfalls to avoid
   1. *Taking things for granted* – A statement of the situation does not necessarily imply that each of the elements is necessarily true; for example, a complaint may be invalid and biased so that all that can be taken for granted is that a complaint has been registered

2. *Considering only one side of a situation* – Wherever possible, indicate several alternatives and then point out the reasons you selected the best one
3. *Failing to indicate follow up* – Whenever your answer indicates action on your part, make certain that you will take proper follow-up action to see how successful your recommendations, procedures or actions turn out to be
4. *Taking too long in answering any single question* – Remember to time your answers properly

IX. AFTER THE TEST

Scoring procedures differ in detail among civil service jurisdictions although the general principles are the same. Whether the papers are hand-scored or graded by machine we have described, they are nearly always graded by number. That is, the person who marks the paper knows only the number – never the name – of the applicant. Not until all the papers have been graded will they be matched with names. If other tests, such as training and experience or oral interview ratings have been given, scores will be combined. Different parts of the examination usually have different weights. For example, the written test might count 60 percent of the final grade, and a rating of training and experience 40 percent. In many jurisdictions, veterans will have a certain number of points added to their grades.

After the final grade has been determined, the names are placed in grade order and an eligible list is established. There are various methods for resolving ties between those who get the same final grade – probably the most common is to place first the name of the person whose application was received first. Job offers are made from the eligible list in the order the names appear on it. You will be notified of your grade and your rank as soon as all these computations have been made. This will be done as rapidly as possible.

People who are found to meet the requirements in the announcement are called "eligibles." Their names are put on a list of eligible candidates. An eligible's chances of getting a job depend on how high he stands on this list and how fast agencies are filling jobs from the list.

When a job is to be filled from a list of eligibles, the agency asks for the names of people on the list of eligibles for that job. When the civil service commission receives this request, it sends to the agency the names of the three people highest on this list. Or, if the job to be filled has specialized requirements, the office sends the agency the names of the top three persons who meet these requirements from the general list.

The appointing officer makes a choice from among the three people whose names were sent to him. If the selected person accepts the appointment, the names of the others are put back on the list to be considered for future openings.

That is the rule in hiring from all kinds of eligible lists, whether they are for typist, carpenter, chemist, or something else. For every vacancy, the appointing officer has his choice of any one of the top three eligibles on the list. This explains why the person whose name is on top of the list sometimes does not get an appointment when some of the persons lower on the list do. If the appointing officer chooses the second or third eligible, the No. 1 eligible does not get a job at once, but stays on the list until he is appointed or the list is terminated.

X. HOW TO PASS THE INTERVIEW TEST

The examination for which you applied requires an oral interview test. You have already taken the written test and you are now being called for the interview test – the final part of the formal examination.

You may think that it is not possible to prepare for an interview test and that there are no procedures to follow during an interview. Our purpose is to point out some things you can do in advance that will help you and some good rules to follow and pitfalls to avoid while you are being interviewed.

What is an interview supposed to test?

The written examination is designed to test the technical knowledge and competence of the candidate; the oral is designed to evaluate intangible qualities, not readily measured otherwise, and to establish a list showing the relative fitness of each candidate – as measured against his competitors – for the position sought. Scoring is not on the basis of "right" and "wrong," but on a sliding scale of values ranging from "not passable" to "outstanding." As a matter of fact, it is possible to achieve a relatively low score without a single "incorrect" answer because of evident weakness in the qualities being measured.

Occasionally, an examination may consist entirely of an oral test – either an individual or a group oral. In such cases, information is sought concerning the technical knowledges and abilities of the candidate, since there has been no written examination for this purpose. More commonly, however, an oral test is used to supplement a written examination.

Who conducts interviews?

The composition of oral boards varies among different jurisdictions. In nearly all, a representative of the personnel department serves as chairman. One of the members of the board may be a representative of the department in which the candidate would work. In some cases, "outside experts" are used, and, frequently, a businessman or some other representative of the general public is asked to serve. Labor and management or other special groups may be represented. The aim is to secure the services of experts in the appropriate field.

However the board is composed, it is a good idea (and not at all improper or unethical) to ascertain in advance of the interview who the members are and what groups they represent. When you are introduced to them, you will have some idea of their backgrounds and interests, and at least you will not stutter and stammer over their names.

What should be done before the interview?

While knowledge about the board members is useful and takes some of the surprise element out of the interview, there is other preparation which is more substantive. It *is* possible to prepare for an oral interview – in several ways:

1) Keep a copy of your application and review it carefully before the interview

This may be the only document before the oral board, and the starting point of the interview. Know what education and experience you have listed there, and the sequence and dates of all of it. Sometimes the board will ask you to review the highlights of your experience for them; you should not have to hem and haw doing it.

2) Study the class specification and the examination announcement

Usually, the oral board has one or both of these to guide them. The qualities, characteristics or knowledges required by the position sought are stated in these documents. They offer valuable clues as to the nature of the oral interview. For example, if the job involves supervisory responsibilities, the announcement will usually indicate that knowledge of modern supervisory methods and the qualifications of the candidate as a supervisor will be tested. If so, you can expect such questions, frequently in the form of a hypothetical situation which you are expected to solve. NEVER go into an oral without knowledge of the duties and responsibilities of the job you seek.

3) Think through each qualification required

Try to visualize the kind of questions you would ask if you were a board member. How well could you answer them? Try especially to appraise your own knowledge and background in each area, *measured against the job sought*, and identify any areas in which you are weak. Be critical and realistic – do not flatter yourself.

4) Do some general reading in areas in which you feel you may be weak

For example, if the job involves supervision and your past experience has NOT, some general reading in supervisory methods and practices, particularly in the field of human relations, might be useful. Do NOT study agency procedures or detailed manuals. The oral board will be testing your understanding and capacity, not your memory.

5) Get a good night's sleep and watch your general health and mental attitude

You will want a clear head at the interview. Take care of a cold or any other minor ailment, and of course, no hangovers.

What should be done on the day of the interview?

Now comes the day of the interview itself. Give yourself plenty of time to get there. Plan to arrive somewhat ahead of the scheduled time, particularly if your appointment is in the fore part of the day. If a previous candidate fails to appear, the board might be ready for you a bit early. By early afternoon an oral board is almost invariably behind schedule if there are many candidates, and you may have to wait. Take along a book or magazine to read, or your application to review, but leave any extraneous material in the waiting room when you go in for your interview. In any event, relax and compose yourself.

The matter of dress is important. The board is forming impressions about you – from your experience, your manners, your attitude, and your appearance. Give your personal appearance careful attention. Dress your best, but not your flashiest. Choose conservative, appropriate clothing, and be sure it is immaculate. This is a business interview, and your appearance should indicate that you regard it as such. Besides, being well groomed and properly dressed will help boost your confidence.

Sooner or later, someone will call your name and escort you into the interview room. *This is it.* From here on you are on your own. It is too late for any more preparation. But remember, you asked for this opportunity to prove your fitness, and you are here because your request was granted.

What happens when you go in?

The usual sequence of events will be as follows: The clerk (who is often the board stenographer) will introduce you to the chairman of the oral board, who will introduce you to the other members of the board. Acknowledge the introductions before you sit down. Do not be surprised if you find a microphone facing you or a stenotypist sitting by. Oral interviews are usually recorded in the event of an appeal or other review.

Usually the chairman of the board will open the interview by reviewing the highlights of your education and work experience from your application – primarily for the benefit of the other members of the board, as well as to get the material into the record. Do not interrupt or comment unless there is an error or significant misinterpretation; if that is the case, do not hesitate. But do not quibble about insignificant matters. Also, he will usually ask you some question about your education, experience or your present job – partly to get you to start talking and to establish the interviewing "rapport." He may start the actual questioning, or turn it over to one of the other members. Frequently, each member undertakes the questioning on a particular area, one in which he is perhaps most competent, so you can expect each member to participate in the examination. Because time is limited, you may also expect some rather abrupt switches in the direction the questioning takes, so do not be upset by it. Normally, a board member will not pursue a single line of questioning unless he discovers a particular strength or weakness.

After each member has participated, the chairman will usually ask whether any member has any further questions, then will ask you if you have anything you wish to add. Unless you are expecting this question, it may floor you. Worse, it may start you off on an extended, extemporaneous speech. The board is not usually seeking more information. The question is principally to offer you a last opportunity to present further qualifications or to indicate that you have nothing to add. So, if you feel that a significant qualification or characteristic has been overlooked, it is proper to point it out in a sentence or so. Do not compliment the board on the thoroughness of their examination – they have been sketchy, and you know it. If you wish, merely say, "No thank you, I have nothing further to add." This is a point where you can "talk yourself out" of a good impression or fail to present an important bit of information. Remember, *you close the interview yourself.*

The chairman will then say, "That is all, Mr. _______, thank you." Do not be startled; the interview is over, and quicker than you think. Thank him, gather your belongings and take your leave. Save your sigh of relief for the other side of the door.

How to put your best foot forward

Throughout this entire process, you may feel that the board individually and collectively is trying to pierce your defenses, seek out your hidden weaknesses and embarrass and confuse you. Actually, this is not true. They are obliged to make an appraisal of your qualifications for the job you are seeking, and they want to see you in your best light. Remember, they must interview all candidates and a non-cooperative candidate may become a failure in spite of their best efforts to bring out his qualifications. Here are 15 suggestions that will help you:

1) Be natural – Keep your attitude confident, not cocky

If you are not confident that you can do the job, do not expect the board to be. Do not apologize for your weaknesses, try to bring out your strong points. The board is interested in a positive, not negative, presentation. Cockiness will antagonize any board member and make him wonder if you are covering up a weakness by a false show of strength.

2) Get comfortable, but don't lounge or sprawl

Sit erectly but not stiffly. A careless posture may lead the board to conclude that you are careless in other things, or at least that you are not impressed by the importance of the occasion. Either conclusion is natural, even if incorrect. Do not fuss with your clothing, a pencil or an ashtray. Your hands may occasionally be useful to emphasize a point; do not let them become a point of distraction.

3) Do not wisecrack or make small talk

This is a serious situation, and your attitude should show that you consider it as such. Further, the time of the board is limited – they do not want to waste it, and neither should you.

4) Do not exaggerate your experience or abilities

In the first place, from information in the application or other interviews and sources, the board may know more about you than you think. Secondly, you probably will not get away with it. An experienced board is rather adept at spotting such a situation, so do not take the chance.

5) If you know a board member, do not make a point of it, yet do not hide it

Certainly you are not fooling him, and probably not the other members of the board. Do not try to take advantage of your acquaintanceship – it will probably do you little good.

6) Do not dominate the interview

Let the board do that. They will give you the clues – do not assume that you have to do all the talking. Realize that the board has a number of questions to ask you, and do not try to take up all the interview time by showing off your extensive knowledge of the answer to the first one.

7) Be attentive

You only have 20 minutes or so, and you should keep your attention at its sharpest throughout. When a member is addressing a problem or question to you, give him your undivided attention. Address your reply principally to him, but do not exclude the other board members.

8) Do not interrupt

A board member may be stating a problem for you to analyze. He will ask you a question when the time comes. Let him state the problem, and wait for the question.

9) Make sure you understand the question

Do not try to answer until you are sure what the question is. If it is not clear, restate it in your own words or ask the board member to clarify it for you. However, do not haggle about minor elements.

10) Reply promptly but not hastily

A common entry on oral board rating sheets is "candidate responded readily," or "candidate hesitated in replies." Respond as promptly and quickly as you can, but do not jump to a hasty, ill-considered answer.

11) Do not be peremptory in your answers

A brief answer is proper – but do not fire your answer back. That is a losing game from your point of view. The board member can probably ask questions much faster than you can answer them.

12) Do not try to create the answer you think the board member wants

He is interested in what kind of mind you have and how it works – not in playing games. Furthermore, he can usually spot this practice and will actually grade you down on it.

13) Do not switch sides in your reply merely to agree with a board member

Frequently, a member will take a contrary position merely to draw you out and to see if you are willing and able to defend your point of view. Do not start a debate, yet do not surrender a good position. If a position is worth taking, it is worth defending.

14) Do not be afraid to admit an error in judgment if you are shown to be wrong

The board knows that you are forced to reply without any opportunity for careful consideration. Your answer may be demonstrably wrong. If so, admit it and get on with the interview.

15) Do not dwell at length on your present job

The opening question may relate to your present assignment. Answer the question but do not go into an extended discussion. You are being examined for a *new* job, not your present one. As a matter of fact, try to phrase ALL your answers in terms of the job for which you are being examined.

Basis of Rating

Probably you will forget most of these "do's" and "don'ts" when you walk into the oral interview room. Even remembering them all will not ensure you a passing grade. Perhaps you did not have the qualifications in the first place. But remembering them will help you to put your best foot forward, without treading on the toes of the board members.

Rumor and popular opinion to the contrary notwithstanding, an oral board wants you to make the best appearance possible. They know you are under pressure – but they also want to see how you respond to it as a guide to what your reaction would be under the pressures of the job you seek. They will be influenced by the degree of poise you display, the personal traits you show and the manner in which you respond.

ABOUT THIS BOOK

This book contains tests divided into Examination Sections. Go through each test, answering every question in the margin. We have also attached a sample answer sheet at the back of the book that can be removed and used. At the end of each test look at the answer key and check your answers. On the ones you got wrong, look at the right answer choice and learn. Do not fill in the answers first. Do not memorize the questions and answers, but understand the answer and principles involved. On your test, the questions will likely be different from the samples. Questions are changed and new ones added. If you understand these past questions you should have success with any changes that arise. Tests may consist of several types of questions. We have additional books on each subject should more study be advisable or necessary for you. Finally, the more you study, the better prepared you will be. This book is intended to be the last thing you study before you walk into the examination room. Prior study of relevant texts is also recommended. NLC publishes some of these in our Fundamental Series. Knowledge and good sense are important factors in passing your exam. Good luck also helps. So now study this Passbook, absorb the material contained within and take that knowledge into the examination. Then do your best to pass that exam.

EXAMINATION SECTION

EXAMINATION SECTION

TEST 1

DIRECTIONS: Each question or incomplete statement is followed by several suggested answers or completions. Select the one that BEST answers the question or completes the statement. *PRINT THE LETTER OF THE CORRECT ANSWER IN THE SPACE AT THE RIGHT.*

Questions 1-5.

DIRECTIONS: Questions 1 through 5 are to be answered on the basis of the following fact pattern.

A restless crowd has gathered on the lower level of the Supreme Courthouse. The judge has not yet descended from chambers and the law clerk is also missing. The forty to fifty person crowd is a mix of jurors, attorneys, and parties.

1. As an initial order of business, what should the court officer be concerned with? 1.____
   A. Taming the crowd
   B. Locating the judge
   C. Locating the law clerk
   D. Sending prospective jurors upstairs to the jury pool room

2. Two attorneys' voices have risen above all the rest. It is unclear whether they are shouting at one another in anger or catching up on old times. They are attracting onlookers as their conversation grows more animated. 2.____
   What is the MOST appropriate action for the court officer to take?
   A. Separate the two attorneys
   B. Ask that they lower their voices or speak privately in another area of the courthouse
   C. Sequester the jurors
   D. Ask that the two attorneys step into the courtroom to resolve their dispute

3. Some of the members of the crowd seem to be holding a single white sheet of paper which appears to be a summons. 3.____
   What is the MOST reasonable next step?
   The court officer should
   A. ask those a summons holders to head upstairs to check in with the clerk
   B. sequester summons holders to the side to confer with one another
   C. ask that those people sued stay put for now
   D. ask the law clerk announce herself to the possible defendants in the room

4. How should the court officer categorize and separate the crowd? 4.____
   A. Separate by the time each person arrived
   B. Separate by those with counsel present
   C. Separate by the reason he or she is at the courthouse
   D. Separate by age, gender, then race

5. In determining where each individual rightfully belongs, the court officer should be MOST familiar with which of the following? 5.____
   A. The location of each judge's chamber
   B. The times when each law clerk is scheduled to arrive at the courthouse
   C. The location of the clerk's desk, courtrooms, and preliminary hearing conference area
   D. The security desk and exits of the courtroom

Questions 6-10.

DIRECTIONS: Questions 6 through 10 are to be answered on the basis of the following fact pattern.

Jury selection has begun. Prospective jurors are gathered in the far courtroom and, after signing in, take their seats and wait to be called for sequestration.

6. During jury pool selection, two prospective jurors start to argue about a recent murder trial that made the New York Post. You should immediately 6.____
   A. shout at them to calm down or else they will be chosen for jury as punishment
   B. intervene to de-escalate the situation
   C. get the attention of the law clerk
   D. inform the judge of the jurors' behavior

7. Three women in the back of the courtroom are overhead chatting. They are being relatively quiet and not disrupting anyone around them. However, one of the women says that she knows who may be on trial today. Her nephew was arrested last night for drinking. If she is picked to serve on the jury, she says she will absolutely try to ensure he is acquitted. 7.____
   You should
   A. interrupt their conversation to inform them they are being inappropriate
   B. interrupt their conversation to inform them that what they plan on doing is illegal
   C. allow them to finish their conversation in peace
   D. allow them to finish their conversation but, if selected, inform the judge of what was overheard

8. Once the jury is selected, which of the following responsibilities will MOST likely be your role? 8.____
   A. Reciting the applicable law of the case
   B. Providing the jury with opening statements
   C. Swearing in the jury
   D. Coordinating the jurors' lunch order

9. One of the jurors asks you how long the trial is scheduled to take. 9.____
What is the MOST appropriate response?
   A. Trials can be extremely lengthy and take several months or take a few hours.
   B. You should pay attention to every aspect of the trial and not worry about how long you'll be here.
   C. Not respond at all as it may create bias in the courtroom.
   D. Civil trials are typically three to five days, while criminal trials are generally five to ten days.

10. After the jury is selected, one of the jurors recognizes the defendant's attorney and begins to scream at him from the jury box. 10.____
You immediately start to
   A. remove the individual from the courtroom
   B. ask him to calm down and reserve his opinion about attorneys for later
   C. physically restrain the juror using force
   D. inform the judge that the juror may be biased in this matter

Questions 111-15.

DIRECTIONS: Questions 11 through 15 are to be answered on the basis of the following fact pattern.

During a civil litigation trial, multiple pieces of evidence must be presented to the jury, the witnesses, and the judge.

11. During opening statements, the plaintiff's attorney mentions that the jury will see and hear over 1,000 pieces of evidence during the trial that will convince them the plaintiff should prevail. Nearing the end of the trial, however, the plaintiff has not produced one piece of physical evidence. 11.____
You should
   A. raise the issue with the judge
   B. remind the attorney during a break that they have not delivered their promise
   C. stay silent
   D. suggest the attorney produce something into evidence

12. During examination of one of the defendant's witnesses, Attorney Bob referred to a piece of evidence as the "receipt from the gas station, marked as #34." When you pick it up from the defendant, you notice the evidence is actually marked as #36. 12.____
Should you intervene to correct the attorney's mistake?
   A. Absolutely not
   B. Yes, but point out to the attorney that it is marked as a different number to give him an opportunity to correct himself
   C. Yes but point out to the jury that the evidence is marked differently so that they are not confused
   D. Yes, but only to the judge in his or her chambers after the trial is complete

13. The two attorneys begin to argue with one another during the trial. How do you intervene? 13.____
    A. Stand between them to signal their behavior will not be tolerated
    B. Issue each of them a stern warning that they will be removed if they do not cease immediately
    C. Allow the judge to intervene first, then follow his or her instructions on how to intervene
    D. Ask the jury to remove themselves from the courtroom

14. As the two attorneys start to become more aggressive, the judge slams his gavel. The attorneys ignore the warning from the court. How would you intervene at this point? 14.____
    A. Physically restrain the plaintiff's attorney
    B. Physically restrain the defendant's attorney
    C. Stand between the two of them, hold out your arms to both sides, and order them to stop speaking directly to one another
    D. Ask the jury to remove themselves from the courtroom

15. During the trial, the defendant mutters an expletive under his breath while the judge gives an order as a show of blatant disrespect for the court. What is the MOST appropriate action to take? 15.____
    A. Allow the judge to sanction the defendant, then escort him or her out of the courtroom
    B. Physically restrain the defendant
    C. Await instruction from the judge on how to intervene
    D. Arrest the individual and remove him or her from the courtroom

16. One of the jurors appears faint and starts to wobble while seated in the jury box. How should you handle the situation? 16.____
    A. Let one of the jurors come to the ailing juror's aid first
    B. Alert the clerk of what you see and ask that the trial be held indefinitely
    C. Politely interject the trial proceedings and ask the juror if he or she is feeling well
    D. Quietly remove the juror from his or her seat, trying not to disrupt the trial proceedings

17. During trial, you believe that you see the defendant winking at one of the jurors. No one else seems to notice their interaction, including the judge and the attorneys. What action would you take? 17.____
    A. Alert the judge in chambers
    B. Tell the law clerk during a break in trial
    C. Interrupt the trial to make all parties aware of the behavior
    D. Confirm with the juror in question that the defendant is winking at her to determine if the feeling is mutual

18. During a sentencing hearing, the convicted defendant seems to be fiddling more than usual. 18.____
Where would you place yourself during the remainder of the hearing?
   A. As close to the judge as possible in the event you may need to protect him or her
   B. As close to the defendant's attorney as possible in the event you may need to protect him or her
   C. As close to the defendant as possible in the event you will need to restrain them
   D. At the back of the courtroom

19. In the trial of a serial killer, many prospective jurors have indicated they feel unsafe. During jury deliberations, you overhear at least two different jurors say that they want to convict the defendant simply because he has seen their faces during the trial. 19.____
What are your next steps?
   A. Interject into the jury room and inform them that their decision on that premise alone is unethical
   B. Interject into the jury room and inform them that their decision on that premise alone is unconstitutional
   C. Alert the judge immediately
   D. Instruct the jury that they do not need to look directly at the defendant in the courtroom

20. During a recess in the trial, the defendant's expert witness is seen chatting with one of the alternate jurors outside the courthouse. While it is unclear what they are talking about, it seems to be a friendly exchange of information. 20.____
What should you do before the court is called back to order?
   A. Tell the juror she must disclose her conversation with the expert witness in open court
   B. Tell the expert witness he must disclose the conversation with the juror in open court
   C. Inform the plaintiff's attorney about the conversation
   D. Inform the judge about the conversation

Questions 21-25.

DIRECTIONS: Questions 21 through 25 are to be answered on the basis of the following fact pattern.

After a TRO is issued to the plaintiff, the ex-wife of the defendant, both parties are free to go. The defendant appeared in court and rigorously opposed his ex-wife's request. His ex-wife already has sole custody of their three children, and he seems incredibly distraught by the judge's grant of her request.

21. How should you allow the parties to exit the courtroom? 21.____
    A. It is permissible and more efficient if everyone exited together.
    B. The defendant should be escorted out of the courtroom through judge's chambers.
    C. The plaintiff and her attorney should be escorted out of the courtroom first.
    D. People are free to choose how they enter and exit a building.

22. After the hearing, you see the plaintiff and the defendant's attorney chatting outside of the courtroom. Should you intervene? 22.____
    A. No, unless the conversation grows heated and someone may need to be restrained
    B. No, but you should make your presence known by moving closer to the two as they converse with one another
    C. No, because the plaintiff is not speaking directly with the defendant
    D. No

23. After the hearing, you see the defendant speaking directly with the law clerk who was present during the hearing. How should you intervene? 23.____
    A. There is no need to intervene since the hearing is over.
    B. There is no need to intervene since the law clerk is not the judge.
    C. You should inform the judge of the conversation, but not intervene in the conversation itself.
    D. You should stop the conversation immediately by announcing that it is inappropriate.

24. In a follow-up hearing, where the plaintiff is requested to extend the TRO, the defendant does not show up. Instead, the defendant's brother appears at the hearing on his behalf. 24.____
    Is the defendant's brother permitted to voice his concerns about extending the TRO?
    The defendant's brother
    A. is not a party to the action and must wait outside of the courtroom during proceedings
    B. is welcome to testify on his brother's behalf
    C. can testify on his brother's behalf as long as he remains calm while doing so
    D. can testify on his brother's behalf so long as the plaintiff's sister can testify on her behalf

25. In judge's chambers, the judge's law clerk indicates that she believes the plaintiff is lying about the defendant's alleged dangerous behavior. The judge does not agree or disagree with the clerk's statement. During proceedings, however, the clerk rolls her eyes and is not taking notes. 25.____
    The MOST appropriate step is to
    A. inform the judge after the hearing and allow the judge to handle the clerk's behavior
    B. ask that the clerk excuse herself if she cannot behave in a professional manner during hearings

C. pause the hearings and demand that the clerk leave the courtroom
D. pause the hearings and allow the clerk to correct her own behavior before the hearings can resume

KEY (CORRECT ANSWERS)

1. A
2. B
3. A
4. C
5. C

6. B
7. D
8. C
9. D
10. A

11. C
12. B
13. C
14. C
15. A

16. C
17. A
18. C
19. C
20. D

21. C
22. B
23. C
24. A
25. A

TEST 2

DIRECTIONS: Each question or incomplete statement is followed by several suggested answers or completions. Select the one that BEST answers the question or completes the statement. *PRINT THE LETTER OF THE CORRECT ANSWER IN THE SPACE AT THE RIGHT.*

Questions 1-5.

DIRECTIONS: Questions 1 through 5 are to be answered on the basis of the following fact pattern.

A trial is set to start at 9:30 A.M. At 9:45 A.M., the judge and the judge's clerk have yet to arrive. At 9:50 A.M., the law clerk enters the courtroom and takes her assigned seat beneath the judge. The judge, however, has still not appeared.

1. Should you leave the courtroom to locate the judge? 1.____
   A. Yes, but only if there is another court officer there to maintain the order of the courtroom
   B. Yes, but only if the law clerk is comfortable maintaining the order of the courtroom on her own
   C. Yes, but only if the jury has not filed into the courtroom yet
   D. No

2. At half past 10 A.M., you try to locate the judge. You see that she has entered her chambers but does not look well. 2.____
   What information do you need to ascertain your next steps?
   Whether the judge
   A. is judicially fit to hear the case
   B. is intoxicated
   C. is feeling well and needs you to adjourn the case for the day
   C. needs physical assistance by way of wheelchair or other device

3. The judge has indicated she is well enough to hear the cases for the day, but needs another few moments to collect herself. She enters her chambers and summons only one of the attorneys from the first trial. 3.____
   What is the LEAST appropriate response?
   A. Collect the attorney as requested
   B. Inform the judge that she will be commencing ex parte communications if you were to do
   C. Refuse and demand the judge recuse herself from proceedings for the day
   D. Confirm the instruction and politely inform the judge this would be inappropriate

4. When you re-enter the courtroom which is still occupied with spectators, attorneys, the parties and the law clerk, who are you MOST likely to inform that the judge does not seem to be feeling well? 4.____
   A. The clerk
   B. The attorneys
   C. The entire courtroom
   D. No one

5. During the swearing-in ceremony of attorneys who passed the Bar exam, one of the attorneys stops you after going through the security check to indicate that her boyfriend is parking the car. Because she is not allowed to have her cellphone on, she cannot inform him to leave his firearm in the car. Which question would be MOST helpful in determining your next step? 5.____
   A. Does your boyfriend have a license to carry a firearm?
   B. Is the weapon loaded?
   C. Is your boyfriend dangerous?
   D. How far away is he?

6. How many alternate jurors are typically sworn in for trial? 6.____
   A. Up to 12
   B. Up to 14
   C. Up to 10
   D. Up to 6

7. A TRO is a _____, while a QDRO is a _____. 7.____
   A. temporary restraining order; qualified domicile relations order
   B. territorial restraining order; qualified domicile relations order
   C. temporary restraining order; qualified domestic revision order
   D. temporary restraining order; qualified domestic relations order

8. There is a shortage of court officer personnel this morning, and two trials are set to start at the District Court. The first trial is a bench trial and involves a no-fault reimbursement claim. The second trial is a jury trial of a twice-convicted child rapist. Your presence is requested at both trials. Which should you cover? 8.____
   A. The bench trial should last a few hours, so you should cover that trial first.
   B. The jury trial has a more pressing need for law enforcement presence, so you should cover that trial in its entirety.
   C. The jury trial has a more pressing need for law enforcement presence, so you should cover the trial at least until the first recess.
   D. You are required to swear in the judge, so you must cover the bench trial.

9. The crowd of people outside the preliminary conference desk is becoming unwieldy. Attorneys are piling out of the small room in droves and seem to be overpowering the sole clerk at the front. What is your role in taming the crowd as it relates to the clerk? 9.____
   A. The clerk should handle the crowd, especially since they are mostly attorneys.
   B. You are responsible for calming the crowd and de-escalating any issues that arise; the clerk deserves an orderly and respectful line.
   C. You are responsible for taming the crowd by yourself and can ask for the clerk's assistance if needed.
   D. You do not need to be in or around the preliminary conference desk at all.

10. As you read the counts of the indictment, one of the jurors begins to cough uncontrollably. Should you continue reading or pause while the juror gathers herself? 10.____
You should
    A. pause and allow the juror to gather herself but not repeat the counts
    B. continue reading the indictment without pause
    C. pause and politely ask the juror if she is okay, then repeat the counts of the indictment from the beginning
    D. remove the juror

11. A twice-convicted felon is being charged with attempted rape of a minor. During a brief recess, one of the jurors returns to the courtroom to quickly grab her purse and makes eye contact with the defendant. 11.____
How do you intervene?
    A. The juror is allowed to make eye contact with the defendant, therefore no intervention is necessary.
    B. You stand in the middle of the two of them to protect the juror.
    C. You report the eye contact to the judge immediately, since bias was clearly created.
    D. You ask the judge to excuse the juror because of her impropriety.

12. Which of the following is MOST deserving of court officer intervention? 12.____
    A. A raucous crowd starting to gather a half mile outside the courthouse
    B. A disorderly jury
    C. An ex parte communication between the judge and one of the attorneys
    D. A motion hearing where one party requests an expedited trial date

13. Which of the following procedures is MOST deserving of a court officer's attention? 13.____
    A. Discovery procedures
    B. Prison handling and escort procedures
    C. Evidentiary exchange procedures
    D. Development of character witness procedures

14. One of Judge Diamond's recent decisions has sparked an outrage in the local community. Approximately one week after the decision, a peaceful and planned protest has begun outside of the courthouse. 14.____
Which of the following is MOST important during the protest?
    A. Securing the safety of Judge Diamond
    B. Controlling the media
    C. Identifying any and all aggressors in the protest
    D. Securing the safety of Judge Diamond's law clerk, Judy

15. Judge Ross is seen discussing Judge Diamond's decision with one of the media outlets covering the protest. 15.____
Which of the following actions should you be the MOST mindful of during Judge Ross's comments?
   A. Any inflammatory words against Judge Diamond
   B. The behavior of the protestors, including any persons who may charge the judge
   C. The behavior of the interviewer who may attack Judge Diamond personally
   D. The behavior of the media more generally who may try to access the courthouse while Judge Ross is speaking to the interviewer

Questions 16-18.

DIRECTIONS: Questions 16 through 18 are to be answered on the basis of the following fact pattern.

While those waiting for the court to open file into the hallway, an argument breaks out between two women and one man. When you intervene between the parties, you discover the two women are arguing over custody of a child – who is standing nearby – and the man is one of their attorneys. Barbara is the biological mother of the child. Tina raised the child from birth. Tina and her attorney, Bill, came with the child to court today.

16. Which party should stay with the child? 16.____
   A. The biological mother, Barbara, of the child should stay with the child while they await for court to begin.
   B. Tina and Bill should stay with the child since she raised the child from birth.
   C. The parties should separate and the child should come with you to a sequestered part of the courthouse.
   D. Tina and Bill should stay with the child as petitioners of the court; Barbara should wait in a separate area away from all three and refrain from contact.

17. Which of the following are Barbara and her attorney MOST likely to request in court? 17.____
   A. A No-Contact Order
   B. Order to Expunge
   C. Order to Impeach
   D. Deposition

18. Should you tell the judge about the behavior of the parties during the hearing? 18.____
   A. You can inform the judge if asked, but not during the hearing itself.
   B. You can inform the judge if asked, but should wait until the hearing is not in session.
   C. Before the hearing is set to begin, you should inform the judge of your encounter with the parties and let the judge decide how to best confront the situation between all involved.
   D. No.

19. Before the start of a trial, which is the court officer MOST likely to administer? Swearing in of the 19.____
    A. judge
    B. judge's clerk
    C. attorneys
    D. jury

Questions 20-25.

DIRECTIONS: Questions 20 through 25 are to be answered on the basis of the following fact pattern.

At Kings County Supreme Court, a trial of a group of alleged rapists has drawn a huge crowd of spectators at each day of the hearings. Two of the defendants are locals of Kings County while the other is a local of Bronx County. The trial date has been set and moved multiple times.

20. In determining which spectators should be allowed into the courthouse to watch the trial, which should be secured FIRST? 20.____
    A. Judge's permission
    B. Clerk's permission
    C. Jury's permission
    D. The mayor's permission

21. Which should NOT be employed in determining which spectators are allowed into the courthouse to watch the trial? 21.____
    A. The age of the spectator
    B. The spectator's affiliation with local media outlets
    C. Gender or race of the spectator
    D. The length of time the spectator has waited for the courthouse to open

22. Which of the following will the defendants MOST likely be charged with? 22.____
    A. An information
    B. A felony
    C. A misdemeanor
    D. An indictment

23. In reading the charge, which of the following is LEAST likely to appear? 23.____
    A. The name of the attorneys of record
    B. The names of the victims
    C. The number of counts of each crime
    D. The name of the judge hearing the case

24. There are likely to be multiples of which during this trial? 24.____
    A. Multiple court officers
    B. Multiple attorneys
    C. Multiple charges
    D. All of the above

25. The venue of the trial is MOST likely to be 25.____
    A. Kings County
    B. Bronx County
    C. Determined by the jury
    D. Determined by the judge

KEY (CORRECT ANSWERS)

1. D
2. C
3. A
4. D
5. A

6. D
7. D
8. B
9. B
10. C

11. A
12. B
13. B
14. A
15. C

16. D
17. A
18. C
19. D
20. A

21. C
22. B
23. B
24. D
25. D

TEST 3

DIRECTIONS: Each question or incomplete statement is followed by several suggested answers or completions. Select the one that BEST answers the question or completes the statement. *PRINT THE LETTER OF THE CORRECT ANSWER IN THE SPACE AT THE RIGHT.*

1. What is one of the MOST effective ways to disperse a large crowd in a courthouse? 1.____
   A. Start yelling that a trial is about to start
   B. Ask the crowd to form one or multiple lines
   C. Inform the crowd that they are being disruptive and should keep the volume of their voices low
   D. There aren't any effective ways to manage a crowd

2. Which of the following is a court officer MOST likely to be volunteered for? 2.____
   A. Domestic violence awareness training
   B. Prisoner escort services
   C. Jury monitoring
   D. All of the above

3. One of the jurors starts to strike up a conversation with you outside of the courtroom. How should you respond? 3.____
   Politely decline to
   A. engage, unless he or she is asking for directions
   B. engage, unless he or she would like to talk about the case
   C. engage, unless he or she knows you personally
   D. engage

4. After a prisoner is escorted into the courtroom, he attempts to kick his attorney. He should 4.____
   A. be removed from the courtroom
   B. be restrained with leg restraints
   C. apologize to his attorney
   D. be forced to stand during the remainder of the proceedings

5. A charge of attempted murder is LEAST likely to accompany a charge of 5.____
   A. murder B. burglary C. robbery D. assault

6. You begin to notice that jurors are growing sleepy and irritable towards the end of a six-week trial. Many jurors have stopped taking notes. Should you inform the law clerk or judge of their behavior? 6.____
   A. The jurors' behavior in this instance does not warrant concern.
   B. You should inform the judge's clerk so he or she can warn the jurors they may miss a critical piece of information.
   C. You should inform the judge so he or she can warn the jurors they may miss a critical piece of evidence.
   D. You should request that the jury remain alert at all times during proceedings.

7. In an attempt to diffuse a heated argument between two attorneys at the New York County Civil Court, which factor should the court officer be MOST mindful of? 7.____
   A. The respective law firms of each attorney
   B. The volume of their voices as it carries throughout the building
   C. The likelihood these attorneys will see one another again on another case
   D. The ability for either attorney to recognize he or she is being warned about their behavior inside a court of law

8. A woman, Leslie, approaches you inside the Supreme Court and says that she has been served with a lawsuit. 8.____
   Which of the following is the MOST appropriate response you can provide to Leslie?
   She should have a copy of the _____ with her and refer to it, which will tell her where she would report within the courthouse.
   A. answer B. complaint C. summons D. information

9. Mary produces the document, but does not know where exactly in the courthouse she should report. What is your NEXT direction? 9.____
   She should
   A. check in at Courtroom A
   B. check in with the clerk's office
   C. check in at the Preliminary Conference desk
   D. wait to be called and have a seat on a nearby bench

10. Who decides whether the jurors are allowed to take notes during the trial? 10.____
    A. The judge
    B. The plaintiff's attorney, since they are bringing the case to court
    C. Jurors are always allowed to take notes during trials
    D. Jurors are never allowed to take notes during trials

11. During a trial, one of the jurors writes a question for one of the witnesses on a piece of paper and hands it to you. 11.____
    What is your NEXT step?
    A. Keep it to yourself; jurors are not allowed to ask a witness questions
    B. Pass the written question to the judge, who may or may not ask the witness the question posed
    C. Decline to receive the written message
    D. Read the question to the witness on the witness stand after cross examination

12. If questions arise during the jury deliberation process, what is the role of the court officer? 12.____
    A. To deliver the written question from the jury foreperson to the judge
    B. To repeat the question orally as told to the court officer by the jury foreperson to the judge
    C. To read the written question in open court with all parties present other than the defendant
    D. To record the written question in the docket

13. In maintaining the security of the courtroom itself, what should the court officer be mindful of as it relates to non-parties to a lawsuit? 13.____
    A. Their interest level in the case
    B. How close they are sitting to the defendant and/or plaintiff
    C. Their demeanor, including a sudden change in demeanor
    D. Their note taking of court proceedings

14. A juror has informed you that she accidentally read information about the case she is serving on while she was at the supermarket last night. How should you respond to her? 14.____
    A. Berate her for not being more diligent in seeking out information about the case
    B. Inform the clerk that the juror should be replaced
    C. Remove the juror from the jury box and replace him or her with an alternate juror yourself
    D. Inform the judge immediately

15. The court officer is MOST likely to participate in which of the following duties? 15.____
    A. Collection of evidence at the scene of the crime
    B. Record court proceedings in the docket
    C. Schedule witnesses for trial, categorized alphabetically by their last name
    D. Assist the judge as necessary with extraneous tasks

16. One of the State's expert witnesses has failed to appear at trial when scheduled. Which document will the judge execute to compel his or her appearance? 16.____
    A. An indictment
    B. An information
    C. An execution
    D. A warrant

17. Which court proceeding takes place closest in time to an arrest? 17.____
    A. Arraignment
    B. Sentencing
    C. Trial
    D. Jury selection

18. Which of the following is LEAST likely to occur at the conclusion of a trial? 18.____
    A. Sentencing
    B. Appeal
    C. Reversal
    D. Plea bargaining

19. It has come to your attention that two of the jurors are related to one another. They are overheard talking about the case outside of the courtroom and in the court hallway. Should you intervene? 19.____
    A. Yes, because someone could overhear their conversation
    B. Yes, because the other jurors should be aware of how they plan on voting
    C. No, because they are siblings
    D. No, because they are outside of the courtroom and talking amongst themselves

20. How many jurors typically serve on a trial? 20.____
    A. 12 B. 18 C. 16 D. 6

21. During jury selection, the judge has already excused 25 prospective jurors for cause. 21.____
    How many more jurors can be excused for cause before reaching the excusal limit?
    A. 5
    B. 10
    C. The judge has reached the limit
    D. There is no excusal limit for "cause"

22. Which of the following is the jury prohibited from doing during a trial on which they are serving? 22.____
    A. Visiting the scene of the alleged crime
    B. Read or listen to news about the trial from outside sources
    C. Research case law that applies to the trial
    D. All of the above

23. Are court officers needed during bench trials? 23.____
    A. No, because heinous offenses are not tried by bench
    B. No, because bench trials are relatively quick
    C. Yes, because bench trials require extra security
    D. Yes, because court officers are needed for a variety of tasks during each trial

24. In New York City, jury trials are conducted at which of the following courts? 24.____
    A. Supreme Court B. New York City Civil Court
    C. New York City Criminal Court D. All of the above

25. A trial involving an alleged assault and battery is MOST likely to occur at which New York City court? 25.____
    A. Town and Village Court B. New York City Civil Court
    C. New York City Criminal Court D. County Court

KEY (CORRECT ANSWERS)

1. B
2. D
3. D
4. A
5. A

6. A
7. D
8. C
9. B
10. A

11. B
12. A
13. C
14. D
15. D

16. D
17. A
18. D
19. A
20. A

21. D
22. D
23. D
24. D
25. C

TEST 4

DIRECTIONS: Each question or incomplete statement is followed by several suggested answers or completions. Select the one that BEST answers the question or completes the statement. *PRINT THE LETTER OF THE CORRECT ANSWER IN THE SPACE AT THE RIGHT.*

1. One device that court officers can employ that others in the court cannot, including the clerks or judges, include 1.____
   A. power to detail
   B. use of force
   C. defensive strategy
   D. all of the above

2. Which of the following parties is LEAST likely to be in the courtroom during every trial? 2.____
   A. Defendant
   B. Court reporter
   C. Attorneys
   D. Translator

3. The order of the steps of a typical trial from first to last is: 3.____
   I. Opening statements
   II. Jury selection
   III. Deliberations
   IV. Oath and preliminary instructions
   The CORRECT answer is:
   A. I, II, III, IV
   B. IV, III, II, I
   C. I, II, IV, III
   D. II, IV, I, III

Questions 4-8.

DIRECTIONS: Questions 4 through 8 are to be answered on the basis of the following fact pattern.

Pre-trial conferences are scheduled for the entire day in courtroom A with Judge Dredd presiding. Each pre-trial conference is scheduled to last 30-45 minutes.

4. During the first pre-trial conference, attorneys Bill and April become agitated with one another. Bill has accused April of ignoring the judge's order and April accuses Bill of hiding key information about the case. 4.____
   How would you diffuse the situation?
   A. The situation most likely does not require diffusing, but if they become more animated you will require they each calm down.
   B. Step between the two parties and demand respect for the court.
   C. Ask the plaintiff's attorney to step into the hallway to cool off for 5-10 minutes.
   D. Ask the defendant's attorney to step into the hallway to cool off for 5-10 minutes.

5. During the second pre-trial hearing, the plaintiff's attorney, John, has called an expert witness to come in and testify. Your role in this process is to 5.____
   A. swear in the witness
   B. Escort the witness to the stand
   C. Record the witness testimony into the docket
   D. Relay the importance of the witnesses' testimony to him or her before they take the stand

6. The second pre-trial conference took longer than the time allotted. The attorneys for the third pre-trial hearing have also seemed to disappear and cannot be located. 6.____
Your NEXT step is to
   A. attempt to locate the attorneys for the hearing
   B. skip the third pre-trial hearing and hear the next conference
   C. issue a warrant for the attorneys' appearance
   D. record the lack of appearance in the docket

7. All of the following are required parties to the pre-trial hearing EXCEPT` 7.____
   A. judge B. attorneys C. jury D. court officer

8. The pre-trial hearing is MOST likely to take place after _____, but before _____. 8.____
   A. arraignment; jury selection
   B. deliberations; closing statements
   C. assignment; adjudication
   D. plea bargain; opening statement

9. During a court recess, you see one of the jurors walking into the judge's chambers. 9.____
You immediately
   A. halt the juror and demand he or she return to the deliberation room
   B. allow the juror to proceed, but ask the judge about the incident later
   C. allow the juror to proceed and assume they know one another personally
   D. allow the juror to proceed but inform the law clerk of the incident

10. When reading an indictment in court, each charge represents a(n) 10.____
   A. allegation of a crime
   B. proven criminal act
   C. evidentiary plea
   D. legal certainty

11. After a defendant has been acquitted, he or she will likely be 11.____
   A. free to leave the courthouse
   B. remanded to federal prison
   C. detained until further notice
   D. formally sentenced

12. Highway Patrol Officer Rowan requests to bring his firearm into the Nassau County Supreme Court as he will be testifying in a case before Judge Pirro. 12.____
Will he be able to?
   A. Yes, as he is licensed to carry the weapon
   B. Yes, as long as he provides proper identification
   C. Yes, if he is willing to discharge it in an emergency
   D. No, he must check his weapon before entering the courtroom

13. Dominic, a defense attorney, has approached you in the hallways of the New York City Civil Court. He is concerned that his client, Don, may become violent during court proceedings. 13.____
How do you handle Dominic's request to closely supervise Don while court is in session?
   A. Inform the judge of Dominic's request and allow proceedings to continue as normal
   B. Ask that another court officer be present during court proceedings

C. Request the judge to sequester the jury while Don is present
D. Ignore Dominic's request for now, until you see how Don behaves yourself

14. Jury sequestration is 14.____
A. extremely common given the complex nature of most criminal trials
B. becoming increasingly common
C. more common in civil cases than in criminal trials
D. rare

15. The judge confides in you that she believes the defendant in an ongoing trial is guilty. 15.____
You have a duty to
A. report the judge to the local authorities
B. inform the clerk's office that the judge is biased
C. there is no duty to report as the judge is free to reserve their opinion of the case
D. there is no duty to report the judge's comment in this instance

16. It is critical after use of force to 16.____
A. document it as well as the circumstance that provided for it
B. recording the reactions of witnesses
C. presenting the judge for reasoning as to why you applied it
D. destroying any contrary evidence

17. During a witness' testimony, which may take place that will likely require your intervention? 17.____
A. Outburst by one of the parties
B. Disruption by the spectators in the courtroom
C. Disagreement by the clerk and stenographer
D. Objection by the judge

18. At arraignment, the defendant is MOST likely to 18.____
A. state his case
B. convince the judge of his or her innocence
C. enter a plea
D. gather information on his or her case from the State's attorney

19. A warrant can be issued for an individual's arrest or for 19.____
A. search of premises outlined in the warrant itself
B. testimony
C. deposition of the arrested individual
D. evidence found at the scene

20. The responsibility to record notes for the judge and listen to issues of law that may need to be researched later are reserved for the 20.____
A. court officer
B. stenographer
C. judge's clerk
D. jury

21. Information about the charges against the defendant, as well as the parties involved in the case, can MOST likely be found in the 21.____
    A. judge's notes
    B. docket
    C. information
    D. discovery report

Questions 22-23.

DIRECTIONS: Questions 22 and 23 are to be answered on the basis of the following fact pattern.

The clerk's office has a line out of the door, with at least eighteen people waiting to be seen. Many of the attorneys are waiting to file documents while some others are waiting for their clients.

22. How would you move the crowd out of the clerk's office? 22.____
    A. Ask that anyone who is waiting for another party to step outside
    B. Ask that anyone who is able to use the automatic filer do so
    C. Ask that only those with a question specifically for the clerk remain in the office
    D. All of the above

23. An example of a question that can only be answered by the court clerk is: 23.____
    A. When the trial is scheduled to start
    B. Where courtroom B is located
    C. The name of the attorney representing the defendant
    D. The name of the judge who hears no-fault cases

24. The opening statements in a trial are delivered by the 24.____
    A. defendant
    B. plaintiff
    C. attorneys
    D. judge

25. The court officer is the MOST likely party to 25.____
    A. dissolve a dispute between two jurors
    B. dissolve a dispute between the judge and the attorneys
    C. dissolve a dispute between spectators
    D. all of the above

KEY (CORRECT ANSWERS)

1.	D	11.	A
2.	D	12.	D
3.	D	13.	B
4.	A	14.	D
5.	B	15.	D
6.	A	16.	A
7.	C	17.	B
8.	A	18.	C
9.	A	19.	A
10.	A	20.	C

21.	B
22.	D
23.	D
24.	C
25.	D

EXAMINATION SECTION

TEST 1

DIRECTIONS: Each question or incomplete statement is followed by several suggested answers or completions. Select the one that BEST answers the question or completes the statement. *PRINT THE LETTER OF THE CORRECT ANSWER IN THE SPACE AT THE RIGHT.*

Questions 1-5.

DIRECTIONS: Questions 1 through 5 are to be answered on the basis of the following fact pattern.

James and Sean started an accounting practice five years ago. Business quickly soured and James and Sean decided to each start their own competing business practices. While James's business flourished, Sean's practice has floundered. Sean believes James spoke poorly about him to their mutual friends, ruining his professional reputation, and went behind his back to steal clients. Sean now wants to sue James civilly.

1. How would Sean begin a civil suit against James? 1.____
   A. Sean needs to file an interpleader to compel James to court.
   B. Sean must file a motion to compel proceedings.
   C. Sean must file a complaint against James in the proper court.
   D. Sean can outline the facts of his case to the clerk who will transcribe the issues.

2. Sean must also file a summons with the clerk. 2.____
   What is the role of the summons in initiating a lawsuit?
   A. It puts the other part on notice that a lawsuit has been filed against them.
   B. It compels discovery in a court of proper jurisdiction.
   C. It requires the other party to answer by initiating a cross-motion.
   D. It gives the other party extended time to file a counterclaim.

3. Sean's attorney and James's attorney begin the process of exchanging information about the witnesses each side plans to call and the evidence that will be presented at trial. 3.____
   This process is called
   A. interrogation B. discovery C. compulsion D. demurrer

4. One of James' and Sean's former clients is moving to London. James' and Sean's attorneys agree to take her deposition now and use it at trial in the event she will not be able to appear. 4.____
   At trial, her testimony will be _____ and part of the record.
   A. read into evidence B. ex parte
   C. sequestered D. assumed credible

5. After being notified that a lawsuit has been filed against him, James has an opportunity to answer the _____ that has been filed against him. 5.____
   A. pleadings
   B. motion to compel
   C. interpleader
   D. complaint

6. Venue refers to the district or county within a state where the 6.____
   A. lawsuit began
   B. lawsuit must be heard
   C. plaintiff resides
   D. plaintiff is domiciled

7. After both parties have agreed on a jury, the jurors are _____ by the court clerk before they are impaneled. 7.____
   A. instructed to take notes
   B. sworn in
   C. fingerprinted
   D. arranged

8. Can the prosecution compel a defendant in a criminal trial to take the stand and testify? 8.____
   A. Yes; he or she must explain what happened in open court
   B. Yes; he or she must take the stand and testify they are invoking their Fifth Amendment right against self-incrimination.
   C. Yes; he or she must take the stand but they can refuse to answer any question they choose
   D. No

9. Criminal charges are brought against a person in all of the following ways, EXCEPT 9.____
   A. citation
   B. information
   C. indictment
   D. subpoena

Questions 10-15.

DIRECTIONS: Questions 10 through 15 are to be answered on the basis of the following fact pattern.

Jason's brother, Andrew, has been arrested. Jason appears at the courthouse as soon as he hears this news. He does not know why Andrew has been arrested, but suspects it may be related to his tumultuous relationship with his ex-girlfriend who has filed a temporary restraining order against Andrew.

10. If Andrew was not arrested on a warrant, when will he be able to file a plea of guilty, not guilty, or no contest? 10.____
   A. At arraignment
   B. At trial
   C. At a preliminary conference
   D. At indictment

11. If Andrew is released from custody without a payment of money on the promise that he will appear for all hearings and for trial, the judge has released Andrew 11.____
   A. on his own recognizance
   B. with time served
   C. after a concurrent term
   D. on exculpatory evidence

12. In the alternative, if the judge sets bail for Andrew's release, he or she does so with the intent of 12.____
    A. punishing Andrew
    B. ensuring Andrew will appear for trial and al pretrial hearings for which he must be present
    C. setting a fine dependent on the type of crime alleged
    D. releasing Andrew into the custody of his responsible brother, Jason

13. Which of the following should NOT be a factor a judge may use in deciding the amount of Andrew's bail? 13.____
    A. The risk of Andrew fleeing
    B. The type of crime Andrew is alleged to have committed
    C. Andrew's age, race, and sex
    D. The safety of the community

14. During Andrew's initial appearance, the judge explains to Andrew that he has a right to a trial by jury. 14.____
    If Andrew does not want a trial by jury, what type of trial will he receive?
    A. An expedited trial
    B. A bench trial
    C. A summation
    D. An information

15. Andrew pleads no contest to the charges in his initial appearance. 15.____
    Andrew is effectively
    A. not admitting guilt or disputing the charge alleged
    B. admitting guilt
    C. denying the charge but admitting he will pay any fines incurred
    D. deferring his plea until a later date

Questions 16-19.

DIRECTIONS: Questions 16 through 19 are to be answered on the basis of the following fact pattern.

Jameson and Avery are neighbors. Jameson moved and purchased a home in the lot next to Avery's lot three months ago. Avery is suing Jameson for building a fence on Avery's property. Jameson attests the fence is actually being built on his own property and there is no boundary dispute. Jameson and Avery are both represented by counsel. A number of motions are filed by each party and discovery has been a lengthy process thus far.

16. Both parties serve each other requests to answer questions in writing under oath. Avery's attorney demands Jameson answer questions about the purchase of his home and dealings with the contractors building the fence. Jameson demands Avery answer questions about the property line dividing their property. 16.____
    This type of discovery is called
    A. interrogatories
    B. demands
    C. summons
    D. written decision

17. Avery's attorney would like to depose the property surveyor, Abe. Can Jameson and/or Jameson's attorney attend Abe's deposition? 17.____
    A. No, because Abe will be Avery's witness
    B. No, because Avery can share the information with Jameson's counsel at a later date
    C. No, because Abe's testimony may not be inadmissible in court so Jameson's presence would be futile
    D. Yes

18. Which of the following will NOT occur at the pre-trial conferenced between the parties? 18.____
    A. A deadline for discovery will be set.
    B. A trial date will be set.
    C. The judge will encourage stipulations between the parties.
    D. The judge will ask for oral arguments.

19. During discovery, both parties ascertain that Jameson built the fence on his side of the property line. Jameson's attorney asks the court to dismiss the case because there is no longer a legally sound basis to proceed. This request to the court is a motion to 19.____
    A. relinquish B. dismiss C. vacate D. suppress

Questions 20-25.

DIRECTIONS: Questions 20 through 25 are to be answered on the basis of the following fact pattern.

A restless crowd has gathered on the lower level of the Nassau County Supreme Courthouse. The judge has not yet descended from chambers and the law clerk is also missing. The 40-50 person crowd is a mix of jurors, attorneys, and parties.

20. As an initial order of business, what should the court officer be concerned with? 20.____
    A. Taming the crowd
    B. Locating the judge
    C. Locating the law clerk
    D. Sending prospective jurors upstairs to the jury pool room

21. Two attorneys' voices have risen above all the rest. It is unclear whether they are shouting at one another in anger or catching up on old times. They are attracting onlookers as their conversation grows more animated. What is the MOST appropriate action for the court officer to take? 21.____
    A. Separate the two attorneys
    B. Ask that they lower their voices or speak privately in another area of the courthouse
    C. Sequester the jurors
    D. Ask that the two attorneys step into the courtroom to resolve their dispute

22. Some of the members of the crowd seem to be holding a single white sheet of paper which appears to be a summons. What is the MOST reasonable next step? The court officer should 22.____
    A. ask those with a summons to head upstairs to check in with the clerk
    B. sequester summons holders to the side to confer with one another
    C. ask that those people sued stay put for now
    D. ask the law clerk to announce herself to the possible defendants in the room

23. How should the court officer categorize and separate the crowd? 23.____
    A. Separate by the time each person arrived
    B. Separate by those with counsel present
    C. Separate by the reason he or she is at the courthouse
    D. Separate by age, gender, then race

24. In determining where each individual rightfully belongs, the court officer should be most familiar with which of the following? 24.____
    A. The location of each judge's chamber
    B. The times when each law clerk is scheduled to arrive at the courthouse
    C. The location of the clerk's desk, courtrooms, and preliminary hearing conference area
    D. The security desk and exits of the courthouse

25. At what juncture should the judge be notified that a large crowd has amassed outside the courtroom? 25.____
    A. Only if he or she asks
    B. After the trial has begun
    C. After the crowd has formed
    D. The clerk should be informed, but not the judge

KEY (CORRECT ANSWERS)

1. C
2. A
3. B
4. A
5. D

6. B
7. B
8. D
9. D
10. A

11. A
12. B
13. C
14. B
15. A

16. A
17. D
18. D
19. B
20. A

21. B
22. A
23. C
24. C
25. C

TEST 2

DIRECTIONS: Each question or incomplete statement is followed by several suggested answers or completions. Select the one that BEST answers the question or completes the statement. *PRINT THE LETTER OF THE CORRECT ANSWER IN THE SPACE AT THE RIGHT.*

Questions 1-4.

DIRECTIONS: Questions 1 through 4 are to be answered on the basis of the following fact pattern.

Steven is on trial for embezzlement. The case is complex; there are eight witnesses for the prosecution and twelve witnesses for the defense, including character witnesses. Steven has filed a cross-claim against his former employer, and plaintiff, ABC Corp., Inc., for defamation of character. Steven maintains that he never stole a dime from ABC Corp., Inc. and wants ABC Corp., Inc. to issue him a public apology when the trial is over.

1. The BEST place to refer back to the testimony of one witness is 1.____
   A. the docket B. the judge's notes
   C. the stenographer's transcript D. clerk notes

2. Steven's attorney presents evidence that his client was not working on the days the theft from ABC Corp. allegedly occurred. 2.____
   What kind of evidence is Steven's counsel presenting to the court?
   A. Alibi B. Exculpatory
   C. Exclusionary D. Exemplary

3. Alexandra, a friend of Steven, testifies for the prosecution in Steven's case. Alexandra testifies that Steven told her that he embezzled money from ABC Corp. 3.____
   Steven's attorney objects to Alexandra's testimony because it is
   A. exculpatory B. hearsay C. untrue D. impeachment

4. At the close of Steven's trial, oral arguments are made by _____ to the court, summarizing their position on the evidence that has been presented and their theories on the case in its entirety. 4.____
   A. jurors B. plaintiffs C. attorneys D. defense

Questions 5-8.

DIRECTIONS: Questions 5 through 8 are to be answered on the basis of the following fact pattern.

April 16 is turning out to be a very busy day at the courthouse. In the morning, three cases were withdrawn by the plaintiff without a hearing, six cases were dismissed without prejudice by the judge, and two cases were settled out of court.

5. How many were decided by the judge on April 16? 5.____
   A. 0 B. 2 C. 6 D. 3

6. How many cases were heard before the judge? 6.____
   A. 3 B. 6 C. 2 D. 8

7. How many cases would the court reporter need to be present for? 7.____
   A. 6 B. 3 C. 2 D. 8

8. How many of the cases were awarded damages? 8.____
   A. 2 B. 6 C. 3 D. 0

Questions 9-12.

DIRECTIONS: Questions 9 through 12 are to be answered on the basis of the following fact pattern.

Miranda has initiated a lawsuit against her former friend, Anne, for breach of contract. Miranda referred Anne's interior design services to Miranda's boss. Anne went to Miranda's boss's house for an initial consultation and, even though Anne agreed to design three rooms in the house, she never followed through with the contract. Miranda is incredibly embarrassed by the entire situation. Anne, however, maintains that she has a reasonable excuse for not finishing the work.

9. In addition to money damages, Miranda would also like the court to compel Anne to execute the contract or, in other words, actually design the rooms. This remedy is deemed 9.____
   A. compulsion under order
   B. specific performance
   C. remedy at law
   D. joint and several liability

10. Miranda alleges that she suffered pain and suffering from Anne's inability to execute the contract. What type of damages are pain and suffering categorized as? 10.____
    A. Punitive B. Special C. Specific D. Compensatory

11. Miranda lives in New York. Anne lives in New Jersey. Miranda's boss lives in Connecticut. When Miranda files suit in New York, the judge initially indicates that she does not have 11.____
    A. authority B. jurisdiction C. venue D. domicile

12. The contract that has allegedly been breached exists between Anne and Miranda's boss, not Miranda. Therefore, there is no legal cause of action for the case to proceed. Miranda's boss is free to file the claim against Anne at a later date if she so chooses. The court will 12.____
    A. dismiss the action without prejudice
    B. deny the action without prejudice
    C. sustain the action
    D. abdicate as necessary

13. Nominal damages are 13.____
    A. damages awarded in name only, indicating no substantial harm was done
    B. damages to recompense the injured for the infliction of emotional distress
    C. damages to recompense the initiator of the lawsuit
    D. a reimbursement of filing fees, awarded to the person who can prove they are injured

14. The type of recovery being sought by the plaintiff is known as the 14.____
    A. order B. punishment C. remedy D. issue

15. Robert approaches the clerk's desk in a panic. He says that he filed a lawsuit against his cousin, Mike, but neglected to add his cousin's friend, Rory, to the suit. What action is Robert attempting to take? 15.____
    A. Amending the complaint
    B. Adding an addendum to the summons
    C. Re-issuing a summons
    D. Redacting the answer

Questions 16-20.

DIRECTIONS: Questions 16 through 20 are to be answered on the basis of the following fact pattern.

Daniel and Patrick sue one another civilly. Daniel sues Patrick for intentional infliction of emotional distress and Patrick countersues Daniel for assault. Both causes of action stem from a physical altercation which took place at a youth hockey game where Daniel and Patrick's sons played against one another. At trial, the judge found that Daniel started the fight and attacked Patrick and found, by extension, that Patrick was not a contributor in the altercation.

Daniel appealed the decision to an appellate court. Daniel's attorney argued that the trial court erred, as a matter of law, in finding that Daniel was the sole initiator of the altercation and ignored evidence to the contrary. Appellate courts generally render decisions by a panel. The panel in Daniel's appeal was comprised of three justices. The appellate court agreed with the trial court's finding of fault.

16. The ultimate disposition of this case was the appellate court 16.____
    A. affirmed the lower court's decision
    B. remanded the lower court's decision
    C. reversed the lower court's decision
    D. acquitted Daniel of all charges

17. An opinion from the entire panel of justices is known as a 17.____
    A. per curiam decision B. affirmative decision
    C. stare decisis D. en banc order

18. One of the judges agrees with the decision of the court, but disagrees with the reasoning of the conclusion. The judge decides to write his own opinion. This is deemed a 18.____
    A. dissenting opinion B. remedial decision
    C. concurring opinion D. recurrent opinion

19. Suppose that one of the judges disagrees entirely with the ruling. 19.____
How will the judgment be altered because of the disagreement?
The judgment
A. is unaffected because the majority voted in agreement with the trial court
B. is unaffected because this judge did not author a dissenting opinion
C. is unaffected because oral arguments were not made before the panel
D. will be overturned

20. The appellate court still requires _____, even if it is established by the trial court, known as original _____. 20.____
A. domicile; venue
B. venue; jurisdiction
C. jurisdiction; jurisdiction
D. jurisdiction; domicile

21. The legal theory upon which a case is based is called a 21.____
A. basis
B. decisis
C. cause of action
D. precedent

Questions 22-25.

DIRECTIONS: Questions 22 through 25 are to be answered on the basis of the following fact pattern.

Last July, Sarah stole Alexis's car and took it for a joyride along Main Street. After a long joyride, Sarah decided to pick up Ashley at Ashley's apartment. Although Ashley asked when Sarah bought a new car, Sarah lied and told Ashley that it was her aunt's car that she borrowed with permission. Sarah and Ashley went on another joyride, this time driving up to 90 miles per hour on the highways around town. After three hours, Ashley asked to go home and Sarah obliged. After Sarah dropped Ashley back off at her apartment, Sarah sped through a busy intersection and crashed the car. The car was totaled.

Alexis has filed a lawsuit against both Sarah and Ashley.

22. Alexis is determined to sue both Sarah and Ashley for conversion, or the wrongful act of dominion or control over another person's property. However, after meeting with her attorney, Alexis decided she may not be able to prove each _____ of the alleged crime against Ashley. 22.____
A. stage
B. element
C. circumstance
D. remedy

23. After Alexis initiated her lawsuit against Sarah and Ashley, Ashley requested the court to remove her from the lawsuit altogether. She attested that she could not have participated in a crime if she did not know the car was stolen. 23.____
Her request to the court will come in the form of a
A. notice
b. motion
C. termination
D. demand

24. Ashley's attorney asks the judge to instruct the jury that it can consider mitigating factors in rendering a verdict against Ashley. 24.____
An example of a mitigating factor in this scenario would MOST likely be:
    A. Ashley does not know Alexis
    B. Sarah is no longer friends with Alexis
    C. Ashley asked Sarah about the origins of the car and Sarah's reply was untruthful
    D. Ashley and Sarah were working in cahoots to steal Alexis's car

25. During the time of the crime, Sarah was a minor. A minor is legally defined as 25.____
    A. someone who cannot think for themselves
    B. anyone under 21
    C. a legally emancipated individual
    D. an infant or individual under the age of legal competence

KEY (CORRECT ANSWERS)

1.	C	11.	B
2.	B	12.	A
3.	B	13.	A
4.	C	14.	C
5.	C	15.	A
6.	B	16.	A
7.	A	17.	A
8.	D	18.	C
9.	B	19.	A
10.	D	20.	C

21.	C
22.	B
23.	B
24.	C
25.	D

TEST 3

DIRECTIONS: Each question or incomplete statement is followed by several suggested answers or completions. Select the one that BEST answers the question or completes the statement. *PRINT THE LETTER OF THE CORRECT ANSWER IN THE SPACE AT THE RIGHT.*

Questions 1-4.

DIRECTIONS: Questions 1 through 4 are to be answered on the basis of the following fact pattern.

A complex civil litigation suit is set to begin between ABC Insurance Corp. and DEF Indemnity Corp. Adam represents ABC Insurance and Jane represents DEF Indemnity Corp. Multiple extensions have been granted to either side to conduct more extensive discovery. At the last conference scheduled before trial, the presiding judge is notably frustrated at the requested delays from both Adam and Jane. The presiding judge would like both parties to stipulate to as many points as possible.

1. Adam and Jane appear in the permanent record as _____ unless either withdrawn or are otherwise removed from the case. 1._____
   A. attorneys in time
   B. attorneys of record
   C. attorneys of the case
   D. permanent attorneys

2. The judge asks whether the parties have attempted to settle this matter in another forum, such as binding 2._____
   A. decision-making
   B. arbitration
   C. neutral court
   D. judgment arena

3. While the judge would like the parties to settle, he quickly realizes that it is not a possibility between these two parties. Adam and Jane continue to argue about various issues, including expert witnesses. Adam argues that Jane's expert witness, who will testify about financial crimes, is a quack. In response, Jane offers that her witness be _____, or testify under oath at a date prior to trial. 3._____
   A. sworn in
   B. indemnified
   C. deposed
   D. saddled

4. Which of the following is the LEAST appropriate behavior of the judge during a pretrial conference? 4._____
   A. Providing advice on Adam and Jane's legal strategy for trial
   B. Asking the parties to stipulate to the facts
   C. Remaining indifferent about the witnesses each party plans to call at trial
   D. Setting a date for trial more than three months away

5. A lawsuit with a single cause of action being breach of contract will be classified as what type of suit? 5._____
   A. Criminal
   B. Divisional
   C. Situational
   D. Civil

6. Sheila's mother passed away last week. She comes to the courthouse and asks about the probate process. You inform her that probate may not be necessary if she is the person named in the will as the individual who will administer her mother's estate. 6.____
This individual is otherwise known as the
   A. administrator B. guarantor C. creditor D. executor

7. Brandy would like her juvenile record expunged. What is she seeking to do? 7.____
She is requesting
   A. her record, or a portion of her record, be removed
   B. her record be sealed
   C. her record be unsealed
   D. to make her record unavailable to creditors

8. Having never met Jamie, a pro se litigant, Judge Smith strikes up a friendly conversation about the recent political climate in the elevator with him on the way to the courtroom. In the courtroom that afternoon, Jamie enters his appearance and says, "You and I are clearly already on the same page, Judge" in open court. Jamie's adversary, Courtney, requests that the judge recuse himself from the case. Why? 8.____
   A. Jamie and Judge Smith's political affiliations are unsavory.
   B. Judge Smith is clearly biased as evidenced by Jamie's comment.
   C. Judge Smith and Jamie have partaken in en banc communications.
   D. Judicial disqualification is appropriate if a conflict of interest would affect a judge's ruling

9. Emily appears at court with a crumbled notice in her hands. The clerk asks that you speak with Emily directly because Emily 9.____
   A. may be in danger of hurting others or herself
   B. may have a legal question that needs answering
   C. is in default and may need to be arrested
   D. would like to apply for a job at the courthouse

10. A conditional release from incarceration is known as 10.____
   A. an expungement B. a restitution
   C. parole D. reduced sentence

11. Tom paid a contractor to cut down a large pine tree in front of his house. The tree had grown so tall that it has started to interfere with the power lines running parallel to the street. As the contractor cut down the tree, a large gust of wind blew and the tree crashed down on top of his neighbor, Dane's, roof. Dane is suing Tom for failure to exercise the degree of care that a reasonable person would have exercised in the same circumstance. 11.____
Dane is suing Tom for
   A. lack of judgment B. breach of contract
   C. negligence D. conversion

12. Lawyers are generally prohibited from asking _____ questions of their own witnesses because they are suggestive, or prompt the witness to answer in a certain way. 12.____
    A. leading B. direct C. cross D. sustainable

13. One process that is generally private, and not heard in open court is(are) 13.____
    A. testimony of expert witnesses
    B. swearing in of jurors
    C. objections
    D. plea bargaining

14. The burden of proof in a civil case is _____ stringent than that in a criminal case. 14.____
    A. less B. more C. equally D. substantially

15. Justin is an attorney for Samuel. During Justin's closing arguments, he states that Samuel is innocent and would never harm another living being. May jurors consider Justin's statement made during closing arguments as evidence or fact? 15.____
    A. Yes, but only if compelling
    B. Yes, but only under the circumstances explained by the judge
    C. Yes, unconditionally
    D. No

16. In reviewing the court transcript, which of the following is the attorney LEAST likely to find? 16.____
    A. The judge's opinion on the case
    B. Testimony of the petitioner
    C. Attorneys of record
    D. Names of the expert witnesses

17. A mandatory injunction has the effect of 17.____
    A. requiring a party to do a particular act
    B. providing the option of a party to do a particular act
    C. requiring a party to report their actions
    D. providing the party an option to report their actions

18. James approaches the clerk's desk and asks how, generally, judges make their decisions on legal matters.
    The MOST correct answer would be based on 18.____
    A. case law, or the body of all court decisions which govern or provide precedent on the same legal issue before the judge
    B. case law, personal opinion and oral arguments by attorneys
    C. case law, oral arguments by attorneys and the defendant's rap sheet
    D. "stare decisis" or that which has already been decided

19. Which of the following individuals is LEAST likely to serve on a jury? 19.____
    A. Susan, who has been called numerous times but never served on a jury
    B. Bill, a supporter of labor unions and freelance political columnist
    C. Gary, who served on a murder trial 10 years ago
    D. Amy, a 16-year-old genius who just finished her junior year of college

20. If a grand jury decides there is enough evidence to move forward with criminal charges against a group or individual, they return a(n) 20.____
A. information B. indictment C. warrant D. seizure

21. Which of the following is MOST likely to cause an outburst in a courtroom? 21.____
A. Reading of the jury instructions
B. Sequestration of the jury
C. Reading of the sentence
D. Plea deal proceedings

22. During a lengthy murder trial, it is discovered that two of the jurors have been romantically involved. They have conspired with one another to enter votes of "not guilty" and attempt to sway other jurors in their favor in an attempt to close out deliberations early. 22.____
What is the likely outcome of the trial?
A. Hung jury
B. Mistrial
C. Acquittal
D. Defensive charge

23. The judge's charge to the jury is also known as 23.____
A. voir dire
B. en banc
C. jury instructions
D. sua sponte

24. Who is MOST likely to deliver the sentence to the convicted? 24.____
A. Bailiff
B. Jury
C. Judge
D. Jury foreperson

25. A motion for directed verdict is made 25.____
A. without the jury present
B. with only the jury foreperson present
C. with the entire jury present
D. with only the alternate jurors present

KEY (CORRECT ANSWERS)

1. B
2. B
3. C
4. A
5. D

6. D
7. A
8. D
9. A
10. C

11. C
12. A
13. D
14. A
15. D

16. A
17. A
18. A
19. D
20. B

21. C
22. B
23. C
24. C
25. A

TEST 4

DIRECTIONS: Each question or incomplete statement is followed by several suggested answers or completions. Select the one that BEST answers the question or completes the statement. *PRINT THE LETTER OF THE CORRECT ANSWER IN THE SPACE AT THE RIGHT.*

Questions 1-6.

DIRECTIONS: Questions 1 through 6 are to be answered on the basis of the following fact pattern.

Damien is accused of heinous crimes against a minor. He is charged with rape of a child, conspiracy to murder, and armed robbery. During the commission of the crime, it is alleged that Damien called his friend, Alex, and asked that he come to the scene of the crime and kill the minor's parents. Damien and Alex are on trial together, but Alex is charged with lesser crimes given that his involvement may have been limited. The trial is lengthy and a large crowd has gathered outside the courtroom each day of testimony.

1. The prosecutors allege that Alex agreed to help Damien commit the crimes because Damien has a propensity for violence and may have threatened to kill Alex if he did not help. The prosecutors are presenting 1.____
   A. evidence B. testimony C. motive D. supposition

2. The intense nature of the court proceedings may require which of the following? 2.____
   A. Increased law enforcement presence
   B. Increased legal analysis
   C. More jurors
   D. More law clerks

3. During the presentation of evidence, the judge is likely to require exhibits be passed to the court officer, who will then present them to the jury, instead of the attorneys, to ensure 3.____
   A. the evidence is not tampered with by the attorneys
   B. a smooth and orderly presentation
   C. the materials are not lost in transit
   D. each item in evidence is numbered correctly

4. Evidence against Damien is presented first. The prosecutor presents testimony from eyewitnesses, other than Alex, that place Damien at the scene of the crime. 4.____
   This evidence is deemed
   A. inculpatory B. explanatory C. involuntary D. dismissive

5. Alex decides to take the stand in his own defense. While on the stand, he declines to invoke his right not to incriminate himself.
Alex is referring to which Constitutional Amendment?
A. Eighth B. Ninth C. Fourth D. Fifth

5.____

6. During the presentation of closing arguments, the victims' stepfather, Bob, becomes enraged. As the defense attorney speaks to the jury, Bob starts screaming and demands justice.
The MOST appropriate response to Bob's disruption of court proceedings is to
A. let Bob calm down on his own
B. eject Bob from the courtroom
C. handcuff Bob
D. allow Bob to continue after a stern warning that he lower his voice

6.____

7. During downtime, which of the following is the LEAST appropriate action a court officer can take?
A. Monitoring courtrooms and hallways for suspicious activity
B. Managing the metal detectors
C. Watching and managing doorways
D. Answering legal questions from the general public

7.____

8. Jessica approaches one of the court officers in the entrance of the Herkimer County Supreme Court and states that she has a disassembled firearm in her vehicle.
The MOST appropriate response to this information is:
A. Make other court officers aware of her admission and monitor Jessica's comings and goings
B. Detain Jessica until police officers arrive
C. Arrange for Jessica to bring the firearm into the courthouse so that it can be locked away in a storage locker
D. Ask Jessica for her license to carry and make a photocopy for court records

8.____

9. Which of the following is MOST likely to occur after opening arguments in a trial?
A. Presentation of evidence B. Jury instructions
C. Closing arguments D. Arraignment

9.____

10. After the judge orders Paul to stay away from Amy in a ruling regarding Amy's request for a temporary restraining order, Paul is overheard in a court hallway that he plans on killing Amy and the judge.
The first party that should be notified is
A. the law clerk B. local police department
C. the jurors in Amy and Paul's trial D. the U.S. Marshals

10.____

Questions 11-15.

DIRECTIONS: Questions 11 through 15 are to be answered on the basis of the following fact pattern.

During a highly publicized and complex trial in the Oswego County Supreme Court, jurors have been isolated from friends and family members. The jurors are staying at the local Ramada Inn. Multiple court officers have been dispatched to the hotel and oversee the transport of the jurors to the courtroom each morning and night.

11. The jurors are being 11.____
   A. sequestered B. influenced C. disposed D. indicted

12. One of the jurors has fallen ill during the trial. Given that one juror can no longer serve, what is the procedure? 12.____
   A. The jury will be comprised of eleven jurors.
   B. The trial will halt until the ill juror feels better.
   C. An alternate juror will serve on the jury.
   D. The jury will go on with six jurors.

13. One of the jurors has been seen texting on his cellphone during the transport to the hotel at night. 13.____
Which is the LEAST appropriate response to this rumor?
   A. Confiscate the juror's phone and inform the judge
   B. Ask to see the juror's text messages so you can delete the text history
   C. Ignore the rumors
   D. Tell the other court officer about the rumor but otherwise ignore it

14. What is the likely outcome of the texting juror? 14.____
The juror will
   A. likely be allowed to remain on the jury
   B. likely be asked to hand over his or her phone and other electronic devices
   C. likely be dismissed form the trial and replaced
   D. be allowed to keep communicating with the outside but will be closely monitored

15. The trial has finally ended and the jury has started deliberations. After nearly two weeks, the jury has been unable to arrive at a decision. 15.____
This is deemed a
   A. final jury B. deliberate jury
   C. mistrial D. hung jury

16. A previously convicted felon, Tim, is on trial for the conspiracy to kill his cellmate in prison. Tim is MOST likely going to be _____ at all times during court proceedings. 16.____
   A. restrained B. redacted
   C. unaccompanied D. redeemed

17. Which of the following is a court officer duty that specifically relates to witness testimony? 17.____
    A. Assisting witnesses leaving the stand
    B. Help witnesses remember their testimony
    C. Relay messages directly from the witnesses to the judge
    D. Engage witnesses in the service of the domestic violence unit if needed

18. As Sarah waits for the judge to enter the courtroom and commence hearings, she opens her purse and pulls out a sandwich and begins to eat it. The court officer informs her that she cannot eat in the courtroom and must leave the building if she want to have food or a beverage. Sarah continues to eat the food and laments that since the judge is not in the courtroom, she should be able to eat. 18.____
    The court officer is MOST likely going to
    A. eject Sarah from the courtroom
    B. allow Sarah to eat until the judge enters the courtroom
    C. allow Sarah to eat as she has a valid point
    D. confiscate Sarah's sandwich

19. Which of the following may require the law clerk's assistance? 19.____
    A. Removal of an unruly individual from the courtroom
    B. Determining which person in a court proceeding is the plaintiff, defendant, or witness
    C. Obtaining personal information from the defendant
    D. Relaying a message to the judge that relates to a personal matter

Questions 20-25.

DIRECTIONS: Questions 20 through 2 are to be answered on the basis of the following fact pattern.

Eric's attorney, Rich, alleges that Eric is not __1__ to stand trial. As a child, Eric was the victim of abuse and as a result may be mentally ill. Eric is accused of murder in the second degree. At trial, Eric's friend, Ross, claims that Eric told him he murdered a young woman. Rich objects to Ross's testimony as it is __2__ and not conclusory of Eric's guilt. Another witness claims that they saw Eric at the scene of the crime, but does not remember seeing Eric with another person. This witness is a twice-convicted felon and is not deemed __3__ by the jury. At the conclusion of the evidence as presented by the attorney, Eric is found guilty.

20. Fill in blank #1: 20.____
    A. mentally well B. competent C. jurisdiction D. venue

21. Fill in blank #2: 21.____
    A. motive B. evidentiary C. hearsay D. realistic

22. Fill in blank #3: 22.____
    A. credible B. justifiable C. plausible D. tangible

23. The victim's family is allowed to make a victim impact statement. At which juncture is the victim impact statement allowed to be heard? 23.____
    A. Sentencing and/or subsequent parole hearings
    B. Prior to jury instructions
    C. After closing arguments
    D. As testimony read into the record

24. Closing arguments enable each party's attorney to 24.____
    A. present new evidence in the trial
    B. summarize the legal and factual points for their side of the case
    C. analyze the jury's reaction to their evidence
    D. provide additional details and analysis to the opinions of the expert witnesses

25. Sylvia asks that a court officer escort her to her car after her foreclosure proceedings. Her foreclosure hearings were not adversarial and Sylvia does not appear to be in imminent harm. The MOST appropriate response to Sylvia's request is to 25.____
    A. ensure there is proper officer coverage inside the courthouse, then escort Sylvia to her car
    B. decline Sylvia's request given that she was only in the courthouse for foreclosure proceedings
    C. decline Sylvia's request as she is not in imminent danger
    D. ignore Sylvia

KEY (CORRECT ANSWERS)

1. C
2. A
3. B
4. A
5. D

6. B
7. D
8. A
9. A
10. B

11. A
12. C
13. C
14. C
15. D

16. A
17. A
18. A
19. B
20. B

21. C
22. A
23. A
24. B
25. A

EXAMINATION SECTION

TEST 1

DIRECTIONS: Each question or incomplete statement is followed by several suggested answers or completions. Select the one that BEST answers the question or completes the statement. *PRINT THE LETTER OF THE CORRECT ANSWER IN THE SPACE AT THE RIGHT.*

Questions 1-4 are based solely on the information in the paragraph below:

A Court Officer shall give reasonable aid to a sick or injured person. He or she shall summon an ambulance, if necessary, by telephoning the Police Department, which shall notify the hospital. He or she shall wait in a place where the arriving ambulance can see him or her, if possible, so as to direct the ambulance attendant to the patient. If the ambulance does not arrive within a half-hour, the Court Officer should call a second time, telling the department that this is a second call. However, if the injured person is conscious, the Court Officer should ask whether such person is willing to go to a hospital before calling for an ambulance.

1. The Court Officer who wishes to summon an ambulance should telephone the 1.______
   A. nearest hospital
   B. Health and Hospitals Corporation
   C. Police Department
   D. nearest police precinct

2. If an ambulance does not arrive within half an hour, the Court Officer should 2.______
   A. ask the person injured if he/she wants to go to the hospital in a cab
   B. call the Police Department
   C. call the nearest police precinct
   D. call the nearest hospital

3. A Court Officer who is called to help a person who has fallen on the courthouse steps and apparently has a broken leg should 3.______
   A. put the leg in traction so the doctor will have no difficulty setting it
   B. ask the person, if he/she is conscious, whether he/she wishes to go to the hospital
   C. attempt to get the story behind the injury
   D. put in a call for an ambulance at once

4. A Court Officer who is present when a witness becomes ill while waiting to testify should 4.______
   A. wait in front of the room until the ambulance arrives
   B. send a bystander to the courtroom to page a doctor
   C. ask the withness if he/she wishes to go to a hospital
   D. call the Court Clerk for instructions

5. "Physical and mental health are essential to the Court Officer." 5.______
According to this statement, a peace officer must be
   A. wise as well as strong
   B. smarter than most people
   C. sound in mind and body
   D. smarter than the average criminal

6. "Teamwork is the basis of successful law enforcement." 6.______
The factor stressed by this statement is
   A. cooperation
   B. determination
   C. initiative
   D. pride

7. "A sufficient quantity of material supplied as evidence enables the laboratory expert to determine the true nature of the substance, whereas an extremely limited specimen may be an abnormal sample containing foreign matter not indicative of the true nature of the material." 7.______
On the basis of this statement alone, it may be concluded that a reason for giving an adequate sample of material for evidence to a laboratory expert is that
   A. a limited specimen spoils more quickly than a larger sample
   B. a small sample may not truly represent the evidence
   C. he or she cannot analyze a small sample correctly
   D. he or she must have enough material to keep a part of it untouched to show in court

8. "The Housing Authority not only faces every problem of the private developer, it must also assume responsibilities of which a private building is free. The authority must account to the community; it must conform to Federal regulations and it must overcome the prejudices of contractors, bankers and prospective tenants against public operations. These authorities are being watched for the first error of judgment or the first evidence of high costs that can be torn to bits before a congressional committee." 8.______
On the basis of this selection, which statement would be most correct?
   A. Private builders do not have the opposition of contractors, bankers and prospective tenants
   B. Congressional committees impede the progress of public housing by petty investigations
   C. A housing authority must deal with all the difficulties encountered by the private builder
   D. Housing authorities are not more immune to errors in judgment than private developers

9. Accident proneness is a subject that deserves much more objective and competent study than it has received to date. In discussing accident proneness, it is important to differentiate between the employee who is a "repeater" and one who is truly accident-prone. It is obvious that any person assigned to work without thorough training is liable to injury until he or she does learn the "how" of it. Few workers left to their own devices develop adequate safe practices, and therefore they must be trained. Only those who fail to respond to proper training should be regarded as accident-prone. The repeater whose accident record can be explained by a correctable physical defect, correctable plant or machine hazards, or by assignment to work for which he or she is not suited because of physical deficiencies or special abilities cannot be fairly called accident-prone. 9.______
According to the passage, people are considered accident-prone if
   A. they have accidents regardless of the fact that they have been properly trained
   B. they have many accidents
   C. it is possible for them to have accidents
   D. they work at a job where accidents are possible

Questions 10 through 12 are based on the following paragraph:

Discontent of some citizens with the practices and policies of local government leads to the creation of local civic associations. Completely outside of government, manned by a few devoted volunteers, understaffed, and with pitifully few dues-paying members, they attempt to arouse widespread public opinion on selected issues by presenting facts and ideas. The findings of these civic associations are widely trusted by the press and public, and amidst the records of rebuffs received are found more than enough achievements to justify what little their activities cost. Civic associations are politically non-partisan. Hence their vitality is drawn from true political independents who in most communities are a trifling minority. Except in a few large cities, civic associations are seldom affluent enough to maintain an office or to afford even a small paid staff.

10. The main reason for the formation of civic associations is to 10.______
   A. provide independent candidates for local public office with an opportunity to be heard
   B. bring about changes in the activities of local government
   C. allow persons who are politically non-partisan to express themselves on local public issues
   D. permit the small minority of true political independents to supply leadership for non-partisan causes

11. The statements that civic associations make on issues of general interest are 11.______
   A. accepted by large segments of the public
   B. taken at face value only by the few people who are truc political independents
   C. questioned as to their accuracy by most newspapers
   D. expressed as a result of aroused widespread public opinion

12. It is most accurate to conclude that since 12.______
    A. they deal with many public issues, the cost of their efforts on each issue is small
    B. their attempts to attain their objectives often fail, little money is contributed to civic associations
    C. they spend little money in their efforts, they are ineffective when they become involved in major issues
    D. their achievements outweigh the small cost of their efforts, civic associations are considered worthwhile

13. "If you are in doubt as to whether any matter is properly mailable, you should ask the postmaster. Even though the post office has not expressly declared any matter to be nonmailable, the sender of such matter may be held fully liable for violation of law if he does actually send nonmailable matter through the mails." 13.______
    Of the following, the most accurate statement made concerning this selection is
    A. nonmailable matter is not always clearly defined
    B. ignorance of what constitutes nonmailable matter relieves the sender of all responsibility
    C. though doubt may exist about the mailability of any matter, the sender is fully liable for any law violation if such matter should be nonmailable
    D. the post office is not explicit in its position on the violation of the nonmailable matter law

Questions 14 through 16 are based on the following paragraph:

What is required is a program that will protect our citizens and their property from criminal and anti-social acts, will effectively restrain and reform juvenile delinquents, and will prevent the further development of anti-social behavior. Discipline and punishment of offenders must necessarily play an important part in any such program. Serious offenders cannot be mollycoddled merely because they are under 21. Restraint and punishment necessarily follow serious anti-social acts. But punishment, if it is to be effective, must be a planned part of a more comprehensive program of treating delinquency.

14. The one goal not included among those listed in the paragraph is to 14.______
    A. stop young people from defacing public property
    B. keep homes from being broken into
    C. develop an intra-city boys baseball league
    D. change juvenile delinquents into useful citizens

15. Punishment is 15.______
    A. not satisfactory in any program dealing with juvenile delinquents
    B. the most effective means by which young vandals and hooligans can be reformed
    C. not used sufficiently when dealing with serious offenders who are under 21
    D. of value in reducing juvenile delinquency only if it is part of a complete program

16. With respect to serious offenders who are under 21 years of age, the paragraph suggests that they 16.______
    A. be mollycoddled
    B. be dealt with as part of a comprehensive program to punish mature criminals
    C. should be punished
    D. be prevented, by brute force if necessary, from performing anti-social acts

17. Statistics tell us that heart disease kills more people than any other illness, and the death rate continues to rise. People over 30 have a 50-50 chance of escaping, for heart disease is chiefly an illness of people in late middle age and advanced years. Since more people in this age group are living today than were some years ago, heart disease is able to find more victims. 17.______
    On the basis of this selection, the statement which is most nearly correct is that
    A. half the people over 30 years of age have heart disease today
    B. more people die of heart disease than of all other diseases combined
    C. older people are the chief victims of heart disease
    D. the rising birth rate has increased the possibility that the average person will die of heart disease

18. Assume that a Court Officer is allowed 25 cents a mile for the use of her automobile for the purpose of conducting defendants to and from court sessions. The first month she drove 416 miles; the second month 328 miles; the third month 2,012 miles; the fourth month 187 miles; the fifth month 713 miles; the sixth month 1,608 miles. Her expenditures for gasoline averaged $2.70 a gallon and her general average of miles per gallon was 16; she used 32 quarts of oil at $1.25 per quart and spent $351.20 on care and general upkeep of her car for the six months. Without considering the depreciation in value of her car, she would have received above her expenditures: 18.______
    A. $36.50
    B. $40
    C. $96.10
    D. $263.20

19. Assume that you borrowed $2,000 on Nov. 1, 1999, for the use of which you were required to pay simple interest semi-annually at seven percent a year. By May 1, 2005, you would have paid interest amounting to 19.______
    A. $140
    B. $280
    C. $700
    D. $770

20. A courtroom contains 72 persons, which is two-fifths of its capacity. The number of persons that the courtroom can hold is 20.______
    A. 28 B. 129 C. 180 D. 200-300

21. The total cost of 30 pencils at 18 cents a dozen, 12 paper pads at 27-1/2 cents each and eight boxes of paper clips at 5-1/4 cents a box is 21.______
    A. more than $10
    B. $1.50
    C. $4.17
    D. $1.52

22. "A" worked five days on overhauling an old car. Then "B" worked four days to finish the job. After the sale of the car, the net profit was $243. They wanted to divide the profit on the basis of time spent by each. A's share of the profit was 22.______
    A. $108
    B. $135
    C. $127
    D. $143

Questions 23-26

DIRECTIONS: Each of the following questions contains four sentences. Select the sentence in each question that is best with respect to grammar and good usage.

23. A. One of us have to make the reply before tomorrow. 23.______
    B. Making the reply before tomorrow will have to be done by one of us.
    C. One of us has to reply before tomorrow.
    D. Anyone has to reply before tomorrow.

24. A. There is several ways to organize a good report. 24.______
    B. Several ways exist in organizing a good report.
    C. To organize a good report, several ways exist.
    D. There are several ways to organize a good report.

25. A. All employees whose record of service ranged between 51 down to 40 years were retired. 25.______
    B. All employees who had served from 40 to 51 years were retired.
    C. All employees serving 40 to 51 years were retired.
    D. Those retired were employees serving 40 to 51 years.

26. A. Of all the employees, he spends the most time at the office. 26.______
    B. He spends more time at the office than that of his employees.
    C. His working hours are longer than or equal to those of other employees.
    D. He devotes as much, if not more, time to his work than the rest of the employees.

Question 27 is based on the following paragraph:

Certain inmate types are generally found in prisons. These types are called gorillas, toughs, hipsters and merchants. Gorillas deliberately use violence to intimidate fearful inmates into providing favors. Toughs are swift to explode into violence against prisoners, because of real or imagined insults. Exploitation of others is not their major goal. Hipsters are bullies who choose victims with caution in order to win acceptance among inmates by demonstrating physical bravery. Their bravery, however, is false. Merchants exploit other inmates through manipulation in sharp trading of goods stolen from prison supplies or in trickery in gambling.

27. Martins frequently beats up Smith and Brooks. Smith and Brooks provide Martins with extra cigarettes and coffee. Martins is a 27.______
    A. tough
    B. gorilla
    C. merchant
    D. hipster

Questions 28 through 30 are based on the following description of the duties of the Court Officer:

Throughout the session of the court, the officer must see that proper order and decorum are maintained in the courtroom. Above all else, silence must be constantly observed, and every possible distraction must be eliminated so as not to delay the most efficient functioning of the court.

The officer must carry out such duties as may be required by the court and clerk. Examples of such duties are directing witnesses to the witness stand and assisting the Court Clerk and counsel in the handling of exhibits. At times, the officer must act as a messenger in procuring any books from the court library that are required by the attorneys and ordered by the Court Clerk.

The enforcement of the rules of the court requires courteous behavior on the part of the Court Officer, although firmness and strictness are necessary when the occasion requires such an attitude.

28. Testimony has been given, the witnesses have been cross-examined and the attorneys have given their summations. Now the judge is charging the jury. A Court Officer has been stationed outside the courtroom door to prevent anyone from entering during the charge. The City Council President arrives, accompanied by a woman, and attempts to enter the courtroom. The Court Officer should 28.______
    A. apologize and explain why they cannot be permitted to enter
    B. permit the man to enter, since he is the City Council President, but exclude the woman
    C. permit them to enter because surely the judge would make an exception for such important people
    D. send a note to the judge to ask whether they may be permitted to enter

29. A witness who is waiting to be called to the stand appears to be very nervous. He wiggles and squirms, stands and stretches, looks over his shoulder at the courtroom door and waves to spectators. The officer should 29.______
    A. tell the witness to leave the courtroom at once
    B. handcuff the witness
    C. ask the witness to please sit still and try to restrain himself
    D. suggest to the judge that he call this witness next

30. During the course of cross-examination, a defendant frequently refers to a book that she claims has had a great influence on her life and that she claims justifies her behavior in the crime for which she is charged. In the jury box, two jurors begin a lively discussion of whether the defendant is quoting accurately. The best action for the Court Officer is to 30.______
    A. ask the Court Clerk for permission to go to the library to get the book
    B. send a messenger to get the book
    C. assure the jurors that the book is being accurately quoted and that only the interpretation is in question
    D. remind the jurors that they are not to converse in the courtroom

31. "Ideally, a correctional system should include several types of institutions to provide different degrees of custody." 31.______
    On the basis of this statement, one could most reasonably say that
    A. as the number of institutions in a correctional system increases, the efficiency of the system increases
    B. the difference in degree of custody for the inmate depends on the types of institutions in a correctional system
    C. the greater the variety of institutions, the stricter the degree of custody that can be maintained
    D. the same type of correctional institution is not desirable for the custody of all prisoners

32. "The enforced idleness of a large percentage of adult men and women in our prisons is one of the direct causes of the tensions that burst forth in riot and disorder." 32.______
    On the basis of this statement, a good reason why inmates should perform daily work of some kind is that
    A. better morale and discipline can be maintained when inmates are kept busy
    B. daily work is an effective way of punishing inmates for the crimes they have committed
    C. law-abiding citizens must work therefore labor should also be required of inmates
    D. products of inmates' labor will in part pay the cost of their maintenance

33. "With industry invading rural areas, the use of the automobile, and the speed of modern communications and transportation, the problems of neglect and delinquency are no longer peculiar to cities but are an established feature of everyday life." 33.______
This statement implies most directly that
    A. delinquents are moving from cities to rural areas
    B. delinquency and neglect are found in rural areas
    C. delinquency is not as much of a problem in rural areas as in cities
    D. rural areas now surpass cities in industry

34. "Young men from minority groups, if unable to find employment, become discouraged and hopeless because of their economic position and may finally resort to any means of supplying their wants." 34.______
The most reasonable of the following conclusions that may be drawn from this statement only is that
    A. discouragement sometimes leads to crime
    B. in general, young men from minority groups are criminals
    C. unemployment turns young men from crime
    D. young men from minority groups are seldom employed

35. "To prevent crime, we must deal with the possible criminals long before they reach the prison. Our aim should be not merely to reform the lawbreakers but to strike at the roots of crime: neglectful parents, bad companions, unsatisfactory homes, selfishness, disregard for the rights of others and bad social conditions." 35.______
The above statement recommends
    A. abolition of prisons
    B. better reformatories
    C. compulsory education
    D. general social reform

36. "There is evidence that shows that comic books which glorify the criminal and criminal acts have a distinct influence in producing young criminals." 36.______
According to this statement
    A. comic books affect the development of criminal careers
    B. comic books specialize in reporting criminal acts
    C. young criminals read comic books exclusively
    D. young criminals should not be permitted to read comic books

37. A study shows that juvenile delinquents are equal in intelligence to but three school grades behind juvenile nondelinquents. On the basis of this information only, it is most reasonable to say that 37.______
    A. a delinquent usually progresses to the educational limit set by intelligence
    B. educational achievement depends on intelligence only
    C. educational achievement is closely associated with delinquency
    D. lack of intelligence is closely associated with delinquency

38. "Prevention of crime is of greater value to the community than the punishment of crime." 38.______
If this statement is accepted as true, greatest emphasis should be placed on
   A. execution
   B. medication
   C. imprisonment
   D. rehabilitation

39. A Court Assistant being instructed in his duties was told by the Court Clerk, "experience is the best teacher." 39.______
The one of the following that most nearly expresses the meaning of this quotation is:
   A. A good teacher will make a hard job look easy
   B. Bad experience does more harm than good
   C. Lack of experience will make an easy job hard
   D. The best way to learn to do a thing is by doing it

40. "Once the purposes or goals of an organization have been determined, they must be communicated to subordinate levels of supervisory staff." 40.______
On the basis of this quotation, the most accurate statement is that
   A. supervisory personnel should participate in the formulation of the goals of an organization
   B. the structure of an organization should be considered in determining the organization's goals
   C. the goals that have been established for the different levels of an organization should be reviewed regularly
   D. information about the goals of an organization should be distributed to supervisory personnel

41. "Close examination of traffic accident statistics reveals that traffic accidents are frequently the result of violations of traffic laws—and usually the violations are the result of illegal and dangerous driving behavior, rather than the result of mechanical defects or poor road conditions." 41.______
According to this statement, the majority of dangerous traffic violations are cause by
   A. poor driving
   B. bad roads
   C. unsafe cars
   D. unwise traffic laws

Questions 42 through 44 are based on the following paragraph:

The supervisor gains the respect of his staff members and increases his influence over them by controlling his temper and avoiding criticizing anyone publicly. When a mistake is made, the good supervisor will talk it over with the employee quietly and privately. The supervisor listens to the employee's story, suggests a better way to do the job, and offers help so the mistake won't happen again. Before closing the discussion, the supervisor should try to find something good to say about other aspects of the employee's work. Some praise and appreciation, along with instruction, is likely to encourage an employee to improve in those areas where he is weakest.

42. A good title that would show the meaning of this entire paragraph would be: 42.______
    A. How to Correct Employee Errors
    B. How to Praise Employees
    C. Mistakes are Preventable
    D. The Weak Employee

43. According to the preceding paragraph, the work of an employee who has made a mistake is more likely to improve if the supervisor 43.______
    A. avoids criticizing him
    B. gives him a chance to suggest a better way of doing the work
    C. listens to the employee's excuses to see if he's right
    D. praises good work at the same time he corrects the mistake

44. When a supervisor needs to correct an employee's mistake, it is important that he 44.______
    A. allow some time to go by after the mistake has been made
    B. do so when other employees are not present
    C. show his influence by his tone of voice
    D. tell other employees to avoid the same mistake

45. "Determination of total, or even partial, guilt and responsibility as viewed by law cannot be made solely on the basis of a consideration of the external factors of the case, but rather should be made mainly in the light of the individual defendant's history and development." 45.______
    The above statement reflects a philosophy of law that requires that
    A. the punishment fit the crime
    B. the individual, rather than the crime, be considered first
    C. motivations behind a crime are relatively unimportant
    D. the individual's knowledge of right and wrong be the sole determinant of guilt

46. A traffic regulation says, "No driver shall enter an intersection unless there is sufficient unobstructed space beyond the intersection to accommodate the vehicle he or she is operating, not withstanding any traffic-control signal indication to the contrary." 46.______
This regulation means that:
    A. a driver should not go through an intersection if there are no parking spaces available on the next block
    B. a driver should not enter an intersection when the traffic light is red
    C. a driver should not enter an intersection if traffic ahead is so badly backed up that he or she would not be able to go ahead and would block the intersection
    D. a driver should ignore traffic signals completely whenever there are obstructions in the road ahead

Questions 47 through 51 are based on the following passage:

A large proportion of people behind bars are not convicted criminals, but people who have been arrested and are being held until their trial in court. Experts have often pointed out that this detention system does not operate fairly. For instance, a person who can afford to pay bail usually will not get locked up.

The theory of the bail system is that the person will make sure to show up in court when he or she is supposed to; otherwise, bail will be forfeited—the person will lose the money that was put up. Sometimes a person who can show that he or she is a stable citizen with a job and a family will be released on "personal recognizance" (without bail). The result is that the well-to-do, the employed and the family men can often avoid the detention system. The people who do wind up in detention tend to be the poor, the unemployed, the single and the young.

47. People who are put behind bars 47.______
    A. are almost always dangerous criminals
    B. include many innocent people who have been arrested by mistake
    C. are often people who have been arrested but have not yet come to trial
    D. are all poor people who tend to be young and single

48. The passage says that the detention system works unfairly against people who are 48.______
    A. rich
    B. old
    C. married
    D. unemployed

49. The passage uses the expression "bail will be forfeited." Even if you had not seen the word *forfeit* before, you could figure out from the way it is used that forfeiting probably means __________ something. 49.______
    A. losing track of
    B. finding
    C. giving up
    D. avoiding

50. When someone is released on personal recognizance, this means that 50.______
    A. the judge knows that the person is innocent
    B. he or she does not have to show up for a trial
    C. he or she has a record of previous convictions
    D. he or she does not have to pay bail

51. Suppose that two men were booked on the same charge at the same time and that the same bail was set for both of them. One man was able to put up bail and was released. The second man was not able to put up bail and was held in detention. The writer of the passage would most likely feel that this result is 51.______
    A. unfair, because it does not have any relationship to guilt or innocence
    B. unfair, because the first man deserves severe punishment
    C. fair, because the first man is obviously innocent
    D. fair, because the law should be tougher on the poor people than on the rich

Questions 52 through 55 are based on the following passage:

The Court Officer has important functions in connection with control of the jury. He or she must confirm that every juror has the proper place in the box and must be constantly on watch to prevent any juror from leaving the jury box while the trial is in progress. Should a juror decide to leave the box while the case is going on, the Court Officer must first inform the judge of the juror's desire to determine whether the judge will grant or refuse the juror's wish. If the judge approves, the trial is stopped and the Court Officer is instructed to accompany the juror while he or she is out of the jury box.

In order to prevent any stoppage or mistrial, the Court Officer must not allow the juror to get out of the range of sight or hearing. The officer must always bear in mind that the juror should be returned as quickly as possible, without any unnecessary delay. The juror must not enter into any conversation with anybody or read any matter that he or she may have or that may be given by another person.

The Court Officer must be particularly careful when placed in charge of a jury that has retired to deliberate. The Court Officer must conduct the jury to the jury room and see to it that no juror talks with anyone on the way. If a juror does talk with someone, the event may afford grounds for a mistrial.

52. A juror has requested and received permission to go to the men's room. As he approaches the door, he takes out a sports magazine he has brought from home as "bathroom literature." The Court Officer should 52.______
    A. permit the juror to read the magazine
    B. check the magazine for papers that might be hidden between the pages, then let the juror read it
    C. offer the juror something of his own to read, something that he knows will not influence the juror in any way
    D. tell the juror that reading in the men's room is not permitted

53. While leading a jury from the courtroom to the jury room, a Court Officer notices a person leaning against a corridor wall making active hand motions as a juror stares intently. The *first* thing for a Court Officer to do is 53.______
    A. tell the juror to look straight ahead and keep walking
    B. step between the juror and the person so as to interrupt the juror's line of vision
    C. ask the juror what he is looking at
    D. call a police officer to arrest the person with the active hands

54. If the Court Officer ascertains that a message has been transmitted by an outside person to a juror, it would be best for the Court Officer to 54.______
    A. keep this information secret
    B. ask the juror what the message was about
    C. deliver the juror to the jury room, then discuss the matter with the Court Clerk
    D. accompany the juror to the judge and tell the judge exactly what the Court Officer observed

55. During the course of testimony, a juror begins to cough uncontrollably. The coughing is loud and distressing. The Court Officer should 55.______
    A. summon a doctor at once
    B. lead the juror from the courtroom as quickly and quietly as possible
    C. bring the juror a glass of water
    D. ask the judge what to do

KEY (CORRECT ANSWERS)

1. C	11. A	21. C	31. D	41. A	51. A
2. B	12. D	22. B	32. A	42. A	52. D
3. B	13. C	23. C	33. B	43. D	53. A
4. C	14. C	24. D	34. A	44. B	54. B
5. C	15. D	25. B	35. D	45. B	55. B
6. A	16. C	26. A	36. A	46. C	
7. B	17. C	27. B	37. C	47. C	
8. C	18. A	28. A	38. D	48. D	
9. A	19. D	29. C	39. D	49. C	
10. A	20. C	30. D	40. D	50. D	

EXAMINATION SECTION
TEST 1

DIRECTIONS: Each question or incomplete statement is followed by several suggested answers or completions. Select the one that BEST answers the question or completes the statement. *PRINT THE LETTER OF THE CORRECT ANSWER IN THE SPACE AT THE RIGHT.*

1. Physical and mental health are essential to the officer. According to this statement, the officer MUST be 1.____

   A. as wise as he is strong
   B. smarter than most people
   C. sound in mind and body
   D. stronger than the average criminal

2. Teamwork is the basis of successful law enforcement. The factor stressed by this statement is 2.____

   A. cooperation
   B. determination
   C. initiative
   D. pride

3. Legal procedure is a means, not an end. Its function is merely to accomplish the enforcement of legal rights. 3.____
   A litigant has no vested interest in the observance of the rules of procedure as such. All that he should be entitled to demand is that he be given an opportunity for a fair and impartial trial of his case. He should not be permitted to invoke the aid of technical rules merely to embarrass his adversary.
   According to this paragraph, it is MOST correct to state that

   A. observance of the rules of procedure guarantees a fair trial
   B. embarrassment of an adversary through technical rules does not make a fair trial
   C. a litigant is not interested in the observance of rules of procedure
   D. technical rules must not be used in a trial

4. One theory states that all criminal behavior is taught by a process of communication within small intimate groups. An individual engages in criminal behavior if the number of criminal patterns which he has acquired exceed the number of non-criminal patterns. This statement indicates that criminal behavior is 4.____

   A. learned
   B. instinctive
   C. hereditary
   D. reprehensible

5. The law enforcement staff of today requires training and mental qualities of a high order. The poorly or partially prepared staff member lowers the standard of work, retards his own earning power, and fails in a career meant to provide a livelihood and social improvement. 5.____
   According to this statement,

   A. an inefficient member of a law enforcement staff will still earn a good livelihood
   B. law enforcement officers move in good social circles
   C. many people fail in law enforcement careers
   D. persons of training and ability are essential to a law enforcement staff

6. In any state, no crime can occur unless there is a written law forbidding the act or the omission in question; and even though an act may not be exactly in harmony with public policy, such act is not a crime unless it is expressly forbidden by legislative statement. According to the above statement, 6.____

   A. a crime is committed with reference to a particular law
   B. acts not in harmony with public policy should be forbidden by law
   C. non-criminal activity will promote public welfare
   D. legislative enactments frequently forbid actions in harmony with public policy

7. The unrestricted sale of firearms is one of the main causes of our shameful crime record. According to this statement, one of the causes of our crime record is 7.____

   A. development of firepower
   B. ease of securing weapons
   C. increased skill in using guns
   D. scientific perfection of firearms

8. Every person must be informed of the reason for his arrest unless he is arrested in the actual commission of a crime. Sufficient force to effect the arrest may be used, but the courts frown on brutal methods.
According to this statement, a person does not have to be informed of the reason for his arrest if 8.____

   A. brutal force was not used in effecting it
   B. the courts will later turn the defendant loose
   C. the person arrested knows force will be used if necessary
   D. the reason for it is clearly evident from the circumstances

9. An important duty of an officer is to keep order in the court.
On the basis of this statement, it is PROBABLY true that 9.____

   A. it is more important for an officer to be strong than it is for him to be smart
   B. people involved in court trials are noisy if not kept in check
   C. not every duty of an officer is important
   D. the maintenance of order is important for the proper conduct of court business

10. Ideally, a correctional system should include several types of institutions to provide different degrees of custody.
On the basis of this statement, one could MOST reasonably say that 10.____

   A. as the number of institutions in a correctional system increases, the efficiency of the system increases
   B. the difference in degree of custody for the inmate depends on the types of institutions in a correctional system
   C. the greater the variety of institutions, the stricter the degree of custody that can be maintained
   D. the same type of correctional institution is not desirable for the custody of all prisoners

11. The enforced idleness of a large percentage of adult men and women in our prisons is one of the direct causes of the tensions which burst forth in riot and disorder. 11.____
On the basis of this statement, a good reason why inmates should perform daily work of some kind is that

A. better morale and discipline can be maintained when inmates are kept busy
B. daily work is an effective way of punishing inmates for the crimes they have committed
C. law-abiding citizens must work, therefore labor should also be required of inmates
D. products of inmates' labor will in part pay the cost of their maintenance

12. With industry invading rural areas, the use of the automobile, and the speed of modern communications and transportation, the problems of neglect and delinquency are no longer peculiar to cities but an established feature of everyday life. 12.____
This statement implies MOST directly that

A. delinquents are moving from cities to rural areas
B. delinquency and neglect are found in rural areas
C. delinquency is not as much of a problem in rural areas as in cities
D. rural areas now surpass cities in industry

13. Young men from minority groups, if unable to find employment, become discouraged and hopeless because of their economic position and may finally resort to any means of supplying their wants. 13.____
The MOST reasonable of the following conclusions that may be drawn from this statement only is that

A. discouragement sometimes leads to crime
B. in general, young men from minority groups are criminals
C. unemployment turns young men from crime
D. young men from minority groups are seldom employed

14. To prevent crime, we must deal with the possible criminal long before he reaches the prison. Our aim should be not merely to reform the law breakers but to strike at the roots of crime: neglectful parents, bad companions, unsatisfactory homes, selfishness, disregard for the rights of others, and bad social conditions. 14.____
The above statement recommends

A. abolition of prisons
B. better reformatories
C. compulsory education
D. general social reform

15. There is evidence which shows that comic books which glorify the criminal and criminal acts have a distinct influence in producing young criminals. 15.____
According to this statement,

A. comic books affect the development of criminal careers
B. comic books specialize in reporting criminal acts
C. young criminals read comic books exclusively
D. young criminals should not be permitted to read comic books

16. Suppose a study shows that juvenile delinquents are equal in intelligence but three school grades behind juvenile non-delinquents. 16.___
On the basis of this information only, it is MOST reasonable to say that

A. a delinquent usually progresses to the educational limit set by his intelligence
B. educational achievement depends on intelligence only
C. educational achievement is closely associated with delinquency
D. lack of intelligence is closely associated with delinquency

17. There is no proof today that the experience of a prison sentence makes a better citizen of an adult. On the contrary, there seems some evidence that the experience is an unwholesome one that frequently confirms the criminality of the inmate. 17.___
From the above paragraph only, it may be BEST concluded that

A. prison sentences tend to punish rather than rehabilitate
B. all criminals should be given prison sentences
C. we should abandon our penal institutions
D. penal institutions are effective in rehabilitating criminals

18. Some courts are referred to as *criminal* courts while others are known as *civil* courts. 18.___
This distinction in name is MOST probably based on the

A. historical origin of the court
B. link between the court and the police
C. manner in which the judges are chosen
D. type of cases tried there

19. Many children who are exposed to contacts and experiences of a delinquent nature become educated and trained in crime in the course of participating in the daily life of the neighborhood. 19.___
From this statement only, we may reasonably conclude that

A. delinquency passes from parent to child
B. neighborhood influences are usually bad
C. schools are training grounds for delinquents
D. none of the above conclusions is reasonable

20. Old age insurance, for whose benefits a quarter of a million city employees may elect to become eligible, is one feature of the Social Security Act that is wholly administered by the Federal government. 20.___
On the basis of this paragraph only, it may MOST reasonably be inferred that

A. a quarter of a million city employees are drawing old age insurance
B. a quarter of a million city employees have elected to become eligible for old age insurance
C. the city has no part in administering Social Security old age insurance
D. only the Federal government administers the Social Security Act

21. An officer's revolver is a defensive, and not offensive, weapon. 21.___
On the basis of this statement only, an officer should BEST draw his revolver to

A. fire at an unarmed burglar
B. force a suspect to confess
C. frighten a juvenile delinquent
D. protect his own life

22. Prevention of crime is of greater value to the community than the punishment of crime. If this statement is accepted as true, GREATEST emphasis should be placed on 22.____

A. malingering
B. medication
C. imprisonment
D. rehabilitation

23. The criminal is rarely or never reformed. Acceptance of this statement as true would mean that GREATEST emphasis should be placed on 23.____

A. imprisonment
B. parole
C. probation
D. malingering

24. The MOST accurate of the following statements about persons convicted of crimes is that 24.____

A. their criminal behavior is almost invariably the result of low intelligence
B. they are almost invariably legally insane
C. they are more likely to come from underprivileged groups than from other groups
D. they have certain facial characteristics which distinguish them from non-criminals

25. Suppose a study shows that the I.Q. (Intelligence Quotient) of prison inmates is 95 as opposed to an I.Q. of 100 for a numerically equivalent civilian group. 25.____
A claim, on the basis of this study, that criminals have a lower I.Q. than non-criminals would be

A. *improper;* prison inmates are criminals who have been caught
B. *proper;* the study was numerically well done
C. *improper;* the sample was inadequate
D. *proper;* even misdemeanors are sometimes penalized by prison sentences

Questions 26-45.

DIRECTIONS: Select the number of the word or expression that MOST NEARLY expresses the meaning of the capitalized word in the group.

26. ABDUCT 26.____

A. lead B. kidnap C. sudden D. worthless

27. BIAS 27.____

A. ability B. envy C. prejudice D. privilege

28. COERCE 28.____

A. cancel B. force C. rescind D. rugged

29. CONDONE 29.____

A. combine B. pardon C. revive D. spice

30. CONSISTENCY 30.____

A. bravery
B. readiness
C. strain
D. uniformity

31. CREDENCE 31.____

A. belief
B. devotion
C. resemblance
D. tempo

32. CURRENT 32.____

A. backward
B. brave
C. prevailing
D. wary

33. CUSTODY 33.____

A. advisement
B. belligerence
C. guardianship
D. suspicion

34. DEBILITY 34.____

A. deceitfulness
B. decency
C. strength
D. weakness

35. DEPLETE 35.____

A. beg B. empty C. excuse D. fold

36. ENUMERATE 36.____

A. name one by one
B. disappear
C. get rid of
D. pretend

37. FEIGN 37.____

A. allow B. incur C. pretend D. weaken

38. INSTIGATE 38.____

A. analyze
B. coordinate
C. oppose
D. provoke

39. LIABLE 39.____

A. careless
B. growing
C. mistaken
D. responsible

40. PONDER 40.____

A. attack B. heavy C. meditate D. solicit

41. PUGILIST 41.____

A. farmer
B. politician
C. prize fighter
D. stage actor

42. QUELL 42.____

A. explode B. inform C. shake D. suppress

43. RECIPROCAL 43.____

A. mutual
B. organized
C. redundant
D. thoughtful

44. RUSE 44.____

A. burn B. impolite C. rot D. trick

45. STEALTHY 45.____

A. crazed B. flowing C. sly D. wicked

Questions 46-50.

DIRECTIONS: Each of the sentences in Questions 46 through 50 may be classified under one of the following four categories:

A. faulty because of incorrect grammar
B. faulty because of incorrect punctuation
C. faulty because of incorrect capitalization or incorrect spelling
D. correct

Examine each sentence carefully to determine under which of the above four options it is best classified. Then, in the space at the right, print the capital letter preceding the option which is the BEST of the four suggested above. Each faulty sentence contains but one type of error. Consider a sentence to be correct if it contains none of the types of errors mentioned, even though there may be other correct ways of expressing the same thought.

46. They told both he and I that the prisoner had escaped. 46.____

47. Any superior officer, who, disregards the just complaints of his subordinates, is remiss in the performance of his duty. 47.____

48. Only those members of the national organization who resided in the Middle west attended the conference in Chicago. 48.____

49. We told him to give the investigation assignment to whoever was available. 49.____

50. Please do not disappoint and embarass us by not appearing in court. 50.____

KEY (CORRECT ANSWERS)

1.	C	11.	A	21.	D	31.	A	41.	C
2.	A	12.	B	22.	D	32.	C	42.	D
3.	B	13.	A	23.	A	33.	C	43.	A
4.	A	14.	D	24.	C	34.	D	44.	D
5.	D	15.	A	25.	A	35.	B	45.	C
6.	A	16.	C	26.	B	36.	A	46.	A
7.	B	17.	A	27.	C	37.	C	47.	B
8.	D	18.	D	28.	B	38.	D	48.	C
9.	D	19.	D	29.	B	39.	D	49.	D
10.	D	20.	C	30.	D	40.	C	50.	C

TEST 2

DIRECTIONS: Each question or incomplete statement is followed by several suggested answers or completions. Select the one that BEST answers the question or completes the statement. *PRINT THE LETTER OF THE CORRECT ANSWER IN THE SPACE AT THE RIGHT.*

1. Suppose a man falls from a two-story high scaffold and is unconscious. You should 1.____

   A. call for medical assistance and avoid moving the man
   B. get someone to help you move him indoors to a bed
   C. have someone help you walk him around until he revives
   D. hold his head up and pour a stimulant down his throat

2. For proper first aid treatment, a person who has fainted should be 2.____

   A. doused with cold water and then warmly covered
   B. given artificial respiration until he is revived
   C. laid down with his head lower than the rest of his body
   D. slapped on the face until he is revived

3. If you are called on to give first aid to a person who is suffering from shock, you should 3.____

   A. apply cold towels
   B. give him a stimulant
   C. keep him awake
   D. wrap him warmly

4. Artificial respiration would NOT be proper first aid for a person suffering from 4.____

   A. drowning
   B. electric shock
   C. external bleeding
   D. suffocation

5. Suppose you are called on to give first aid to several victims of an accident. First attention should be given to the one who is 5.____

   A. bleeding severely
   B. groaning loudly
   C. unconscious
   D. vomiting

6. If an officer's weekly salary is increased from $480 to $540, then the percent of increase is ______ percent. 6.____

   A. 10 B. 11 1/9 C. 12 1/2 D. 20

7. Suppose that one-half the officers in a department have served for more than ten years and one-third have served for more than 15 years. Then, the fraction of officers who have served between ten and fifteen years is 7.____

   A. 1/3 B. 1/5 C. 1/6 D. 1/12

8. In a city prison there are four floors on which prisoners are housed. The top floor houses one-quarter of the inmates, the bottom floor houses one-sixth of the inmates, one-third are housed on the second floor. The rest of the inmates are housed on the third floor. If there are 90 inmates housed on the third floor, the TOTAL number of inmates housed on all four floors together is 8.____

   A. 270 B. 360 C. 450 D. 540

9. Suppose that ten percent of those who commit serious crimes are convicted and that fifteen percent of those convicted are sentenced for more than 3 years. 9.____
The percentage of those committing serious crimes who are sentenced for more than 3 years is ______ percent.

A. 15 B. 1.5 C. .15 D. .015

10. Assume that there are 1,100 employees in a city agency. Of these, 15 percent are officers, 80 percent of whom are attorneys; of the attorneys, two-fifths have been with the agency over five years. 10.____
Then, the number of officers who are attorneys and have over five years experience with the agency is MOST NEARLY

A. 45 B. 53 C. 132 D. 165

11. An employee who has 500 cartons of supplies to pack can pack them at the rate of 50 an hour. After this employee has worked for 1/2 hour, he is joined by another employee who can pack 45 cartons an hour. 11.____
Assuming that both employees can maintain their respective rates of speed, then the TOTAL number of hours required to pack all the cartons is

A. 4 1/2 B. 5 C. 5 1/2 D. 6 1/2

12. Thirty-six officers can complete an assignment in 22 days. Assuming that all officers work at the same rate of speed, the number of officers that would be needed to complete this assignment in 12 days is 12.____

A. 42 B. 54 C. 66 D. 72

Questions 13-15.

DIRECTIONS: Questions 13 through 15 are to be answered on the basis of the table below. Data for certain categories have been omitted from the table. You are to calculate the missing numbers if needed to answer the questions.

	2007	2008	Numerical Increase
Correction Officers	1,226	1,347	
Court Officers		529	34
Deputy Sheriffs	38	40	
Supervisors			
	2,180	2,414	

13. The number in the *Supervisors* group in 2007 was MOST NEARLY 13.____

A. 500 B. 475 C. 450 D. 425

14. The LARGEST percentage increase from 2007 to 2008 was in the group of 14.____

A. Correction Officers
B. Court Officers
C. Deputy Sheriffs
D. Supervisors

15. In 2008, the ratio of the number of Correction Officers to the total of the other three categories of employees was MOST NEARLY 15.____

A. 1:1 B. 2:1 C. 3:1 D. 4:1

16. A directed verdict is made by a court when 16.____

A. the facts are not disputed
B. the defendant's motion for a directed verdict has been denied
C. there is no question of law involved
D. neither party has moved for a directed verdict

17. Papers on appeal of a criminal case do NOT include one of the following: 17.____

A. Summons
B. Minutes of trial
C. Complaint
D. Intermediate motion papers

18. A pleading titled *Smith vs. Jones, et al* indicates 18.____

A. two plaintiffs
B. two defendants
C. more than two defendants
D. unknown defendants

19. A District Attorney makes a *prima facie* case when 19.____

A. there is proof of guilt beyond a reasonable doubt
B. the evidence is sufficient to convict in the absence of rebutting evidence
C. the prosecution presents more evidence than the defense
D. the defendant fails to take the stand

20. A person is NOT qualified to act as a trial juror in a criminal action if he or she 20.____

A. has been convicted previously of a misdemeanor
B. is under 18 years of age
C. has scruples against the death penalty
D. does not own property of a value at least $500

21. A court clerk who falsifies a court record commits a(n) 21.____

A. misdemeanor
B. offense
C. felony
D. no crime, but automatically forfeits his tenure

22. Insolent and contemptuous behavior to a judge during a court of record proceeding is punishable as 22.____

A. civil contempt
B. criminal contempt
C. disorderly conduct
D. a disorderly person

23. Offering a bribe to a court clerk would not constitute a crime UNLESS the 23.____

A. court clerk accepted the bribe
B. bribe consisted of money
C. bribe was given with intent to influence the court clerk in his official functions
D. court was actually in session

24. A defendant comes to trial in the same court in which he had previously been defendant in a similar case. 24.____
The court officer should

A. tell him, *Knew we'd be seeing you again*
B. tell newspaper reporters what he knows of the previous action
C. treat him the same as he would any other defendant
D. warn the judge that the man had previously been a defendant

25. Suppose in conversation with you, an attorney strongly criticizes a ruling of the judge and you believe the attorney to be correct. 25.____
You should

A. assure him you feel the same way
B. tell him the judge knows the law
C. tell him to ask for an exception
D. refuse to discuss the matter

26. Assume that you are a court officer. A woman sees you in the hall and attempts to register a complaint that her husband raped her two hours earlier. 26.____
Which one of the following is the MOST appropriate action for you to take FIRST in this case?

A. Refer her to Family Court.
B. Advise her that her husband has not committed any crime.
C. Ask her for additional information about the circumstances surrounding her allegation so that you may refer her to the proper office or agency.
D. Have her sign a criminal information in the court.

27. Which one of the following is the BEST example of a privileged communication which is NOT admissible as evidence in a court of law without the consent of the communicator? 27.____

A. Client to his accountant
B. Informant to a law enforcement officer
C. Parent to his child
D. Defendant to his spouse

28. A court officer has many contacts with the public. In these contacts, it is MOST important that he 28.____

A. be brief and complete in his answers
B. be courteous and helpful
C. go along with what they ask
D. know the law

29. Suppose a witness becomes engaged in a very heated argument with an attorney who is cross-examining him. The court officer should 29.____

A. ask the attorney to avoid exciting the witness
B. ask the judge if he wishes any action to be taken
C. await the judge's order before interceding
D. caution the witness to be more respectful

30. Suppose that you are a court officer stationed at the door of the courtroom to prevent anyone from entering while the judge is charging the jury. A man whom you recognize as a City Councilman, accompanied by a woman, attempts to enter the courtroom. The BEST action for you to take is to 30.___

A. apologize and explain why they cannot be permitted to enter
B. permit the man to enter since he is a Councilman but exclude the woman
C. permit them to enter since the judge would surely make an exception for them
D. send a note in to the judge to find if they may be permitted to enter

31. It is desirable that a court officer acquire a knowledge of the procedures of the court to which he is assigned MAINLY because such knowledge will help him 31.___

A. become familiar with anti-social behavior
B. discharge his duties properly
C. gain insight into causes of crime
D. in any personal legal proceeding

32. Since he is a city employee, a court officer who refuses to waive immunity from prosecution when called on to testify in court automatically terminates his employment. From this statement ONLY, it may be BEST inferred that 32.___

A. a court officer is a city employee
B. all city employees are court officers
C. city employees may be fired only for malfeasance
D. court attendants who waive immunity may not be prosecuted

33. Referees of the Civil Court are former judges of this court who have served at least ten years and whose term of office terminated at the age of 55 or over, or any judge who has served in a court of record and has retired. According to this statement, a person can be a referee of the Civil Court ONLY if he 33.___

A. has been a judge
B. has retired
C. has served at least 10 years in the court
D. meets certain age requirements

34. Assume that you are assigned to a jury room where you are to guard the jury until 4 P.M. Your relief does not arrive and the jury is still deliberating. Of the following, the BEST action for you to take is to 34.___

A. ask the foreman of the jury to assume responsibility until your relief arrives
B. find out what the jurors may need, get it, and then lock them in for the night
C. inform your supervisor but remain on duty until you are relieved
D. wait until 5 P.M., your usual closing time, and then leave if the relief has not arrived by then

35. When, at a trial, a piece of evidence is tagged as *Exhibit A,* the CHIEF purpose is to 35.___

A. assure its return to the owner
B. make it possible to examine it for fingerprints without chance of error
C. make it possible to identify and refer to it easily
D. prevent the defendant from denying he had it

36. In one case, a mistrial was declared because the indictment used the pronoun he instead of she. 36.____
The MOST useful information a court attendant can derive from this statement is that

A. accuracy is important
B. mistrial is a legal term
C. one must always use good grammar
D. to misrepresent is criminal

37. Suppose a newspaper reporter asks you for information about what happened at a trial where the judge had ordered the courtroom cleared of reporters and spectators. 37.____
You should

A. give him the information he wants
B. refer him to the judge for information
C. refuse to talk to him unless reporters from other papers are present
D. give him misleading information

38. Assume that you are the court officer on duty outside the judge's chambers in the court house. One day, one of the judges informs you that he will be too busy that day to see any visitors, and he tells you to refer them to his secretary for new appointments. Later in the day, an important visitor comes in and asks to see the judge about urgent business. 38.____
Of the following, the BEST course of action for you to take in this situation is to

A. ask the visitor to come back another day when the judge may be able to see him
B. call the judge on the phone and tell him that the visitor has urgent business to discuss with him
C. refer the visitor to one of the other judges who may be present in chambers
D. tell the visitor that the judge is not available, but his secretary may be able to help him or make a new appointment

39. To gain a verdict against X in a trial, it was necessary to show that he could have been at Y Street at 5 P.M. 39.____
It was proven that he was seen at Z Street at 4:45 P.M. The question that MUST be answered to show whether the verdict should be against X is:

A. How long does it take to get from Z Street to Y Street?
B. In what sort of neighborhood is Y Street located?
C. Was X acting suspiciously on the day in question?
D. Who was with X when he was seen at Z Street at 4:45 P.M.?

40. If, at the instructions of the judge, a court officer calls the name of a defendant in a lawsuit and the person does not answer, the court officer should FIRST 40.____

A. ask the judge if he called the person's name correctly
B. call the person's name again
C. look outside the doors of the courtroom for the defendant
D. tell the judge the person doesn't answer

41. When X is accused of having cheated Y of a sum of money and Y is proven to have been deprived of the money, there is an additional requirement for a verdict against X. 41.____
The additional requirement is to prove that

A. the money was stolen from Y
B. X had the money after Y had it
C. X had the money before Y had it
D. X cheated Y of the money

42. Assume that you are on duty in a courtroom and during the judge's absence one of the witnesses for a pending case becomes very angry about the delay. 42.____
Of the following, the BEST action for you to take is to

A. listen to him until he calms down and then explain the reason for the delay
B. tell him your court is no different from any other court
C. walk away from him so that you will not get involved in a dispute
D. warn him that the judge may be back at any minute and will hold him in contempt

43. Assume that you are assigned to the post outside judge's chambers in the court house. A visitor tells you he has an appointment with Judge Jones who is expected to arrive shortly. He asks for permission to wait in the judge's office which is unoccupied at the present time. 43.____
For you to permit him to wait there would be

A. *wise;* the judge would no doubt wish to speak to the man privately
B. *wise;* it would keep the anteroom where you are stationed clear, allowing other employees to work without any disturbance
C. *unwise;* it is rude to allow a visitor to sit alone in an office
D. *unwise;* there may be confidential material on the judge's desk or bookcases

44. A court officer shall not receive a gift from any defendant or other person on the defendant's behalf. 44.____
The BEST explanation for this rule is that

A. acceptance of a gift has no significance
B. defendants cannot usually afford gifts
C. favors may be expected in return
D. gifts are only an expression of good will

45. When a jury is selected, the attorney for each side has a right to refuse to accept a certain number of prospective jurors without giving any reason therefor. 45.____
The reason for this is MAINLY that

A. attorneys can exclude persons likely to be biased even though no prejudice is admitted
B. persons who will suffer economically by being summoned for jury duty can be excused forthwith
C. relatives of the litigants can be excused thus insuring a fair trial for each side
D. there will be a greater number of people from which the jury can be selected

46. Where the defendant in a criminal case is too poor to afford counsel, the court will assign one and he will be paid by the government. 46.____
The principle BEST established by this statement is that

A. it is improper for the government to provide both prosecuting and defending counsel in a trial
B. laws are usually violated because of poverty and defendants are too poor to employ counsel
C. only wealthy law violators may hope to be represented by competent counsel
D. the government is obligated to shield the innocent as well as punish the guilty

47. If a visitor to the court asks foolish questions, the BEST action for the court officer to take is to 47.____

A. answer in a brusque manner to discourage further foolish questions
B. refer the questioner to his supervisor
C. answer them the same way as he would any other questions
D. ignore them since the person doesn't really expect an answer

48. A man plus a uniform makes a good court officer. This statement is FALSE because 48.____

A. a court officer is also required to wear a badge
B. a good court officer is not made merely by putting on a uniform
C. it makes no mention of the fact that the uniform must be neat
D. patrolmen as well as court officers wear uniforms

49. It is a frequent misconception that court officers can be recruited from those registers established for the recruitment of city police or firemen. While it is true that many common qualifications are found in all of these, specific standards for court work are indicated, varying with the size, geographical location, and policies of the court. According to this paragraph ONLY, it may BEST be inferred that 49.____

A. a successful court officer must have some qualifications not required of a policeman or fireman
B. qualifications which make a successful patrolman will also make a successful fireman
C. the same qualifications are required of a court officer regardless of the court to which he is assigned
D. the successful court officer is required to be both more intelligent and stronger than a fireman

50. One of the duties of a court officer is to assist the public with their problems. A PROPER exercise of this duty by a court officer would be for the officer to 50.____

A. advise members of the public to settle their differences out of court
B. advise a member of the public how to fill out forms required by the court
C. lend money to a member of the public to pay the required court fees
D. recommend a lawyer to a member of the public who does not have one

KEY (CORRECT ANSWERS)

1.	A	11.	C	21.	C	31.	B	41.	D
2.	C	12.	C	22.	B	32.	A	42.	A
3.	D	13.	D	23.	C	33.	A	43.	D
4.	C	14.	D	24.	C	34.	C	44.	C
5.	A	15.	A	25.	D	35.	C	45.	A
6.	C	16.	A	26.	C	36.	A	46.	D
7.	C	17.	D	27.	D	37.	B	47.	C
8.	B	18.	C	28.	B	38.	D	48.	B
9.	B	19.	B	29.	C	39.	A	49.	A
10.	B	20.	B	30.	A	40.	B	50.	B

EXAMINATION SECTION
TEST 1

DIRECTIONS: Each question or incomplete statement is followed by several suggested answers or completions. Select the one that BEST answers the question or completes the statement. *PRINT THE LETTER OF THE CORRECT ANSWER IN THE SPACE AT THE RIGHT.*

Questions 1-3.

DIRECTIONS: Questions 1 through 3 are to be answered on the basis of the following paragraph.

The Jingle-Dress dance is a popular competitive dance performed at intertribal powwows. The costume of the Jingle-Dress dancer is adorned with small metal cones. The cones are made from chewing tobacco lids, which are rolled into cylinders and sewn onto the dress. During the dance, these tin cones strike one another to produce a soft, rhythmic sound. The dancer blends complicated footwork with a series of gentle hops, causing the cones to jingle in time to the drumbeat.

1. The purpose of the cones in the Jingle-Dress dance is to 1.____

   A. shine and sparkle during the dance
   B. produce a soft, rhythmic sound
   C. aid the dancer with the complicated footwork required by the dance
   D. make use of recycled tobacco can lids

2. The dancer causes the cones to make sounds by 2.____

   A. making large cones to sew onto the dress
   B. sewing the cones as close to another as possible
   C. jumping up and down as quickly as possible
   D. combining footwork with gentle hops

3. The Jingle-Dress dance is performed as a 3.____

   A. ceremonial dance at semi-annual powwows
   B. healing dance at intertribal powwows
   C. competitive dance at intertribal powwows
   D. costume dance at annual powwows

Questions 4-6.

DIRECTIONS: Questions 4 through 6 are to be answered on the basis of the following paragraph.

Although volleyball is a unique sport, it shares one important similarity with other well-known sports. Like most sports, the ability to win doesn't just depend on a team's ability to score the most points, but on its ability to make the fewest number of errors. In volleyball, a team cannot score unless it is serving. Serving errors, therefore, are extremely costly since losing the serve also means granting your opponent a scoring opportunity.

4. To win a volleyball game, it is MOST important to make sure your team 4.____

   A. makes the fewest number of errors
   B. plays good defense
   C. grants scoring opportunities to your opponents
   D. serves first

5. What important similarity does volleyball share with other sports? 5.____

   A. It's exciting to watch.
   B. Winning depends on a powerful serve.
   C. A volleyball team cannot score unless it is serving.
   D. The winning team usually commits the fewest errors.

6. Serving errors are costly in a volleyball game because they 6.____

   A. count as an error against your team
   B. provide your opponent with a scoring opportunity
   C. place your team in a receiving position
   D. can result in a delay-of-game penalty

Questions 7-8.

DIRECTIONS: Questions 7 and 8 are to be answered on the basis of the following paragraph.

Throughout history, solar eclipses have sometimes caused great fear and anxiety. Some cultures believed eclipses predicted the end of the world. Many older cultures believed a dragon was swallowing the sun and, in order to save the sun, people made as much noise as possible to frighten the dragon away. When the sun returned, whole and bright, the noise-makers celebrated their success.

7. Why have eclipses caused such anxiety throughout history? 7.____

   A. People believed they signaled the end of the world
   B. No one knows what causes them
   C. Because people make so much noise when they appear
   D. Because watching one can harm the eyes

8. Why did ancient cultures often make noise during an eclipse? 8.____

   A. People were frightened in the darkness
   B. To celebrate the arrival of the eclipse
   C. To summon the dragon who would swallow the sun
   D. To chase away the dragon they thought had swallowed the sun

Questions 9-11.

DIRECTIONS: Questions 9 through 11 are to be answered on the basis of the following paragraph.

In the films of the 1940s, most American Indians appeared as enemies. They spoke broken English and blocked civilization's progress. During this same time, however, a group of Navajo Indians used their unique language to develop a code for the U.S. military which would become one of the most successful codes in military history. During World War II, this group, known as the Navajo Code Talkers, played a key role in many of the most crucial victories fought by the U.S. military in the Pacific.

9. What role did the Navajo Code Talkers play in World War II? They 9.____

   A. appeared as enemies in many films
   B. spoke broken English and blocked civilization's progress
   C. developed a military code which helped win the war in the Pacific
   D. used their unique language to block civilization's progress

10. In films from the 1940s, American Indians were most often depicted as enemies by 10.____

   A. speaking broken English and blocking civilization's progress
   B. speaking only in their native Navajo tongue
   C. using their language to develop secret codes
   D. trying to block crucial American victories in the Pacific

11. The Navajo Code Talkers used their language to 11.____

   A. block civilization's progress
   B. fight Hollywood stereotypes
   C. defeat their enemies in other tribes
   D. develop one of the most effective U.S. military codes in history

Questions 12-13.

DIRECTIONS: Questions 12 and 13 are to be answered on the basis of the following paragraph.

In the last several years, judges throughout the country have attracted controversy by practicing *creative sentencing*. The term refers to the judges' tendency for offering defendants what they consider valid alternatives to jail sentences. For example, to qualify for probation, one defendant had to wear a tee shirt that announced his status as a criminal on probation. An abusive husband had to donate his car to a shelter for battered women. In one case, a judge gave a woman found guilty of child abuse a chance to avoid jail if she would voluntarily allow Norplant, a form of birth control, to be implanted in her arm.

12. What does the term *creative sentencing* refer to? 12.____

   A. Various judicial controversies
   B. Judges who offer defendants alternatives to jail sentences

C. Defendants who are forced to undergo humiliating punishments in addition to jail sentences
D. Judges who have the power to determine how much time a defendant spends in jail

13. Creative sentencing is considered controversial because the 13.___

A. judges are overstepping the bounds of their power by forcing defendants to submit to these punishments
B. defendants have no opportunity to defend themselves
C. alternatives offered to defendants are often surprising and odd
D. judges have been forced to these extreme measures because of prison overcrowding

Questions 14-16.

DIRECTIONS: Questions 14 through 16 are to be answered on the basis of the following paragraph.

When examined closely, Earth's position in the solar system is something of a miracle. If it were closer to the sun, the heat would be so intense that water would be vaporized. If it were farther away, water would be frozen. Of all the planets in the solar system, only Earth and Mars share the temperature band which allows water to exist in the three states which are necessary to produce and sustain life. But only Earth is surrounded by a protective ozone layer which aids water in making the transition between these three states.

14. Why is Earth's position in the solar system something of a miracle? 14.___

A. If it were closer to the sun, water would vaporize.
B. If it were farther from the sun, water would freeze.
C. It exists in the narrow temperature band which allows water to exist in the three states necessary to sustain life.
D. It exists in the narrow temperature band which allows a protective ozone layer to form around the planet.

15. What is the difference between Earth and Mars? 15.___

A. Mars is surrounded by a protective ozone layer.
B. Earth is surrounded by a protective ozone layer.
C. Only Earth exists within the narrow temperature band which allows water to exist in the three states necessary to sustain life.
D. Only Mars exists within the narrow temperature band which allows water to exist in the three states necessary to sustain life.

16. The ozone layer is important to the production and sustenance of life because it 16.___

A. helps water make the transition between the three forms necessary to sustain life
B. keeps water from being vaporized by the sun's harmful rays
C. keeps water from being frozen when the sun sets
D. keeps water from leaving the atmosphere

Questions 17-19.

DIRECTIONS: Questions 17 through 19 are to be answered on the basis of the following paragraph.

During the seventeenth century, sailors at sea often suffered from muscle weakness and unexplained bleeding. This disease often proved fatal until the discovery that sailors who ate oranges and lines either didn't get sick, or suffered a much milder form of the illness. As a result, the British navy required every ship to provide lemons and limes for the entire crew. By accident, it had discovered that the vitamin C contained in the citrus fruits prevented scurvy.

17. What disease did sailors at sea often suffer from? 17.____

A. Malnourishment
B. Overdoses of vitamin C
C. Muscle weakness and unexplained bleeding
D. Scurvy

18. How is the disease prevented? 18.____

A. Consumption of vitamin C
B. Consumption of fresh water
C. Hard work
D. Bed rest

19. The cure for scurvy was discovered 19.____

A. as a result of careful testing in laboratories
B. through the accidental discovery that sailors who consumed vitamin C didn't grow ill
C. through the accidental discovery that sailors who consumed vitamin C often grew ill
D. as a result of years of study and experimentation

Questions 20-22.

DIRECTIONS: Questions 20 through 22 are to be answered on the basis of the following paragraph.

Unlike dogs, cats are typically a solitary animal species who avoid social interaction, but they do display specific social responses to each other upon meeting. When two cats meet who are strangers, their first actions and gestures determine who the *dominant* cat will be. If a cat desires dominance or sees the other cat as a threat to its territory, it will stare directly at the intruder with a lowered tail. If the other cat responds with a similar gesture, or with the strong defensive posture of an arched back, laid-back ears, and raised tail, a fight or chase is likely if neither cat gives in. This is unlikely, however; before such a point of open hostility is reached, one of the cats will usually take the *submissive* position of crouching down while looking away from the other cat.

20. A cat signals its dominance over another cat by 20.____

A. crouching down and looking away from the other cat
B. arching its back and raising its tail
C. staring directly at the other cat and lowering its tail
D. chasing the other cat

21. Cats usually greet each other by 21.____

A. displaying specific social responses
B. staring directly at one another
C. raising their tails
D. arching their backs

22. Why is it unlikely for cats who are strangers to reach a point of open hostility with one another? 22.____

A. Cats are solitary animals.
B. One of the cats usually runs away.
C. One of the cats usually takes a submissive position before they reach the point of open hostility.
D. The two cats generally stare at each other with lowered tails until the hostility passes.

Questions 23-25.

DIRECTIONS: Questions 23 through 25 are to be answered on the basis of the following paragraph.

Between the nineteenth and twentieth centuries, the area in America known as the Great Plains underwent startling changes. At the beginning of the nineteenth century, there were few settlements. One could walk for miles without seeing a house. By the end of the century, settlements had sprung up all over. More and more people began to seek their fortunes in this area. In 1800, the Plains were covered by herds of buffalo. These huge animals were the natural cattle of the Plains. By 1900 the buffalo had almost disappeared, however, and the tribes who had roamed the Plains in pursuit of the buffalo had been forced to live on reservations.

23. When did these changes occur on the Great Plains? 23.____

A. Between the 1700s and the 1800s
B. Between the 1800s and the 1900s
C. During the 1900s
D. Between 1850 and 1950

24. What caused the sudden increase in the number of settlements on the Great Plains? 24.____

A. The disappearance of the buffalo
B. The disappearance of the Plains tribes
C. An increased desire to hunt buffalo for sport
D. An increased number of people seeking their fortunes in the area

25. What happened to the Plains tribes after the buffalo disappeared? 25.____
They

A. were forced to live on reservations
B. were all killed
C. died of starvation
D. moved farther west, away from the settlers

Questions 26-28.

DIRECTIONS: Questions 26 through 28 are to be answered on the basis of the following paragraph.

One important line of thinking about stress focuses on the differences between Type A and Type B personalities. Type A individuals are extremely competitive, are very devoted to work, and have a strong sense of time urgency. They are likely to be aggressive, impatient, and very work-oriented. Type B individuals are less competitive, less devoted to work, and have a weaker sense of time urgency. These individuals are less likely to experience conflict with other people and more likely to have a balanced, relaxed approach to life.

26. Type B individuals are likely to display which of the following characteristics? 26.____

A. A strong sense of time urgency
B. Devotion to work
C. A balanced approach to life
D. Aggressiveness

27. Type A individuals are likely to display which of the following characteristics? 27.____

A. A balanced approach to life
B. Passivity
C. Contentment
D. A strong sense of time urgency

28. These personality types help researchers study which of the following problems? 28.____

A. Stress
B. Apathy
C. Criminal behavior
D. Underachievement

Questions 29-36.

The paragraphs which follow contain blank spaces with numbers corresponding to the questions. Each of the corresponding questions contains one lettered choice whose meaning fits in the space. Place the letter of the correct choice in the answer space to the right of the question.

Most successful job interviews (29) three basic steps. Step 1 lasts about three minutes and (30) when you first introduce yourself. Those people who have a firm handshake, who maintain eye contact, smile, and seem friendly, are the (31) successful during this phase. Step 2 is the (32) phase. This is the point at which interviewees (33) their skills and work to *sell* themselves. Step 3 comes at the (34) of the interview and, like Step 1, lasts only a few minutes. After the employer says, *We'll call you,* successful interviewees are quick (35) respond, *I'll get in touch with you if I don't hear from you in a few days.* This final gesture conveys (36).

29. A. lack B. mimic 29.___
C. follow D. end with

30. A. begins B. ends C. stalls D. fails 30.___

31. A. least B. mostly C. more D. most 31.___

32. A. least challenging B. most boring 32.___
C. longest D. shortest

33. A. brag about B. explain C. enunciate D. lie about 33.___

34. A. middle B. outset C. beginning D. end 34.___

35. A. to B. at C. with D. for 35.___

36. A. insistence B. impatience 36.___
C. enthusiasm D. hope

Questions 37-40.

The idea of duty is important to the followers of Hinduism, the major (37) in India. In fact, the many duties prescribed by Hinduism make it a way of life that (38) each day. From an early age, children learn that nothing is more important (39) doing one's duty. In fact doing (40) duty is, in itself, a form of worship.

37. A. belief B. religion 37.___
C. system D. political institution

38. A. organizes B. disrupts 38.___
C. produces D. destabilizes

39. A. if B. with C. of D. than 39.___

40. A. your B. his C. one's D. its 40.___

Questions 41-46.

Strong emotions are accompanied (41) physiological changes. When we are extremely fearful or angry, for example, (42) heartbeat speeds up, our pulse races, and our breathing rate tends to increase. The body's metabolism (43), burning up sugar in the bloodstream and fats in the tissues at a faster rate. The salivary glands become less active, making the mouth feel (44). The sweat glands may overreact, (45) a dripping forehead, clammy hands, and cold sweat. Finally, the pupils may (46), producing the wide-eyed look that is characteristic of both terror and rage.

41. A. with B. to C. beside D. by 41.___

42. A. your B. our C. the D. a 42.___

43. A. accelerates B. slows down C. works D. stays the same 43.____

44. A. hot B. cold C. wet D. dry 44.____

45. A. with B. showing C. producing D. fearing 45.____

46. A. dilate B. enlarge C. blacken D. disappear 46.____

Questions 47-52.

Increased numbers of women are (47) going to college and graduating with degrees in law and medicine. More women than ever before are (48) careers and earning as much as men. Many career women who are married have also achieved economic equality (49) their husbands. The number of women in elected office has also increased, and a large majority of Americans are now willing to vote for a qualified (50) for president. A growing number of women are entering the military, with the U.S. now having more female soldiers than any other (51). These are all signs that women have made significant headway toward (52) equality.

47. A. now B. then C. yet D. not 47.____

48. A. leaving B. changing C. avoiding D. pursuing 48.____

49. A. to B. with C. at D. for 49.____

50. A. Republican B. candidate C. woman D. man 50.____

51. A. woman B. country C. man D. branch 51.____

52. A. racial B. economic C. religious D. gender 52.____

Questions 53-56.

Understanding does not mean manipulating someone to agree (53) your point of view. Although a manipulative person views understanding as having someone else come around to his or her opinion, an understanding person conveys a sense of open-mindedness and (54). A communicator who is understanding does (55) insist upon agreement. He or she understands that, in order to be understood, you must also (56) others.

53. A. to B. at C. with D. for 53.____

54. A. acceptance B. exclusion C. anger D. elation 54.____

55. A. always B. not C. sometimes D. generally 55.____

56. A. disagree with B. judge C. love D. understand 56.____

Questions 57-62.

DIRECTIONS: Questions 57 through 62 are to be answered on the basis of the following facts.

Apollo Elementary School serves students in grades kindergarten through fifth. The school library is located in the center of the school. Classrooms surround the library, forming a large circle. Throughout the school day, teachers bring their classes into the library to conduct research and reading activities. There are usually several classes using the library at any one time.

The school librarian is Mrs. Samuels. She is a tall, middle-aged woman with brown hair and green eyes. Her part-time assistant is Velma Thomas. Velma is a student at the local community college, where she studies library science.

On the afternoon of Wednesday, April 11, Mrs. Simon brought her fourth-grade class to the library at approximately 1:50 P.M. Mrs. Samuels was already working with a third-grade class, so Velma began assisting the fourth grade students. A young girl from Mrs. Simon's class asked Velma how to find her book in the card catalog. As Velma guided the girl through the procedure, she noticed that one of the third graders had drifted away from his class and was attempting to reach a book by standing on one of the bookshelves.

Just as Velma called to the boy, he lost his footing and fell. Mrs. Samuels rushed to his side and checked him for injuries. The boy had a slight bruise on his wrist, but was otherwise uninjured.

57. Who checked the boy for injuries after his fall? 57.___

A. Mrs. Samuels
B. Velma Thomas
C. Mrs. Simon
D. The third grade teacher

58. Who is the school librarian? 58.___

A. Mrs. Samuels
B. Velma Thomas
C. Mrs. Simon
D. She is not named in this passage

59. On what day of the week did the incident occur? 59.___

A. Monday B. Tuesday C. Wednesday D. Friday

60. In what grade was the boy who fell from the shelf? 60.___

A. Fifth B. Fourth C. Third D. Second

61. What grade does Mrs. Simon teach? 61.___

A. Fifth B. Fourth C. Third D. Second

62. What grades does Apollo Elementary serve? 62.____

A. First through fifth
B. First through sixth
C. Kindergarten through fourth
D. Kindergarten through fifth

Questions 63-68.

DIRECTIONS: Questions 63 through 68 are to be answered on the basis of the following facts.

There is a small hot dog cart located in the outdoor plaza of the Smith County Courthouse. The cart sells Polish hot dogs, sausages, bratwurst, soft pretzels, and soda. In the mornings between 7:00 and 9:30, fresh coffee and danishes are also sold. Employees of the court and other nearby businesses often purchase their lunch there, and eat on the plaza benches and tables.

The cart opens at 7:00 A.M. and closes at 3:00 P.M. during weekdays. It does not operate on weekends. It is owned and operated by Luisa Gonzalez, who is a 21-year-old college student with brown hair and brown eyes. Her father is Martin Gonzalez, a retired police officer, and he often works with her. At approximately 12:00 P.M. on October 3, Court Officer Laura Innes stopped at the cart to buy her lunch. After paying Luisa, Laura moved to the condiment table, located just to the right of the cart. She noticed Martin Gonzalez struggling to pour a large tub of boiling water into the hot dog steamer. Before she could move to help him, however, Martin lost his grip and dropped the tub of water, splashing himself.

The Court Officer administered first aid, and Martin was taken to St. Luke's hospital. He had received second degree burns on his arms and feet and was not able to return to the hot dog cart for three weeks.

63. What hospital was Martin taken to? 63.____

A. St. Mark' s
B. St. Peter' s
C. St. Mary' s
D. St. Luke' s

64. What part of his body did Martin burn? 64.____
His

A. arms and feet
B. arms
C. feet and ankles
D. arms and face

65. Who owns the hot dog cart? 65.____

A. Martin Gonzalez
B. Luisa Gonzalez
C. Laura Innes
D. Luke Martin

66. During what hours does the cart operate on weekends? 66.____

A. 7:00 A.M. to 3:00 P.M.
B. 9:30 A.M. to 3:00 P.M.
C. 7:00 A.M. to 9:30 A.M.
D. The cart does not operate on weekends

67. Where is the hot dog cart located? 67.___
On the ______ of the courthouse.

A. first floor
B. roof
C. outdoor plaza
D. third floor

68. Who was first to administer first aid to Martin? 68.___

A. Laura Innes
B. Luisa Gonzalez
C. Luke Martin
D. Paramedics

Questions 69-74.

DIRECTIONS: Questions 69 through 74 are to be answered on the basis of the following facts.

The offices of Judge Anjelica Chen are located on the third floor of the Peak County Courthouse. The offices of Judge Benjamin Laurence are also located on the third floor of the courthouse, across a courtyard. The windows of these offices face one another.

Judge Chen keeps her pet parrot, Mabel, in her offices. Although Mabel has a cage, Judge Chen keeps the door open, allowing Mabel to perch on bookshelves and lamps while the Judge finishes paperwork late in the evenings. Judge Laurence has no pets, but he often feeds pigeons from his window, sprinkling breadcrumbs along his sill.

On the evening of Tuesday, May 2, Court Officer Roger Crawford heard a scream from Judge Chen's office. He arrived to find the judge searching frantically through her office for Mabel, who had apparently disappeared. The window to the judge's office was open. The court officer assisted the judge in her search. At approximately 7:30, nearly 45 minutes after he had arrived in Judge Chen's office, the court officer heard someone hollering from the other side of the building.

Officer Crawford rushed toward the noise and found Judge Laurence in his office, trying to fend off the bright parrot flying back and forth across his office. The court officer summoned Judge Chen, who calmed Mabel and led her back to her cage.

69. Where was Mabel found? 69.___

A. In Judge Chen's office
B. In Judge Laurence's office
C. In the courtyard
D. In her cage

70. What kind of bird is Mabel? 70.___

A. Pigeon
B. Canary
C. Chickadee
D. Parrot

71. Where is Judge Chen's office located? 71.___
______ Judge Laurence's office.

A. Below
B. Next to
C. Across from
D. Above

72. Why does Judge Laurence leave breadcrumbs on his window-sill? 72.____

A. To feed pigeons
B. To feed Mabel
C. To feed squirrels
D. To keep food litter out of his office

73. How long did Judge Chen and Officer Crawford look for Mabel before they heard Judge Laurence yelling in his office? 73.____
_______ minutes.

A. 30 B. 45 C. 60 D. 15

74. Why does Judge Chen leave Mabel's cage door open? 74.____

A. To allow Mabel to escape
B. To allow Mabel a clearer view of Judge Laurence's windowsill
C. Judge Chen does not leave Mabel's cage door open
D. To allow Mabel to perch on bookshelves and lamps while the Judge finishes her paperwork

Questions 75-80.

DIRECTIONS: Questions 75 through 80 are to be answered on the basis of the following facts.

The Hickory Ridge Courthouse is located just across the street from the Hickory Ridge Public Library. Employees begin arriving at the courthouse at approximately 7:00 A.M. each weekday morning. The library opens at 9:00 A.M. and closes at 5:00 P.M. each weekday. Both the courthouse and the library have bicycle stands in front of them. Bicyclists lock their bikes to the stands while they run their errands and conduct their business.

Court Officer Melinda Thompson eats her lunch each day at a small cafe next to the library. The cafe caters mainly to employees of the library and courthouse. It operates from 11:00 A.M. to 3:00 P.M. each day.

On the afternoon of August 11, the court officer observed a young man with a backpack lock his bike to a stand in front of the library. The young man had blond hair, green eyes, and long sideburns. Approximately 30 minutes after the young man entered the library, a dark-haired man emerged from the cafe where the court officer was eating her lunch. The man had a beard, and was of medium build. He walked to the bicycle stand and began jiggling a lock on one of the bikes.

The court officer recognized the bicycle as the same one the blond-haired young man had locked to the stand. By the time the court officer reached the bicycle stand, the second man had already broken the lock. Although she called for him to stop, he rode away on the young man's bicycle. Her excellent description, however, helped police locate the bicycle thief and the bicycle a short time later.

75. What time does the library open? 75.____

A. 7:00 A.M. B. 9:00 A.M. C. 11:00 A.M. D. 3:00 P.M.

76. Where is the cafe located? 76.____

A. Next to the courthouse
B. Across from the library
C. Next to the library
D. Between the library and the courthouse

77. Who stole the bicycle? 77.____

A. The blond-haired man
B. The dark-haired man
C. The man with the backpack
D. The man with the long sideburns

78. What hours is the cafe open? 78.____

A. 11:00 A.M. to 3:00 P.M.
B. 9:00 A.M. to 5:00 P.M.
C. 7:00 A.M. to 5:00 P.M.
D. 7:00 A.M. to 3:00 P.M.

79. When do employees begin arriving at the courthouse each day? 79.____

A. 7:00 A.M. B. 9:00 A.M. C. 10:00 A.M. D. 11:00 A.M.

80. What did the bicycle thief do when the court officer ordered him to stop? 80.____

A. He stopped.
B. He rode away.
C. He threw down the bicycle and ran.
D. He insisted the bicycle was his.

Questions 81-87.

DIRECTIONS: Questions 81 through 87 are to be answered on the basis of the following facts.

The Jade Market is located on the first floor of the Angel County Courthouse. The courthouse is located across the street from San Gabriel High School. Jade Market sells newspapers, magazines, sandwiches, beverages, and sodas. In the mornings, between 7:00 A.M. and 9:00 A.M., the market is frequented mostly by employees of the courthouse. In the afternoons, between 1:45 and 2:45, the small market is crowded with teenagers wearing cumbersome backpacks. Classes at San Gabriel High School end at 1:30 P.M.

Jade Market is operated by James Chang, who is 55 years old, with graying black hair and brown eyes. His wife, Lola, also helps at the market during the afternoon and evening hours.

On the afternoon of Thursday, September 1, Court Officer Mason Stewart stopped at Jade Market to buy a newspaper and some coffee. While he was talking with Lola Chang, twelve to fifteen high school students walked into the market. They moved noisily up and down the narrow aisles. They each carried a heavy backpack. As they walked through the store, their packs often knocked items from the shelves.

As the court officer watched the students, he noticed one young woman knock several magazines from the magazine stand located at the back of the store. Several other students walked past the magazine stand before the young woman was able to turn around and pick the magazines up. The young woman had blond hair and brown eyes, and she carried a red backpack. When she returned to the stand, Officer Stewart saw that she only replaced one magazine.

When the court officer approached the girl about the missing magazines, she insisted that she had not seen them. He asked her to wait at the front counter, which she did. Officer Stewart studied the magazine stand for a brief moment, and then bent down to peer beneath it. He saw the magazines lying there, where they had been accidentally kicked by the other passing students. The young woman helped gather the magazines, and then left the store after apologizing to Mr. and Mrs. Chang.

81. What hours is the market open? 81.____

    A. 7:00 A.M. to 2:45 P.M.
    B. 7:00 A.M. to 9:00 A.M.
    C. 7:00 A.M. to 1:30 P.M.
    D. The passage doesn't contain this information

82. Where were the missing magazines found? 82.____

    A. Inside the girl's backpack
    B. On the magazine stand
    C. Beneath the magazine stand
    D. They were never found

83. What did the girl do when Officer Stewart asked her about the missing magazines? She 83.____

    A. ran from the store
    B. denied stealing them
    C. confessed
    D. ran to the front counter

84. Where is the Jade Market located? 84.____

    A. On the first floor of the courthouse
    B. On the third floor of the courthouse
    C. Next to Angel High School
    D. In the plaza of Angel High School

85. When does Lola Chang work in the market? 85.____

    A. All day
    B. Afternoons
    C. Afternoons and evenings
    D. The passage doesn't contain this information

86. On what day of the week did the incident occur? 86.____

    A. Monday B. Tuesday C. Wednesday D. Thursday

87. What time are students at San Gabriel High School dismissed from class? 87.___

A. 1:30 P.M.
B. 1:45 P.M.
C. 2:45 P.M.
D. The passage does not contain this information

Questions 88-89.

DIRECTIONS: Questions 88 and 89 are to be answered on the basis of the following facts.

Procedure: The Service Station at the Friendly Car Dealership has a policy which allows customers to drop off their cars the night before they are to be worked on. This allows customers the convenience of not having to take time off from work to have their cars serviced. Cars must be dropped off between 9 P.M. and 11 P.M. the night before. Keys must be labeled with the make and license plate number of the car to which they belong. They are then placed into envelopes and dropped into a locked drop box outside the service station office. Cars must be picked up by 9:00 P.M. on the day repairs are completed. If the car cannot be picked up on that day, other arrangements must be made with the service department by 3:00 P.M. of that day.

Situation: Sarah Stone drops her car off at 10:45 P.M. the night before it is to be serviced. She labels her key, places it in the envelope and leaves it in the drop box. Her car is repaired by 11:00 A.M. the next morning. Because Sarah has to catch up on a backlog of work, she is unable to pick her car up before 6:00 P.M. on the day after the repairs have been completed.

88. Based on the above procedure, which one of the following statements regarding Stone's actions is correct? 88.___
Stone

A. should have dropped her car off before 10:45 P.M. the night before it was to be serviced
B. should have given her keys to someone in the service department instead of dropping them in a box
C. should have notified the service department of her plans by 3:00 P.M. on the day the car was repaired
D. did everything according to proper procedure

89. If Stone wishes to pick her car up at 8:00 P.M. the day the repairs are completed, which of the following things must she do? 89.___
She

A. must make special arrangements with the service department
B. must wait until the following morning to pick up her car
C. must make a special appointment to pick up her car after hours
D. does not need to do anything

Questions 90-91.

DIRECTIONS: Questions 90 and 91 are to be answered on the basis of the following facts.

Procedure: Notification of absence due to illness must be made between 9:00 A.M. and 10:00 A.M. on the first day of illness. Illness which results in more than four days of consecutive absence must be confirmed by a doctor's note stating the nature of the illness and the approximate date of return to work.

Situation: Officer Janus Lee becomes sick on the night of June 25 while at home. At 10:15 on the morning of June 26, Lee notifies his office that he will not be in. On July 4, Lee submits a doctor's note confirming and identifying his illness and stating that Lee will return to work on July 5.

90. Based on the above procedure, which one of the following statements regarding Lee's actions is correct? 90.____
Officer Lee

A. should have notified his office of his absence by 10:00 A.M. on the morning of June 26
B. should have notified his office of his absence by 10:00 A.M. on the morning of June 25
C. should have submitted the doctor's note on June 26
D. followed the procedure correctly

91. Officer Lee's note from the doctor states that he will be absent from the office from June 26 through July 4. Which of the following notification procedures should he follow on those days? 91.____

A. Officer Lee must notify his office of his absence on each morning between June 26 and July 4 by 10:00 A.M.
B. Officer Lee's doctor must notify his office of Officer Lee's absence on each morning between June 26 and July 4 by 10:00 A.M.
C. Officer Lee must contact his office periodically between June 26 and July 4 to notify them of his progress.
D. Once he has submitted his doctor's note, Officer Lee does not need to notify his office any further so long as he returns to work on July 5.

Questions 92-93.

DIRECTIONS: Questions 92 and 93 are to be answered on the basis of the following facts.

Procedure: Court officers in Montgomery County who work overtime are awarded compensation time instead of overtime pay. Each hour of over-time is equal to one hour of compensation time. In order to use compensation time, court officers must submit a written vacation request two weeks in advance of the desired time off. The request must contain the beginning and ending dates of the requested vacation. It must be signed by the officer's supervisor before the officer may utilize the compensation time.

Situation: Officer Sabrina Hellman wishes to use compensation time for a vacation beginning October 1 and ending October 10. The vacation will require 7 days of compensation time. Officer Hellman submits her vacation request on September 24. The request contains the beginning and ending dates of her desired vacation.

92. Based on the above procedure, which of the following statements regarding Officer Hellman's actions is correct? 92.___
Officer Hellman

A. should have submitted her vacation request by September 17
B. should have submitted her vacation request by September 1
C. should have submitted the beginning and ending dates of her vacation
D. followed the procedures correctly

93. How many hours of overtime must Officer Hellman have in order to accumulate 100 hours of compensation time? 93.___

A. 50 B. 75 C. 150 D. 100

Questions 94-95.

DIRECTIONS: Questions 94 and 95 are to be answered on the basis of the following facts.

Procedure: Court officers in Salinas County who work overtime are awarded compensation time instead of overtime pay. Each hour of overtime is equal to one hour of compensation time. At the end of each calendar year, compensation time which has not been used is automatically erased unless employees submit a written request to have their compensation time rolled over to the next year. Rollover requests must be submitted no later than November 1. They must contain the employee's name, social security, and the total number of compensation hours s/he wishes to rollover.

Situation: Officer Larry Bernstein accumulated 20 hours of compensation time during calendar year 2008. In addition to that, he has 40 hours of compensation time which was rolled over from 2007. On October 30, Officer Bernstein submits a written request asking that his remaining compensation time be rolled over to calendar year 2009.

94. Based on the above procedure, which of the following statements regarding Officer Bernstein's actions is correct? Officer Bernstein 94.___

A. should have submitted his rollover request by November 1, 2008
B. should have submitted his vacation request by October 1, 2008
C. should have submitted the total number of hours he wanted to be rolled over
D. followed the procedures correctly

95. Based on the above procedure and situation, how many hours of compensation time can Officer Bernstein expect to be rolled over to calendar year 2009? 95.___

A. 20 B. 40 C. 60 D. 80

Questions 96-97.

DIRECTIONS: Questions 96 and 97 are to be answered on the basis of the following facts.

Procedure: Court officers in Salinas County who work overtime are awarded compensation time instead of overtime pay. Each hour of overtime is equal to one hour of compensation time. If a court officer is laid off or chooses to leave his or her employment as a court officer with the county, and he or she has compensation time remaining, then he or she can choose one of two options. The first option is for the employee to use the remaining compensation time as paid vacation time. This would allow the officer to cease his or her duties early, but still be paid until the end of his or her regular employment. In order to utilize this option, employees must submit a written request 30 days before the start of the paid vacation. The second option is for the employee to remain through the end of his or her regular employment, and receive a check for any remaining compensation time. In order to utilize this option, employees must submit a written request 90 days before the scheduled departure date.

Situation: Officer Glen Regan is due to retire at the end of calendar year 2008. Through the course of his career as a court officer, Glen has accumulated 200 hours of compensation time. This equals approximately 25 standard working days.

96. If Officer Regan decides that he would like to retire early, he should submit a written request by _______ 1, 2008. 96.____

A. December B. November C. October D. September

97. If Officer Regan decides to receive a check for his unused compensation time, he should submit a written request by _______ 1, 2008. 97.____

A. December B. November C. October D. September

Questions 98-100.

DIRECTIONS: Questions 98 through 100 are to be answered on the basis of the following facts.

Procedure: Court officers in James County are granted 10 paid sick days each year. Sick days are to be used only in the case of unforeseen illness. Employees are also granted 5 paid personal days. Officers who work overtime are also granted compensation time instead of overtime pay. Each hour of overtime is equal to one hour of compensation time. In order to use a sick day, employees must notify a supervisor by 10:00 A.M. on the day of their absence. In order to use a personal day, employees must notify a supervisor two working days in advance. In order to use a compensation-time day, employees must notify a supervisor two weeks in advance.

Situation: Court Officer Carla Lewis has a doctor and a dentist appointment on Monday, October 5.

98. In order to use a compensation day for these appointments, by what date must Carla notify her supervisor? 98.____

A. Friday, September 4
B. Monday, September 14
C. 10:00 A.M. October 5
D. Thursday, September 1

99. If Officer Carla Lewis wants to use a personal day for these appointments, by what date must she notify her supervisor? 99.____

A. Friday, September 4
B. Monday, September 14
C. 10:00 A.M. October 5
D. Thursday, October 1

100. If Officer Carla Lewis wants to use a sick day for these appointments, by what date must she notify her supervisor? 100.___

A. 10:00 A.M. on October 5
B. Monday, September 14
C. She cannot use a sick day for these appointments
D. She does not have to notify her supervisor until after she returns to work

KEY (CORRECT ANSWERS)

1.	B	21.	A	41.	D	61.	B	81.	D
2.	D	22.	C	42.	B	62.	D	82.	C
3.	C	23.	B	43.	A	63.	D	83.	B
4.	A	24.	D	44.	D	64.	A	84.	A
5.	D	25.	A	45.	C	65.	B	85.	C
6.	B	26.	C	46.	B	66.	D	86.	D
7.	A	27.	D	47.	A	67.	C	87.	A
8.	D	28.	A	48.	D	68.	A	88.	C
9.	C	29.	C	49.	B	69.	B	89.	D
10.	A	30.	A	50.	C	70.	D	90.	A
11.	D	31.	D	51.	B	71.	C	91.	D
12.	B	32.	C	52.	D	72.	A	92.	A
13.	C	33.	B	53.	C	73.	B	93.	D
14.	C	34.	D	54.	A	74.	D	94.	D
15.	B	35.	A	55.	B	75.	B	95.	C
16.	A	36.	C	56.	D	76.	C	96.	B
17.	D	37.	B	57.	A	77.	B	97.	C
18.	A	38.	A	58.	A	78.	A	98.	B
19.	B	39.	D	59.	C	79.	A	99.	D
20.	C	40.	C	60.	C	80.	B	100.	C

EXAMINATION SECTION

TEST 1

DIRECTIONS: Each question or incomplete statement is followed by several suggested answers or completions. Select the one that BEST answers the question or completes the statement. *PRINT THE LETTER OF THE CORRECT ANSWER IN THE SPACE AT THE RIGHT.*

1. While waiting for jury selection, one of the prospective jurors asks you how long a typical trial lasts. 1.____
   Which of the following is the MOST appropriate response?
   A. Trials can be lengthy.
   B. The length of trials varies widely, but every aspect of it is important.
   C. Civil trials typically last three to five days, while criminal trials are generally five to ten days.
   D. Decline to respond for fear of appearing biased.

2. One of the jurors appears faint and starts to wobble while seated in the jury box. 2.____
   How should you handle the situation?
   A. Let one of the other jurors come to the ailing juror's aid first.
   B. Alert the court officer of what you see and ask that the trial be held indefinitely.
   C. Politely interject the trial proceedings and ask the juror if he or she is feeling well.
   D. Alert the court officer who may or may not escort the juror out of the courtroom.

3. During trial, you believe that you see the defendant winking at one of the jurors. No one else seems to notice their interaction, including the judge. 3.____
   Which of the following actions would you take?
   A. Alert the judge in chambers
   B. Tell the court officer during a break in trial
   C. Interrupt the trial to make all parties aware of the behavior
   D. Confirm with the juror in question that the defendant is winking at her to determine if the feeling is mutual

4. During a recess in the trial, the defendant's expert witness is seen chatting with one of the alternate jurors outside the courthouse. While it is unclear what they are talking about, it seems to be a friendly exchange of information. 4.____
   What should you do before the court is called back to order?
   A. Tell the juror she must disclose her conversation with the expert witness in open court
   B. Tell the expert witness he must disclose the conversation with the juror in open court
   C. Inform the plaintiff's attorney about the conversation
   D. Inform the judge about the conversation

Questions 5-7.

DIRECTIONS: Questions 5 through 7 are to be answered on the basis of the following fact pattern.

After a TRO is issued to the plaintiff, the ex-wife of the defendant, both parties are free to go. The defendant appeared in court and rigorously opposed his ex-wife's request. His ex-wife already has sole custody of their three children and he seems incredibly distraught by the judge's grant of her request.

5. In a follow-up hearing, where the plaintiff is requesting to extend a TRO, the defendant does not show up. Instead, the defendant's brother appears at the hearing on his behalf. Is the defendant's brother permitted to voice his concerns about extending the TRO? 5.____
The defendant's brother
   A. is not a party to the action and must wait outside of the courtroom during proceedings.
   B. is welcome to testify on his brother's behalf
   C. can testify on his brother's behalf as long as he remains calm while doing so
   D. can testify on his brother's behalf so long as the plaintiff's sister can testify on her behalf

6. A TRO is a _____ restraining order, while a QDRO is a qualified _____ order. 6.____
   A. temporary; domicile relations
   B. territorial; domicile relations
   C. temporary; domestic revision
   D. temporary; domestic relations

7. How many alternate jurors are typically sworn in for trial? 7.____
   A. Up to 12
   B. Up to 14
   C. Up to 10
   D. Up to 6

Questions 8-10.

DIRECTIONS: Questions 8 through 10 are to be answered on the basis of the following fact pattern.

While those waiting for the court to open file into the hallway, an argument breaks out between two women and one man. When you intervene between the parties, you discover the two women are arguing over custody of a child – who is standing nearby – and the man is one of their attorneys. Barbara is the biological mother of the child. Tina raised the child from birth. Tina and her attorney, Bill, came with the child to court today.

8. Which party should stay with the child? 8.____
   A. The biological mother, Barbara, of the child should stay with the child while they await for court to begin.
   B. Tina and Bill should stay with the child since she raised the child from birth.

C. The parties should separate and the child should come with you to a sequestered part of the courthouse.
D. Tina and Bill should stay with the child as petitioners of the court, Barbara should wait in a separate area away from all three and refrain from contact.

9. Which of the following are Barbara and her attorney MOST likely to request in court? 9.____
A. An order of protection
B. Order to expunge
C. Order to impeach
D. Deposition

10. Should you tell the judge about the behavior of the parties during the hearing? 10.____
A. You can inform the judge if asked, but not during the hearing itself.
B. You can inform the judge if asked, but should wait until a hearing is not in session.
C. Before the hearing is set to begin, you should inform the judge of your encounter with the parties and let the judge decide how to best confront the situation between all involved.
D. No.

Questions 11-14.

DIRECTIONS: Questions 11 through 14 are to be answered on the basis of the following fact pattern.

At district court, a trial of a group of alleged rapists has drawn a huge crowd of spectators at each day of the hearings. Two of the defendants are locals of Nassau County, while the other is a local of Richmond County. The trial date has been set and moved multiple times.

11. Which of the following will the defendants MOST likely be charged with? 11.____
A. An information
B. A felony
C. A misdemeanor
D. An indictment

12. In reading the charge, which of the following is LEAST likely to appear? 12.____
A. The name of the attorneys of record
B. The names of the victims
C. The number of counts of each crime
D. The name of the judge hearing the case

13. There are likely to be multiples of which during this trial? 13.____
A. Multiple court officers
B. Multiple attorneys
C. Multiple charges
D. All of the above

14. The venue of the trial is MOST likely to be 14.____
A. Nassau County
B. Richmond County
C. Determined by the jury
D. Determined by the judge

Questions 15-17.

DIRECTIONS: Questions 15 through 17 are to be answered on the basis of the following fact pattern.

In the Supreme Court Foreclosure Part, a variety of parties are awaiting for hearings to begin. Homeowners, attorneys, creditors, and trustees anxiously talk amongst themselves. Based on your knowledge of foreclosure procedures, answer the following questions.

15. As you approach the foreclosure part, a woman rushes toward you. She is incredibly upset and begins to cry as soon as she begins speaking. She tells you that she cannot wait any longer for her hearing to begin because her mother just had an accident and she must rush to the hospital. 15.____
If she misses her court date, what should she be MOST concerned with as it relates to her foreclosure case?
    A. Having to reschedule her court date to defend herself
    B. Defaulting and, therefore, her creditor(s) prevailing against her
    C. Answering a motion to show cause from the bank
    D. Answering a complaint from the bank

16. One of the most frequent questions you are asked is whether a bank can accelerate the mortgage loan against a homeowner/borrower after the homeowner has made a few late payments. 16.____
Acceleration is
    A. requiring a borrower to immediately pay off the balance of the loan
    B. the amount of money owed on the mortgage
    C. the document showing the ownership of a mortgage or deed of trust
    D. the basic repayment plan the homeowner/borrower initially agreed to when purchasing the home

17. Homeowners in foreclosure sometimes file simultaneously for bankruptcy. 17.____
The automatic stay is a function unique to bankruptcy.
An automatic stay is defined as
    A. a large lump sum payment due as the last payment on a loan
    B. an injunction automatically issued by the bankruptcy court when someone files for bankruptcy
    C. an optional injunction that requires creditors to call the debtor and seek a settlement
    D. another term meaning "to stay a motion" or to hold a request from the court temporarily

18. Dave approaches the clerk's desk and asks how, generally, judges make their decisions on legal matters. The MOST correct answer would be based on 18.____
    A. case law, or the body of all court decisions which govern or provide precedent on the same legal issue before the judge
    B. case law, personal opinion and oral arguments by attorneys
    C. case law, oral arguments by attorneys, and the defendant's rap sheet
    D. "stare decisis" or that which has already been decided

19. Which hearing below will MOST likely be heard in the Commercial Division of the Suffolk County Supreme courthouse? 19.____
    A. Divorce petition between Bill and Amy
    B. A custody dispute between Jim and John
    C. A business dispute between ABC Corp. and XYZ, Inc.
    D. A petition for expungement of a stockbroker's record

20. Richard may face criminal charges for allegedly embezzling thousands of dollars from his company's business account. 20.____
    If a grand jury decides there is enough evidence to move forward with criminal charges against Richard, they
    A. return an information
    B. return an indictment
    C. issue a warrant
    D. issue a seizure

21. At trial, the prosecutor asks many pointed questions at Richard. The prosecutor believes Richard is lying on the stand. 21.____
    When an attorney attempts to reduce the credibility of the other side's witness, they are said to be trying to _____ the witness on the stand.
    A. objectify
    B. anger
    C. impeach
    D. frustrate

22. During a lengthy trial, four jurors conspire with one another to enter votes of "not guilty" and hatch a plan to sway other jurors in their favor in an attempt to close out deliberations early. 22.____
    What is the likely outcome of the trial?
    A. Hung jury
    B. Mistrial
    C. Acquittal
    D. Defensive charge

23. The judge's charge to the jury is also known as 23.____
    A. closing statements
    B. quid pro quo
    C. jury instructions
    D. sua sponte

24. Who is the only party responsible for delivering the sentence to the convicted? 24.____
    A. Bailiff
    B. Jury
    C. Judge
    D. Jury foreperson

25. A motion for directed verdict is made 25.____
    A. without the jury present
    B. with only the jury foreperson present
    C. with the entire jury present
    D. with only the alternate jurors present

KEY (CORRECT ANSWERS)

1. C
2. D
3. A
4. D
5. A

6. D
7. D
8. D
9. A
10. C

11. B
12. B
13. D
14. D
15. B

16. A
17. B
18. A
19. C
20. B

21. C
22. B
23. C
24. C
25. A

TEST 2

DIRECTIONS: Each question or incomplete statement is followed by several suggested answers or completions. Select the one that BEST answers the question or completes the statement. *PRINT THE LETTER OF THE CORRECT ANSWER IN THE SPACE AT THE RIGHT.*

1. Juror #12 is a close friend of your brother's, Tom. Tom starts to strike up a conversation with you outside of the courtroom. 1.____
   How should you respond?
   A. Politely decline to engage, unless he or she is asking for directions
   B. Politely decline to engage, unless he or she would like to talk about the case
   C. Politely decline to engage, unless he or she knows you personally
   D. Engage in the conversation remaining mindful of the appearance of bias and immediately ceasing the conversation if the trial at hand comes up

2. A charge of attempted murder is LEAST likely to accompany a charge of 2.____
   A. murder B. burglary C. robbery D. assault

Questions 3-4.

DIRECTIONS: Questions 3 and 4 are to be answered on the basis of the following fact pattern.

Mary approaches you inside the Albany County Supreme Court and says that she has been served with a lawsuit. She is confused about the entire lawsuit process and is confused as to what area of the courthouse she should be in. She believes, but is not entirely sure, that her sister may be suing her over money she lent her then subsequently lost gambling in the casino.

3. Which of the following is the MOST appropriate response you can provide Mary with regard to her being served? 3.____
   She should have a copy of the _____ with her and refer to it, which will tell her where she would report within the courthouse.
   A. answer B. complaint C. summons D. information

4. Mary produces the document and asks you if there is anything she can do to respond to the lawsuit. 4.____
   What is the MOST appropriate answer?
   She should
   A. file an answer, and perhaps seek legal counsel
   B. seek legal counsel
   C. check in at the Preliminary Conference desk
   D. file an injunction, and perhaps seek legal counsel

5. Who decides whether the jurors are allowed to take notes during the trial? 5.____
   A. The judge
   B. The plaintiff's attorney, since they are bringing the case to court
   C. Jurors are always allowed to take notes during trials
   D. Jurors are never allowed to take notes during trials.

6. During a trial, one of the jurors writes a question for one of the witnesses on a piece of paper and hands it to the court officer. 6.____
What is the CORRECT procedure?
The court officer
   A. may, but is not required to, pass the written question to the judge
   B. must pass the written question to the judge, who may or may not ask the witness the question posed
   C. must decline receipt of the written message
   D. passes the written question to the court assistant who may or may not read the question aloud

7. If questions arise during the jury deliberation process, what is the role of the court officer? 7.____
   A. To deliver the written question from the jury foreperson to the judge
   B. To repeat the question orally as told to the court officer by the jury foreperson to the judge
   C. To read the written question in open court with all parties present other than the defendant
   D. To record the written question in the docket

8. A juror has informed you that she accidentally read information about the case she is serving on while she was at the supermarket last night. 8.____
How should you respond to her?
   A. Berate her for not being more diligent in seeking out information about the case
   B. Inform the court officer that the juror should be replaced
   C. Remove the juror from the jury box and replace him or her with an alternate juror yourself
   D. Inform the judge immediately

9. Which court proceeding takes place CLOSEST in time to an arrest? 9.____
   A. Arraignment
   B. Sentencing
   C. Trial
   D. Jury selection

10. Which of the following is LEAST likely to occur at the conclusion of a trial? 10.____
   A. Sentencing
   B. Appeal
   C. Reversal
   D. Plea bargaining

11. You overhear two jurors talking about the case in the hallway during recess. From their conversation, it appears that they are related to one another. 11.____
You should
   A. do nothing as it's none of your business
   B. make sure no one else hears them
   C. simply tell them not to discuss the case between themselves
   D. tell the judge

12. How many jurors typically serve on a criminal trial?
    A. 12 B. 18 C. 16 D. 6

13. During jury selection, the judge has already excused 25 prospective jurors for cause. How many more jurors can be excused for cause before reaching the excusal limit? 13.____
    A. 5
    B. 10
    C. The judge has reached the limit
    D. There is no excusal limit "for cause"

14. Which of the following is the jury usually prohibited from doing during a trial on which they are serving? 14.____
    A. Visiting the scene of the alleged crime
    B. Read or listen to news about the trial from outside sources
    C. Research case law that applies to the trial
    D. All of the above

15. In New York City, jury trials are conducted at which of the following courts? 15.____
    A. Supreme Court B. New York City Civil Court
    C. New York City Criminal Court D. All of the above

16. A trial involving an alleged assault and battery is MOST likely to occur at which New York City court? 16.____
    A. Town and Village Court B. New York City Civil Court
    C. New York City Criminal Court D. County Court

17. In vacating a default, which must the petitioner file FIRST? 17.____
    A. Notice of motion B. Emergency affidavit
    C. Legal back D. Injunction

18. Order the steps of a typical trial from first to last. 18.____
    I. Opening statements II. Jury selection
    III. Deliberations IV. Oath and preliminary instructions
    The CORRECT answer is:
    A. I, II, III, IV B. IV, III, II, I C. I, II, IV, III D. II, IV, I, III

19. On appeal, three justices hear a case that was already decided in the lower courts. The issue before them is a complicated issue involving a determination of legal guardian. 19.____
    An opinion from the entire panel of justices is known as a(n)
    A. per curiam decision B. affirmative decision
    C. stare decisis D. en banc order

20. One of the judges agrees with the decision of the court, but disagrees with the reasoning of the conclusion. This judge decides to write his own opinion. 20.____
    This is deemed a
    A. dissenting opinion B. remedial decision
    C. concurring opinion D. recurrent opinion

21. Suppose that one of the judges disagrees entirely with the ruling. How will the judgment be altered because of the disagreement? The judgment 21.____
    A. is unaffected because the majority voted in agreement with the trial court
    B. is unaffected because this judge did not author a dissenting opinion
    C. is unaffected because oral arguments were not made before the panel
    D. will be overturned

22. The appellate court still requires _____, even if it is established by the trial court, known as original _____. 22.____
    A. domicile; venue
    B. venue; jurisdiction
    C. jurisdiction; jurisdiction
    D. jurisdiction; domicile

23. The legal theory upon which a case is based is called a 23.____
    A. basis
    B. decisis
    C. cause of action
    D. precedent

24. Sarah and her friend, Ashley, burglarized a number of homes in Kings County over the summer. They were only apprehended after one of their other friends overheard them talking about their crimes. At the time, both Sarah and Ashley were 18 and legally minors. A minor is legally defined as: 24.____
    A. In New York, a minor is anyone under the age of 18
    B. Anyone under 18
    C. A legally emancipated individual
    D. An infant or individual under the age of legal competence

25. The BEST place to refer back to the testimony of one witness is 25.____
    A. the docket
    B. the judge's notes which can be obtained freely from chambers
    C. the stenographer's transcript
    D. clerk notes which, in some instances, are available online

KEY (CORRECT ANSWERS)

1. D
2. A
3. B
4. B
5. A

6. B
7. A
8. D
9. A
10. D

11. D
12. A
13. D
14. D
15. D

16. C
17. A
18. D
19. A
20. C

21. A
22. C
23. C
24. D
25. C

TEST 3

DIRECTIONS: Each question or incomplete statement is followed by several suggested answers or completions. Select the one that BEST answers the question or completes the statement. *PRINT THE LETTER OF THE CORRECT ANSWER IN THE SPACE AT THE RIGHT.*

1. The pre-trial hearing is MOST likely to take place after _____, but before _____. 1.____
   A. arraignment; jury selection
   B. deliberations; closing statements
   C. assignment; adjudication
   D. plea bargain; opening statement

2. During a court recess, you see one of the jurors walking into the judge's chambers. You immediately 2.____
   A. halt the juror and demand he or she return to the deliberation room
   B. allow the juror to proceed, but ask the judge about the incident later
   C. allow the juror to proceed and assume they know one another personally
   D. allow the juror to proceed, but inform the court officer of the incident

3. When reading an indictment in court, each charge represents a(n) 3.____
   A. allegation of a crime
   B. proven criminal act
   C. evidentiary plea
   D. legal certainty

4. After a defendant has been acquitted, he or she will likely be 4.____
   A. free to leave the courthouse
   B. remanded to federal prison
   C. detained until further notice
   D. formally sentenced

5. Jeremiah, a defense attorney, has approached you in the hallways of the New York Civil Court. He is concerned that his client, Dave, may become violent during court proceedings. 5.____
   How do you handle Jeremiah's request to closely supervise Dave while court is in session?
   A. Inform the judge of Jeremiah's request and allow proceedings to continue as normal
   B. Ask that a court officer be present during court proceedings
   C. Request the judge to sequester the jury while Dave is present
   D. Ignore Jeremiah's request for now, until you see how Dave behaves yourself

6. Jury sequestration is 6.____
   A. extremely common given the complex nature of most criminal trials
   B. becoming increasingly common
   C. more common in civil cases than in criminal trials
   D. rare

7. At arraignment, the defendant is MOST likely to 7.____
   A. state his case
   B. convince the judge of his or her innocence
   C. enter a plea
   D. gather information on his or her case from the State's attorney

8. A warrant can be issued for an individual's arrest or for 8.____
   A. search of premises outlined in the warrant itself
   B. testimony
   C. deposition of the arrested individual
   D. evidence found at the scene

9. The responsibility to record notes for the judge and listen to issues of law that may need to be researched later are reserved for the 9.____
   A. court officer B. stenographer
   C. judge's clerk D. jury

10. Information about the charges against the defendant, as well as the parties involved in the case, can MOST likely be found in the 10.____
   A. judge's notes B. docket
   C. information D. discovery report

11. The opening statements in a trial are delivered by the 11.____
   A. defendant B. plaintiff C. attorneys D. judge

12. When the judge sustains the objection of an attorney who is asking a question of the witness on the stand, the witness must 12.____
   A. answer the question as asked
   B. wait for counsel to re-phrase the question in a proper form or ask another question before answering
   C. refuse to answer the question
   D. the witness may step down

13. An expert is permitted to 13.____
   A. review the plaintiff's evidence, draw a reasonable conclusion and give testimony to that effect
   B. review the defendant's evidence, draw a reasonable conclusion and submit his or her opinion in writing to the judge
   C. give his or her opinion based on the facts in evidence and provide the reasoning for that opinion
   D. provide an opinion in open court

14. Prosecutor and defense counsel have both made closing arguments in the trial of Samuel Smith Jones. Mr. Jones is being tried for capital murder for the alleged murder of his mother and sister. 14.____
   Which party is entitled to a rebuttal in closing arguments?
   A. The prosecutor
   B. The defense
   C. The defense, but only after the plaintiff has given their closing argument
   D. The defense, but only if the plaintiff waives their right to make a closing argument

15. When a jury cannot agree on a verdict, a(n) _____ occurs and the result is a _____. 15._____
    A. mistrial; acquittal
    B. mistrial; hung jury
    C. hung jury; mistrial
    D. acquittal; mistrial

16. Nominal damages are 16._____
    A. damages awarded in name only, indicating no substantial harm was done
    B. damages to recompense the injured for the infliction of emotional distress
    C. damages to recompense the initiator of the lawsuit
    D. a reimbursement of filing fees, awarded to the person who can prove they are injured

17. The type of recovery being sought by the plaintiff is known as the 17._____
    A. order
    B. punishment
    C. remedy
    D. issue

18. Robert approaches the clerk's desk in a panic. He says that he filed a lawsuit last week against his cousin, Mike, but neglected to add his cousin's friend, Rory, to the suit. 18._____
    Robert must _____ the compliant.
    A. amend
    B. refile
    C. re-serve
    D. redact

19. In a foreclosure action, which of the following will the borrower MOST likely be asked about in terms of securing a second or third mortgage? 19._____
    A. Business terms
    B. Collateral
    C. Damages
    D. Remedy

20. Maya has asked you about Article 7A proceedings. 20._____
    Article 7A hearings allow
    A. tenants being foreclosed upon to file a class action against the landlord
    B. at least 1/3 of tenants to ask the court to appoint an administrator to run the building in select circumstances
    C. tenants to forego paying the rent when living conditions in the building become inhabitable
    D. tenants to book their landlord from collecting rent when living conditions in the building become inhabitable

21. The Housing Court, sometimes referred to as Landlord and Tenant Court, is held at the 21._____
    A. Town and Village Court
    B. New York City Civil Court
    C. New York City Criminal Court
    D. County Court

22. Without an attorney, how much money can one sue for in Town or Village Courts, outside of New York City? 22._____
    A. Up to $3,000
    B. Up to $5,000
    C. Up to $2,500
    D. Up to $2,000

23. Judith wants to sue her neighbor, Samantha, in small claims court after Samantha borrowed Judith's lawnmower and refused to return it. Judith has begun a petition in small claims court for recovery of the lawnmower. How will the case proceed? 23.____
    A. The case will not go forward, because only money damages can be sought in small claims court.
    B. The case will not go forward, because small claims court cannot compel Samantha to return the lawnmower.
    C. The case will not go forward, because the lawnmower exceeds the small claims court limit.
    D. Judith will likely prevail.

24. Daniel wants to file for probate of his father's estate. The filing fee is based on 24.____
    A. Daniel's assets
    B. Daniel's age
    C. The size of the estate
    D. The age at which Daniel's father passed

25. Family court will hear each of the following cases EXCEPT 25.____
    A. custody and visitation
    B. adoption
    C. juvenile delinquency
    D. estate

KEY (CORRECT ANSWERS)

1.	A	11.	C
2.	A	12.	B
3.	A	13.	C
4.	A	14.	A
5.	B	15.	C
6.	D	16.	A
7.	C	17.	C
8.	A	18.	A
9.	C	19.	B
10.	B	20.	B

21.	B
22.	A
23.	A
24.	C
25.	D

TEST 4

DIRECTIONS: Each question or incomplete statement is followed by several suggested answers or completions. Select the one that BEST answers the question or completes the statement. *PRINT THE LETTER OF THE CORRECT ANSWER IN THE SPACE AT THE RIGHT.*

1. Jason is currently a student at SUNY Buffalo. He is worried that his recent conviction will affect his financial aid package with the college. How will Jason's conviction of drug possession affect his financial aid? It will 1.____
   A. remain unaffected
   B. remain unaffected as long as Jason is represented by counsel
   C. automatically be cancelled for a period of time
   D. be cancelled indefinitely

2. Who is responsible for drafting the Pre-Sentence report that judges use in sentencing convicted defendants? 2.____
   A. Defendant's attorney
   B. Probation officer
   C. Court assistant
   D. Judge's law clerk

3. Restitution cannot be made for 3.____
   A. breach of contract
   B. assault and battery
   C. lost wages
   D. future losses

4. In a bench trial, the _____ serves as the ultimate fact finder. 4.____
   A. jury
   B. judge
   C. bailiff
   D. law clerk

5. The role of the bankruptcy trustee is to represent the 5.____
   A. interest of the bankruptcy estate and the creditors of the debtor
   B. debtor against all creditors
   C. largest creditor of the debtor
   D. smallest creditor of the debtor

6. The bankruptcy estate typically includes _____ at the time of the filing. 6.____
   A. all property of the debtor, including interests in property
   B. the home where the debtor resides
   C. the home and personal vehicle of the debtor
   D. all personal property, but not real property, of the debtor

7. When a party to a lawsuit cannot afford the cost of the lawsuit, the Court 7.____
   A. may permit that party to proceed without being required to pay for court costs
   B. disallows payment for foreclosure proceeds
   C. does not require that party to pay for filing fees
   D. requires that party to settle the matter in ADR

8. An answer is a formal response to which document? 8.____
   A. indictment B. discovery C. complaint D. summons

9. Ishmael sued his former employer, Igor, for loss of wages. Igor lost the case and now wishes to appeal the ruling. 9.____
   When Igor appeals the case, he becomes an
   A. appellee B. appellant C. respondent D. defendant

10. Damiano has been sentenced to six years for armed robbery and ten years for grand larceny. He is sentenced to serve his prison terms concurrently. 10.____
    What is the MAXIMUM amount of time he will spend behind bars?
    A. Six years B. Sixteen years
    C. Ten years D. Four years

11. What does the exclusionary rule exclude in a criminal trial? 11.____
    A. Testimony that is deemed hearsay by a judge in a court of competent jurisdiction
    B. Evidence obtained in violation of a defendant's constitutional or statutory rights
    C. Depositions that are unsworn or not notarized
    D. Affidavits that are unsworn or not notarized

12. David is being arraigned and needs to enter a plea for the crime he allegedly committed while he was with his friend, Robert. Robert pleads guilty during his arraignment yesterday, but David has been advised by his attorney to plead no contest, also known as 12.____
    A. nolo contendere B. pro se C. quid pro quo D. qui tam

13. Adoptions can be heard in which two courts? 13.____
    A. Family court and surrogate court
    B. Foreclosure court and family court
    C. Family court and commercial court
    D. Family court and court of claims

14. Which party may NOT file a paternity petition? 14.____
    A. The child's mother
    B. The man who believes he may be the father of the child
    C. The child or the child's guardian
    D. The child's teacher or other close associate

15. Amy was married to Bob at the time her child was born. John believes he is the father of Amy's baby. 15.____
    Who is presumed to be the father of Amy's child?
    A. Bob
    B. John
    C. Neither can be presumed; a DNA test must be administered in this circumstance
    D. Neither can be presumed; each has to petition the court separately

16. Parties that represent themselves during court hearings are referred to as _____ litigants. 16.____
A. qui tam B. pro se C. en banc D. quid quo pro

17. Normally, guardianship petitions must be filed in _____ court. 17.____
A. family B. surrogates C. probate D. civil

18. At what age can a child's own preference be taken under consideration in guardianship or custody hearings? 18.____
A. 12 B. 14 C. 17 D. 16

19. Civil litigation claims against the State of New York or other State-related agencies are heard exclusively in the 19.____
A. Civil Court
B. Criminal Court
C. Court of Claims
D. Surrogate Court

20. Preliminary conferences are automatically scheduled by the Court within _____ days after a Request for Judicial Intervention (RJI). 20.____
A. 30 B. 45 C. 50 D. 55

21. There are two junior attorneys that have been sent to cover the preliminary conference of their case *Abe v. Gabe* in part 22 of the court. Both attorneys approach the clerk's desk to ask what the "return date" on a motion refers to. The return date is the date the 21.____
A. motion will be conferenced and/or orally argued at the discretion of the court
B. attorneys must return for more information
C. attorneys must return with the clients
D. attorneys must return to complete discovery

22. Decisions made on motions and pro se litigants must be 22.____
A. mailed or a copy provided of the decision
B. made available for photocopy or fax
C. made available for scan, but not photocopied or faxed
D. uploaded to the court website so it can be easily accessed online

23. A stipulation of settlement represents a formal agreement between the 23.____
A. judge and the parties resolving the case
B. litigants and their attorneys resolving the dispute
C. clerk and the litigants representing a near end to the dispute at issue
D. judge and the clerk representing a notation of the resolution

24. A motion to vacate a default in foreclosure part represents an attempt by the homeowner or borrower to 24.____
A. reverse the court's finding of default
B. reverse the court's finding of dereliction
C. obtain a new hearing
D. reschedule a hearing due to a missed court date

25. The Personal Appearance Part in the Civil Court is where which types of cases are heard? 25.____
Cases where
A. one or both parties are self-represented
B. the plaintiff is self-represented
C. the defendant is self-represented
D. clerk is the fact finder

KEY (CORRECT ANSWERS)

1.	C	11.	B
2.	B	12.	A
3.	D	13.	A
4.	B	14.	D
5.	A	15.	A
6.	A	16.	B
7.	A	17.	A
8.	C	18.	B
9.	B	19.	C
10.	C	20.	B

21.	A
22.	A
23.	B
24.	A
25.	A

EXAMINATION SECTION

TEST 1

DIRECTIONS: Each question or incomplete statement is followed by several suggested answers or completions. Select the one that BEST answers the question or completes the statement. *PRINT THE LETTER OF THE CORRECT ANSWER IN THE SPACE AT THE RIGHT.*

Questions 1-5.

DIRECTIONS: Questions 1 through 5 are to be answered on the basis of the following passage.

The jury could not decide the verdict in the case of *The People of New York vs. Tim Jones*. One of the main reasons why the jury was deadlocked was because the jury found the presentation of the evidence by the prosecutor and the defense was quite confusing. One of the major focal points in the case was the __(1)__ of __(2)__ against the defendant, Tim Jones. When the jury initially came back to the courtroom and announced they could not come to a decision, the judge asked that the jury return to __(3)__. Three hours later, after still not arriving at a decision, the judge declared the jury to be a hung jury. Because it was a jury trial and not a __(4)__ trial, the court polled the jury.

1. The CORRECT word to fill in space number 1 is 1.____
   A. admissibility B. entertainment
   C. exclusion D. branding

2. The CORRECT word to fill in space number 2 is 2.____
   A. documents B. testimony C. ex parte D. voir dire

3. The CORRECT word to fill in space number 3 is 3.____
   A. deliberations B. group C. court D. bench

4. The CORRECT word to fill in space number 4 is 4.____
   A. bench B. regular C. heightened D. closed

5. A _____, unlike a hung jury, is an invalid trial caused by a fundamental error. 5.____
   A. erroneous trial B. deadlocked jury
   C. bilateral trial D. mistrial

Questions 6-7.

DIRECTIONS: Questions 6 and 7 are to be answered on the basis of the following passage.

Two former friends are embattled in a legal dispute whereby one friend, James, accuses the other, Robin, of negligence and fraud. In addition to a complaint, James also submitted an __(6)__ accounting the events that led up to the lawsuit. James is not represented by counsel. Robin, however, is represented by an attorney. James is considered a __(7)__ litigant.

6. The CORRECT word to fill in space number 6 is 6.____
A. motion B. document C. affidavit D. complaint

7. The CORRECT word to fill in space number 7 is 7.____
A. represented B. pro se C. individual D. per diem

8. Testimony is a type of _____, which is more broadly defined as information presented and/or used to persuade the fact finder to decide the case in favor of one side or the other. 8.____
A. evidence
B. conference
C. pre-hearing motion
D. deposition

9. Erin is accused of following her former boss home, burglarizing his home and assaulting him. The crimes are serious, especially the charge of assault which is punishable by imprisonment for more than one year. Consequently, Erin will be charged with at least one _____. 9.____
A. felony
B. misdemeanor
C. offense
D. civil crime

10. A _____ is a body of 16-23 citizens who listen to evidence of criminal allegations, which is presented by the prosecutors, and determine whether there is probable cause to believe an individual committed an offense. 10.____
A. jury
B. alternate jury
C. grand jury
D. exculpatory hearing

11. The same body returns an _____ if there is probable cause to believe an individual committed an offense. 11.____
A. indictment B. information C. conviction D. acquittal

12. If the same is presented by a government body, the body returns an _____. 12.____
A. information B. verdict C. ex-parte D. ramification

Questions 13-16.

DIRECTIONS: Questions 13 through 16 are to be answered on the basis of the following passage.

Stacy appears at the Nassau County Courthouse to support her cousin, Dave, who is on trial for attempted robbery. While Stacy knows Dave is innocent, the testimony presented by the prosecutor is convincing. The prosecutor calls four different witnesses who testified they saw Dave point a gun at an elderly gentleman and demand that he turn over his wallet and cellphone. The defense __(13)__ and does not present any evidence. The prosecutor and defense then both presented their __(14)__ to the jury, which summarized their cases __(15)__.

13. The CORRECT word to fill in space number 13 is 13.____
A. persists B. re-examines C. rests D. repositions

14. The CORRECT word to fill in space number 14 is 14.____
    A. closing argument
    B. opening arguments
    C. summaries
    D. depositions

15. The CORRECT word to fill in space number 15 is 15.____
    A. in brief
    B. in totality
    C. amicus
    D. sua sponte

16. Which part of the trial did Stacy miss? 16.____
    A. Closing argument
    B. Opening argument
    C. Evidence presentation
    D. Direct examination

Questions 17-20.

DIRECTIONS: Questions 17 through 20 are to be answered on the basis of the following passage.

During jury deliberations, two jurors cannot seem to agree. Melissa feels strongly that the defendant is innocent and continues to argue with another juror, Jim, who strongly believes the defendant is guilty of a __(17)__ , which is a crime punishable by death. Melissa argues that much of the evidence presented during the trial was __(18)__ and should not be considered because it creates a __(19)__ against the defendant.

17. The CORRECT word to fill in space number 17 is 17.____
    A. capital offense
    B. delinquency
    C. delinquent crime
    D. obstructionist offense

18. The CORRECT word to fill in space number 18 is 18.____
    A. admissible
    B. triable
    C. presentable
    D. inadmissible

19. The CORRECT word to fill in space number 19 is 19.____
    A. demands
    B. bias
    C. recant
    D. confusion

20. What is the term used to described the outcome if Melissa, Jim, and the other jurors do not agree on a verdict? 20.____
    A. Suspended jury
    B. Hung jury
    C. Dreaded jury
    D. Misguided jury

Questions 21-25.

DIRECTIONS: Questions 21 through 25 are to be answered on the basis of the following passage.

The pre-trial process, like the actual trial, takes place in multiple __(21)__. Hearings are scheduled by __(22)__ between the parties and the judge. If the factfinder is not a judge, the __(23)__ is selected in a separate process called voir dire. __(24)__ are argued in court before a trial begins, in which an issue relating to the case is decided. Finally, the trial begins once a __(25)__ has been set. Even then, the case may settle before the start of opening statements.

21. The CORRECT word to fill in space number 21 is 21.____
    A. parts B. pieces C. units D. slices

22. The CORRECT word to fill in space number 22 is 22.____
    A. schedules B. calendars C. conference D. telephone

23. The CORRECT word to fill in space number 23 is 23.____
    A. jury B. panel C. composition D. attorneys

24. The CORRECT word to fill in space number 24 is 24.____
    A. Motions B. Witnesses
    C. Issue statements D. Stipulations

25. The CORRECT word to fill in space number 25 is 25.____
    A. trial date B. defendant
    C. judge D. final conference

KEY (CORRECT ANSWERS)

1.	A	11.	A
2.	B	12.	A
3.	A	13.	C
4.	A	14.	B
5.	D	15.	A
6.	C	16.	B
7.	B	17.	A
8.	A	18.	D
9.	A	19.	B
10.	C	20.	B

21.	A
22.	C
23.	A
24.	A
25.	A

TEST 2

DIRECTIONS: Each question or incomplete statement is followed by several suggested answers or completions. Select the one that BEST answers the question or completes the statement. *PRINT THE LETTER OF THE CORRECT ANSWER IN THE SPACE AT THE RIGHT.*

Questions 1-3.

DIRECTIONS: Questions 1 through 3 are to be answered on the basis of the following passage.

In a divorce proceeding, Alice and Tom have each filed for __(1)__ of their son, Jack. Alice wants Jack to live with her full time, and Tom has asked the court for the same. In their petitions, each party has outlined why living with them would be in the __(2)__ of the child. The family court judge has taken account of all the evidence and is currently deliberating on the final __(3)__.

1. The CORRECT word to fill in space number 1 is 1.____
   A. physical custody
   B. alimony
   C. child support
   D. restraining order

2. The CORRECT word to fill in space number 2 is 2.____
   A. best interests
   B. sustaining interests
   C. limited interests
   D. maternal wishes

3. The CORRECT word to fill in space number 3 is 3.____
   A. issue B. order C. motion D. request

4. A _____ is a sworn statement containing facts about a child involved in a case, including the full name of the child, date of birth, current and past residences, and other information as may be required by law. 4.____
   A. surrogates certificate
   B. custody affidavit
   C. remembrance order
   D. restraining order

Questions 5-7.

DIRECTIONS: Questions 5 through 7 are to be answered on the basis of the following passage.

Bill is on the witness stand providing details on when he last saw Kevin. Bill and Kevin do not know one another. Bill believes that he saw Kevin in the bank two months ago, just before the bank was robbed. Kevin is accused of writing bad checks. Bill's attorney questions him on the stand, then Kevin's attorney questions Bill on the stand. Kevin does not take the stand in his own defense.

5. Kevin's attorney will _____ Bill. 5.____
   A. examine
   B. decipher
   C. impeach
   D. cross-examine

6. Bill is providing which of the following? 6.____
   A. Testimony
   B. Interrogatory
   C. Illustrative examination
   D. Demonstration

7. Kevin is exercising his right against 7.____
   A. self-inducement
   B. judgment
   C. self-incrimination
   D. perjury

8. In a criminal case, one of the major issues is whether the defendant had a guilty mind, or _____. Without it, the charge from second degree murder would drop to manslaughter, given the lack of premeditation. 8.____
   A. anger reduction
   B. mens rea
   C. exclusionary rule
   D. per diem application

Questions 9-11.

DIRECTIONS: Questions 9 through 11 are to be answered on the basis of the following passage.

Mary brought a wrongful death __(9)__ against a manufacturer of antibiotic ointment after her husband applied the ointment to an open wound on his knee and became fatally ill. In her lawsuit, Mary alleges that the manufacturer knew certain shipments of the ointment had been tainted and did not issue a recall to consumers. After a lengthy trial, the court awarded her punitive __(10)__. Assume that the manufacturer Mary sued was ABC, Inc. The manufacturer of the ointment Mary's husband used, however, is Ointment, Inc. The judge __(11)__ the case __(12)__, allowing Mary to bring the suit again after the correct manufacturer was identified.

9. The CORRECT word to fill in space number 9 is 9.____
   A. action
   B. exercise
   C. request
   D. application

10. The CORRECT word to fill in space number 10 is 10.____
    A. funds
    B. null award
    C. compensatory
    D. damages

11. The CORRECT word to fill in space number 11 is 11.____
    A. dismissed
    B. acquitted
    C. relieved
    D. excused

12. The CORRECT word to fill in space number 12 is 12.____
    A. without prejudice
    B. knowingly
    C. erroneously
    D. with prejudice

13. A tort action would most likely be filed and litigated in _____ court, rather than criminal court. 13.____
    A. Civil
    B. Surrogate's
    C. Supreme
    D. District

14. Newlyweds Richard and Erica are in the process of closing on their new home in Bronx County. An examination of public records to determine the state of a title and confirm that the seller of a property is its legal owner is deemed a 14.____
A. title search
B. seizure
C. lien in assets
D. forfeiture

15. Ronnie was convicted of assault with a deadly weapon in Orange County Supreme Court and sentenced to eleven years imprisonment. The verdict in Ronnie's case was 15.____
A. nolo contendere
B. moot
C. arraigned
D. guilty

16. Eric's hearing, stemming from an alleged petty larceny, was scheduled for Friday at 3 P.M. At noon, Eric's mother informed him that his grandmother had passed. Eric rushed to the hospital in disbelief, missing his hearing. Eric's attorney was not informed by Eric that he would not be able to attend the hearing. Eric's _____ will certainly be detrimental to his case. 16.____
A. failure to appear
B. failed deposition
C. failed interrogatory
D. failed hearing

17. During a break, one of the jurors in the *Tim James v. Alpha, Inc.* spots one of the courthouse judges speaking to a lawyer in the Tim James case. The juror has witnessed a possible 17.____
A. ex-parte communication
B. domiciled conversation
C. un-docketed conversation
D. delinquent conversation

Questions 18-20.

DIRECTIONS: Questions 18 through 20 are to be answered on the basis of the following passage.

In a __(18)__, the attorneys for the Estate of Abe Smith and Red Bank, Inc. are attempting to determine the scope of possible trial. The Estate of Abe Smith is suing the bank for mismanagement of the estate's funds.

18. The CORRECT word to fill in space number 18 is 18.____
A. probationary hearing
B. pretrial conference
C. protective order hearing
D. pleading

19. Red Bank, Inc. is identified as the _____ in the case. 19.____
A. litigant
B. plaintiff
C. appellant
D. defendant

20. The case will MOST likely be heard in _____ Court. 20.____
A. Criminal
B. Surrogate's
C. Bankruptcy
D. Family

21. To avoid trial, Benjamin agrees to a _____ which requires that he serve three years in jail, followed by five years of probation. 21.____
A. dismissal
B. reduced issue
C. plea bargain
D. unilateral contract

22. Jamal and Nicole want to legally separate. Jamal and Nicole are both represented by attorneys. Jamal's attorney, Sam, went to law school with Nicole's attorney, Barbara. Who are the litigants in this case? 22.____
    A. Jamal only
    B. Jamal and Nicole
    C. Nicole only
    D. Sam and Barbara

Questions 23-25.

DIRECTIONS: Questions 23 through 25 are to be answered on the basis of the following passage.

A jury is selected in a criminal trial in Suffolk County Supreme Court. Each __(23)__ as selected from a larger pool and subjected to __(24)__, or the process of questioning each prospective juror about their qualifications to serve on a panel. After the trial concludes, the judge delivers formal instructions, or the __(25)__ on the law before the jury can begin their official deliberations.

23. The CORRECT word to fill in space number 23 is 23.____
    A. party
    B. juror
    C. representative
    D. attorney

24. The CORRECT word to fill in space number 24 is 24,____
    A. voir dire
    B. peremptory challenge
    C. exclusionary rule
    D. exclusion-based bias

25. The CORRECT word to fill in space number 25 is 25.____
    A. jury charge
    B. mandate
    C. directive
    D. affirmative response

KEY (CORRECT ANSWERS)

1. A
2. A
3. B
4. B
5. D

6. A
7. C
8. B
9. A
10. D

11. A
12. A
13. C
14. A
15. D

16. A
17. A
18. B
19. D
20. B

21. C
22. B
23. B
24. A
25. A

EXAMINATION SECTION

TEST 1

DIRECTIONS: Each question or incomplete statement is followed by several suggested answers or completions. Select the one that BEST answers the question or completes the statement. *PRINT THE LETTER OF THE CORRECT ANSWER IN THE SPACE AT THE RIGHT.*

Questions 1-3.

DIRECTIONS: Questions 1 through 3 are to be answered on the basis of the following passage.

Bryan accused his uncle, Jeremy, of petty larceny after he discovered $300 in cash was missing from his car's glove compartment. As a defense, Jeremy testified that he left the car windows rolled down while he ran errands and, therefore, it was possible that someone else stole the money. Bryan initiated the lawsuit against Jeremy after Jeremy refused to give Bryan $300.

1. The dispute is BEST deemed a(n) 1.____
   A. congenial dispute
   B. adversarial proceeding
   C. stipulated matter
   D. raised issue

2. Bryan and Jeremy would have recounted their respective statement of the facts in which of the following documents? 2.____
   A. Affidavit B. Notice C. Subpoena D. Warrant

3. Assume that Jeremy wants to change his accounting of the events that led to the theft from Bryan's car. Jeremy would need to _____ his statement of facts. 3.____
   A. relieve B. amend C. recount D. rename

4. Jared's mother is accused of child abuse. At her arraignment, Jared begins yelling obscenities at the judge. Jared is held in 4.____
   A. grievance
   B. collateral estoppel
   C. contempt of court
   D. recognizance

5. Attorneys in a libel and defamation lawsuit are not prepared for their pretrial conference. The attorneys, jointly, petition the court for a _____, which would allow for a postponement of the hearing and provide each side with more time to gather information for trial. 5.____
   A. hearing adjustment
   B. continuance
   C. leverage
   D. codicil

6. Given that Lindsay has been found guilty of mail fraud, a federal crime and felony, she is now considered a _____ felon. 6.____
   A. convicted B. contrived C. imperiled D. contracted

Questions 7-9.

DIRECTIONS: Questions 7 through 9 are to be answered on the basis of the following passage.

Tim and Lisa are in the midst of a contentious legal battle. Tim has accused Lisa, his former employer, of paying him less than minimum wage. Lisa, an owner of a local restaurant, maintains that Tim was paid in accordance with the laws of New York State. As part of __(7)__, Tim was asked by Lisa's attorney to turn copies of all paystubs during his employment at the restaurant. Tim never complied; instead he stopped responding to all requests from Lisa's attorney and the judge. Additionally, he stopped __(8)__ at court hearings. Consequently, the judge issued a __(9)__ in Lisa's favor.

7. The CORRECT word to fill in space number 7 is 7.____
   A. discovery B. investigation
   C. interrogatories D. motions

8. The CORRECT word to fill in space number 8 is 8.____
   A. recounting B. revisiting C. defending D. appearing

9. The CORRECT word to fill in space number 9 is 9.____
   A. default judgment B. support judgment
   C. cause of action D. in rem motion

10. A subordinate employee to the clerk who is empowered to act in the place of the clerk in the official business of the court is also known as the 10.____
   A. regular clerk B. municipal judge
   C. supervisory magistrate D. deputy clerk

11. A divorce decree is equivalent to a(n) 11.____
   A. order of the court B. void certificate
   C. effective disclaimer D. dismissal order

Questions 12-13.

DIRECTIONS: Questions 12 and 13 are to be answered on the basis of the following passage.

Robert was ordered to pay child support three years ago. Since then, Robert has not missed any payments, as they are deducted automatically from his paycheck, but he has recently lost his job. Robert would like to petition the court for a downward __(12)__ of the child support law.

12. The CORRECT word to fill in space number 12 is 12.____
   A. modification B. recipient C. treatment D. restitution

13. Robert is subject to 13.____
   A. garnishee B. indictment C. incarceration D. garnishment

Questions 14-15.

DIRECTIONS: Questions 14 and 15 are to be answered on the basis of the following passage.

The judge in the Bronx County Criminal Court has asked her clerk to take notes during the trial of The People vs. Joe Smith. More specifically, the judge requested that the clerk record any factor that may reduce the severity of the crime raised by the defense. Mr. Smith is accused of armed robbery and attempted arson. The prosecutor asked Mr. Smith if he was of sound mind during the incident, whether he was at the scene of the crime during the night in question, and whether he was with anyone while the crime was being committed. Mr. Smith denied knowing anything about the robbery or the arson.

14. The judge has asked the clerk to identify 14.____
   A. mitigating factors
   B. letters testamentary
   C. litigant application(s)
   D. raison d'etre

15. Which of the following has Mr. Smith NOT provided in his testimony? 15.____
   A. Jurisdiction
   B. Alibi
   C. Plea bargain
   D. Indemnification

Questions 16-19.

DIRECTIONS: Questions 16 through 19 are to be answered on the basis of the following passage.

Lily and Dan Johnson are suing the landscaping company that used to mow their lawn. The landscaping company is owned by Richard. The Johnsons did not sign a contract for Richard's company to mow their lawn, but two of Richard's workers continued to mow the Johnson's lawn for the entire summer of 2016. Lily received a bill for $2,000 in May of 2016 and disputes the bill. Richard countersued, claiming the Johnson's did not honor the contract that was rightfully in place for mowing services. The Court estopped Richard's company from performing all landscaping activities for the Johnsons and their respective parties.

16. What is the cause of action for Richard's claim? 16.____
   A. Fraud
   B. Breach of contract
   C. Libel
   D. Negligence

17. Who are the cross-claimants in this case? 17.____
   A. Richard's company
   B. Lily and Dan
   C. Richard and Richard's contractors
   D. There are no cross-claimants in this matter

18. Which parties are consanguineous, or related by blood? 18.____
   A. Lily and Dan
   B. Lily and Richard
   C. Dan and Richard
   D. None of the parties

19. What did the court order Richard's company to do? 19.____
    A. Stop landscaping activities
    B. Stop mailing bills to the Johnsons
    C. Stop engaging the Johnsons in conversations about landscaping
    D. Continue landscaping activities

Questions 20-22.

DIRECTIONS: Questions 20 through 22 are to be answered on the basis of the following passage.

The Southern District Court of New York is a court of __(20)__ jurisdiction, meaning that the court only has jurisdiction over actions authorized by law. In a class action suit, heard at the District Court, there are more than one hundred plaintiffs that are suing a New York-based manufacturer of a particular drug. Some plaintiffs claim that the drug causes death while others claim the drug is illegally manufactured. All claims have been __(21)__ in the class action suit. One requirement in a class action suit is that the class be represented by the same __(22)__.

20. The CORRECT word to fill in space number 20 is 20.____
    A. limited B. unlimited C. timely D. wholly

21. The CORRECT word to fill in space number 21 is 21.____
    A. consolidated B. remarkable C. accepted D. stipulated

22. The CORRECT word to fill in space number 22 is 22.____
    A. litigants B. judge C. jury D. counsel

Questions 23-25.

DIRECTIONS: Questions 23 through 25 are to be answered on the basis of the following passage.

During cross-examination by Jackson, Katie stated that she witnessed someone leaving the scene of an accident in a red car. The driver, she said, was a male with blond hair like the defendant, Adam. During the direct examination by Carl, Katie said the driver had blondish–reddish hair.

23. Who is Adam's attorney? 23.____
    A. Carl
    B. Jackson
    C. Katie
    D. Adam is not represented by counsel

24. In which court is this trial MOST likely to be held? 24.____
    A. Civil B. Criminal C. Surrogates D. Family

25. Who is Katie's attorney? 25.____
    A. Jackson
    B. Carl
    C. Katie is not represented by counsel
    D. It is unclear if Katie has an attorney

KEY (CORRECT ANSWERS)

1.	B	11.	A
2.	A	12.	A
3.	B	13.	D
4.	C	14.	A
5.	B	15.	B
6.	A	16.	B
7.	A	17.	D
8.	D	18.	D
9.	A	19.	A
10.	D	20.	A

21.	A
22.	D
23.	B
24.	B
25.	D

TEST 2

DIRECTIONS: Each question or incomplete statement is followed by several suggested answers or completions. Select the one that BEST answers the question or completes the statement. *PRINT THE LETTER OF THE CORRECT ANSWER IN THE SPACE AT THE RIGHT.*

1. A case that has been decided is declared _____ by the court. 1.____
   A. adjudicated B. annulled
   C. detrimental D. acknowledged

Questions 2-4.

DIRECTIONS: Questions 2 through 4 are to be answered on the basis of the following passage.

Three different individuals approach the clerk's desk at different times, each in need of assistance in filing their lawsuit. Amy wants to respond to a notice that she received in the mail that names her as a party in a lawsuit. Bill wants to start a lawsuit and name a party. Carl wants to respond to a lawsuit in which he has been named, and sue the person that sued him. Amy, Bill, and Carl each want to know what they would need to get started.

2. Amy needs to file a(n) 2.____
   A. letter B. response C. answer D. reply

3. Bill needs to file a(n) 3.____
   A. immediate interrogatory B. complaint
   C. affiant D. codicil

4. Carl is MOST likely seeking to file a 4.____
   A. counterclaim B. restitution claim
   C. defamatory issuance D. interlocutory demand

5. If a jury finds that there is insufficient evidence to convict, the recorded verdict is not guilty and the case results in a(n) 5.____
   A. reversal B. acquittal C. recusal D. repository

Questions 6-8.

DIRECTIONS: Questions 6 through 8 are to be answered on the basis of the following passage.

At the close of a bench trial, the defendant, John Ash, was found not guilty. The plaintiff in the case against Mr. Ash, Mr. Steel, wants to appeal the verdict. Mr. Steel's friend, Mr. Smith, wants to file a brief in support of her friend. Mr. Smith is an attorney and her brief would take the form of a memorandum of law.

6. Mr. Steel is which of the following in the appellate case? 6.____
   A. Appellate B. Appellee C. Appellant D. Affirmation

7. If Mr. Ash was found guilty, could Mr. Steel file an appeal? 7.____
   A. Yes, any party can appeal any verdict.
   B. Yes, Mr. Steel has an affirmative right to appeal a verdict he is a party to.
   C. No, Mr. Steel can only appeal in federal court.
   D. No, Mr. Steel would not need to file an appeal if Mr. Ash was found guilty.

8. Mr. Smith is seeking to file a(n) 8.____
   A. amicus brief
   B. dissertation brief
   C. motion in limine
   D. motion of law

9. During arraignment, the defendant may choose to have one of two types of trials. A jury trial will consist of 6-12 jurors, with _____ while a _____ trial will be decided by a single judge. 9.____
   A. alternates; brief
   B. alternate jurors; bench
   C. alternative jurors; trustee
   D. alternate jurors; hearing

10. A _____ bankruptcy can occur in two circumstances; the debtor can be a business or an individual involved in business and the debts are for business purposes. 10.____
   A. liquidation
   B. reorganization
   C. business
   D. restitution

Questions 11-12.

DIRECTIONS: Questions 11 through 12 are to be answered on the basis of the following passage.

As is standard procedure in many divorce cases, the judge presiding over Brian and Kate's divorce has asked that the parties attempt to settle matters in __(11)__, or the dispute resolution process in which an impartial third party assists the parties to reach a mutually acceptable settlement. Both Brian and Kate request additional time to decide on whether to complete that process, which is granted by the judge.

11. The CORRECT word to fill in space number 11 is 11.____
   A. arbitration
   B. mediation
   C. dispute training
   D. mandamus

12. Which of the following was MOST likely granted by the judge? 12.____
   A. Adjournment
   B. Adjudication
   C. Allegation
   D. Acknowledgment

13. The clerk is responsible for calling the cases scheduled for the day, also termed a 13.____
   A. calendar call
   B. document review
   C. docketing
   D. case certification

Questions 14-16.

DIRECTIONS: Questions 14 through 16 are to be answered on the basis of the following passage.

In an effort to speed matters along in the courtroom, Judge Johnson would like the clerks to begin summarizing the hearings on the daily docket at the beginning of each day. Judge Johnson asks that pleadings submitted by pro se parties be given special attention. Specifically, the judge wants to know if any of the pleadings are defective on their face. If so, the judge would like the clerk to assist the litigants in correcting the pleadings before the hearing so as not to waste the court's time.

14. Pro se litigants are those 14.____
   A. who represent themselves in any kind of case
   B. that represent others on a pro bono basis
   C. that represent family members for a small fee or on a volunteer basis
   D. who represent themselves under anonymity

15. Which of the following are considered pleadings? 15.____
   A. Motion to dismiss
   B. Answer
   C. Complaint
   D. All of the above

16. A defective complaint would be one that 16.____
   A. listed the parties' names
   B. did not state a cause of action
   C. did not list a location of the action
   D. contains a notary public stamp

Questions 17-19.

DIRECTIONS: Questions 17 through 19 are to be answered on the basis of the following passage.

As documents are filed with the Court, they are stamped with a __(17)__ date which usually indicates the date a motion will be heard in court. Jamie is at the clerk's desk and wants to know if this date is picked and asks the clerk for guidance.

17. The CORRECT word to fill in space number 17 is 17.____
   A. blank
   B. expedited
   C. return
   D. sealant

18. Which of the following should be considered in the selection of the above date? 18.____
   I. Notice to the other parties.
   II. Day of the week the proper court hears motions
   III. Convenience of the clerk
   IV. Will of the attorneys

   The CORRECT answer is:
   A. None of the above
   B. I, II, III
   C. I, IV
   D. I and II

19. Motions to the court must include which of the following? 19.____
    A. Full address of the courthouse
    B. Relief sought
    C. Part, room, and time the motion will be heard
    D. All of the above

Questions 20-25.

DIRECTIONS: Questions 20 through 25 are to be answered on the basis of the following passage.

Harper hired Janelle to write articles for Harper's online magazine. Harper paid Janelle for two articles, then ceased paying Janelle. In Civil Court, Janelle sued Harper for fraud and breach of contract. In a countersuit, Harper sued Janelle for defamation. The clerk is asked to first confer with the parties about a date for __(20)__ or a conference with the judge to discuss discovery and possible settlement. Harper is representing herself at trial as she cannot afford an attorney, while Janelle is represented by Jane. Janelle submits an affidavit to the court, swearing to the events that led up to her filing a suit against Janelle.

20. The CORRECT word to fill in space number 20 is 20.____
    A. pretrial
    B. pre-sentence investigation
    C. restraining order hearing
    D. show cause hearing

21. Harper is _____ and considered a _____ litigant. 21.____
    A. incapable; pro se
    B. injunction; pro bono
    C. indigent; pro se
    D. incarcerated; per diem

22. If Harper were to prevail in her suit, which of the following is she MOST likely to recover? 22.____
    A. Janelle's imprisonment
    B. Janelle's probation
    C. Payment of fines
    D. Asset seizure and forfeiture

23. If Janelle were to prevail in her suit against Harper, which of the following is she LEAST likely to recover? 23.____
    A. Back-payment for the articles written
    B. Punitive damages for fraud and breach of contract
    C. Monetary damages for breach of contract
    D. Harper's imprisonment

24. Which of the following is likely to be entered into evidence? 24.____
    A. Employment contract(s)
    B. Paystubs
    C. Articles written and websites where the articles were published
    D. All of the above

25. Who is the affiant in Janelle's affidavit? 25.____
    A. Harper
    B. Harper's attorney
    C. Janelle
    D. Janelle's attorney

KEY (CORRECT ANSWERS)

1. A
2. C
3. B
4. A
5. B

6. C
7. D
8. A
9. B
10. C

11. B
12. A
13. A
14. A
15. D

16. B
17. C
18. D
19. D
20. A

21. C
22. C
23. D
24. D
25. C

EXAMINATION SECTION

TEST 1

DIRECTIONS: Each question or incomplete statement is followed by several suggested answers or completions. Select the one that BEST answers the question or completes the statement. *PRINT THE LETTER OF THE CORRECT ANSWER IN THE SPACE AT THE RIGHT.*

Questions 1-6.

DIRECTIONS: Questions 1 through 6 are to be answered SOLELY on the basis of the numbered boxes on the Arrest Report and paragraph below.

ARREST REPORT

1. Arrest Number	2. Precinct of Arrest		3. Date/Time of Arrest	4. Defendant's Name		5. Defendant's Address
6. Defendant's Date of Birth	7. Sex	8. Race	9. Height	10. Weight	11. Location of Arrest	12. Date and Time of Occurrence
13. Location of Occurrence	14. Complaint Number		15. Victim's Name		16. Victim's Address	17. Victim's Date of Birth
18. Precinct of Complaint	19. Arresting Officer's Name		20. Shield Number		21. Assigned Unit Precinct	2. Date of Complaint

On Friday, December 13 at 11:45 P.M., while leaving a store at 235 Spring Street, Grace O'Connell, a white female, 5'2" 130 lbs., was approached by a white male, 5'11", 200 lbs., who demanded her money and jewelry. As the man ran and turned down River Street, Police Officer William James, Shield Number 31724, assigned to the 14th Precinct, gave chase and apprehended him in front of 523 River Street. The prisoner, Gerald Grande, who resides at 17 Water Street, was arrested at 12:05 A.M., was charged with robbery, and taken to the 13th Precinct, where he was assigned Arrest Number 53048. Miss O'Connell, who resides at 275 Spring St., was given Complaint Number 822460.

1. On the basis of the Arrest Report and the above paragraph, the CORRECT entry for Box Number 3 should be 1.____
   A. 11:45 P.M.,12/13
   B. 11:45 P.M., 12/14
   C. 12:05 A.M., 12/13
   D. 12:05 A.M., 12/14

2. On the basis of the Arrest Report and the above paragraph, the CORRECT entry for Box Number 21 should be 2.____
   A. 12th Precinct
   B. 14th Precinct
   C. Mounted Unit
   D. 32nd Precinct

3. On the basis of the Arrest Report and the above paragraph, the CORRECT entry for Box Number 11 should be 3.____
   A. 235 Spring St.
   B. 523 River St.
   C. 275 Spring St.
   D. 17 Water St.

4. On the basis of the Arrest Report and the above paragraph, the CORRECT entry for Box Number 2 should be 4.____
   A. 13th Precinct
   B. 14th Precinct
   C. Mounted Unit
   D. 32nd Precinct

5. On the basis of the Arrest Report and the above paragraph, the CORRECT entry for Box Number 13 should be 5.____
   A. 523 River St.
   B. 17 Water St.
   C. 275 Spring St.
   D. 235 Spring St.

6. On the basis of the Arrest Report and the above paragraph, the CORRECT entry for Box Number 14 should be 6.____
   A. 53048 B. 31724 C. 12/13 D. 82460

Questions 7-10.

DIRECTIONS: Questions 7 through 10 are to be answered SOLELY on the basis of the following information.

You are required to file various documents in file drawers which are labeled according to the following pattern:

DOCUMENTS

MEMOS		LETTERS		REPORTS		INQUIRIES	
File	Subject	File	Subject	File	Subject	File	Subject
84PM1	(A-L)	84PC1	(A-L)	84PR1	(A-L)	84PQ1	(A-L)
84PM2	(M-Z)	84PC2	(M-Z)	84PR2	(M-Z)	84PQ2	(M-Z)

7. A letter dealing with a burglary should be filed in the drawer labeled 7.____
   A. 84PM1 B. 84PC1 C. 84PR1 D. 84PQ2

8. A report on *Statistics* should be found in the drawer labeled 8.____
   A. 84PM1 B. 84PC2 C. 84PR2 D. 84PQ2

9. An inquiry is received about parade permit procedures. It should be filed in the drawer labeled 9.____
   A. 84PM2 B. 84PC1 C. 84PR1 D. 84PQ2

10. A police officer has a question about a robbery report you filed. You should pull this file from the drawer labeled 10.____
    A. 84PM1 B. 84PM2 C. 84PR1 D. 84PR2

Questions 11-18.

DIRECTIONS: Questions 11 through 18 are to be answered SOLELY on the basis of the following information.

Below are listed the code number, name, and area of investigation of six detective units. Each question describes a crime.

For each question, choose the option (A, B, C, or D) which contains the code number for the detective unit responsible for handling that crime.

DETECTIVE UNITS

Unit Code No.	Unit Name	Unit's Area of Investigation
01	Senior Citizens Unit	All robberies of senior citizens 65 years or older
02	Major Case Unit	Any bank robbery; a commercial robbery where value of goods or money stolen is over $25,000
03	Robbery Unit	Any commercial, non-bank robbery where the value of the stolen goods or money is $25,000 or less; robberies of individuals under 65 years of age
04	Fraud and Larceny Unit	Confidence games and pickpockets
05	Special Investigations Unit	Burglaries of premises where the value of goods removed or monies taken is $15,000 or less
06	Burglary Unit	Burglaries of premises where the value of goods removed or monies taken is over $15,000

11. Mrs. Green calls the precinct and reports that her apartment was burglarized while she was on vacation and that precious jewelry and silverware, valued at $27,000, were taken. 11.____
To which unit code number should her complaint be referred?
A. 05 B. 02 C. 03 D. 06

12. Sylvia Bailey, Manager of the Building and Loan Savings Bank, reports that a man handed one of her tellers a note stating, *This is a robbery*. He had a gun and demanded money. The teller gave the man $500 in small bills, and the man then left. 12.____
To which unit code should the complaint be referred?
A. 02 B. 06 C. 03 D. 05

13. Mrs. Miniver, a 67-year-old widow, states that she was beaten and robbed by two men in the elevator of her apartment building. 13.____
To which unit code number should the complaint be referred?
A. 06 B. 01 C. 03 D. 02

14. Mr. Whipple, Manager of T.V.A. Supermarket, reports that during the night someone entered the store and removed merchandise valued at $12,500. 14.____
To which unit code number should the complaint be referred?
A. 05 B. 03 C. 06 D. 02

15. Mr. Gold, owner of Gold's Jewelry Exchange, reports that two men, armed with shotguns, robbed his store and removed money and jewelry valued at $28,000. 15.____
To which unit code number should the complaint be referred?
A. 05 B. 03 C. 06 D. 02

16. Mr. Watson, a 62-year-old man, was walking in Central Park when he was approached by a man with a knife and was robbed of $72. 16.____
To which unit code number should the complaint be referred?
A. 01 B. 06 C. 03 D. 02

17. The Ace Jewelry Manufacturing Company was broken into over the weekend when the building was closed. The owner stated that $35,000 in gold, silver, diamonds, and jewelry were taken. 17.____
To which unit code number should the complaint be referred?
A. 02 B. 03 C. 06 D. 05

18. Mrs. Vargas, 62, reports that she gave Mr. Greene of the Starlite Realty Corporation $1,000 to locate a new apartment for her family. A week went by, and she never heard from Mr. Greene. She called the Starlite Realty Corporation, and they informed her that Mr. Greene never worked for Starlite Realty Corporation and that they have no record of the $1,000 deposit of Mrs. Vargas. 18.____
To which unit code number should the complaint be referred?
A. 04 B. 03 C. 01 D. 05

Questions 19-24.

DIRECTIONS: Questions 19 through 24 consist of sentences which contain examples of correct or incorrect English usage. Examine each sentence with reference to grammar, spelling, punctuation, and capitalization. Choose one of the following options that would be BEST for correct English usage:
A. The sentence is correct.
B. There is one mistake.
C. There are two mistakes.
D. There are three mistakes.

19. Mrs. Fitzgerald came to the 59th Precinct to retreive her property which were stolen earlier in the week. 19.____

20. The two officer's responded to the call, only to find that the perpatrator and the victim have left the scene. 20.____

21. Mr. Coleman called the 61st Precinct to report that, upon arriving at his store, he discovered that there was a large hole in the wall and that three boxes of radios were missing 21.____

22. The Administrative Leiutenant of the 62nd Precinct held a meeting which was attended by all the civilians, assigned to the Precinct. 22.____

23. Three days after the robbery occured the detective apprahended two suspects and recovered the stolen items. 23.____

24. The Community Affairs Officer of the 64th Precinct is the liaison between the Precinct and the community; he works closely with various community organizations, and elected officials. 24.____

Questions 25-32.

DIRECTIONS: Questions 25 through 32 are to be answered on the basis of the following paragraph, which contains some deliberate errors in spelling and/or grammar and/or punctuation. Each line of the paragraph is preceded by a number. There are 9 lines and 9 numbers.

Line No.	Paragraph Line
1	The protection of life and property are, one of
2	the oldest and most important functions of a city.
3	New York city has its own full-time police Agency.
4	The police Department has the power an it shall
5	be there duty to preserve the Public piece,
6	prevent crime detect and arrest offenders, suppress
7	riots, protect the rites of persons and property, etc.
8	The maintainance of sound relations with the community they
9	serve is an important function of law enforcement officers.

25. How many errors are contained in line one? 25.____
    A. One B. Two C. Three D. None

26. How many errors are contained in line two? 26.____
    A. One B. Two C. Three D. None

27. How many errors are contained in line three? 27.____
    A. One B. Two C. Three D. None

28. How many errors are contained in line four? 28.____
    A. One B. Two C. Three D. None

29. How many errors are contained in line five? 29.____
A. One B. Two C. Three D. None

30. How many errors are contained in line six? 30.____
A. One B. Two C. Three D. None

31. How many errors are contained in line seven? 31.____
A. One B. Two C. Three D. None

32. How many errors are contained in line eight? 32.____
A. One B. Two C. Three D. None

Questions 33-40.

DIRECTIONS: Questions 33 through 40 are to be answered on the basis of the material contained in the INDEX OF CRIME IN CENTRAL CITY, U.S.A. 2011-2020 appearing below. Certain information is various columns is deliberately left blank.
The correct answer (A, B, C, or D) to these questions requires you to make computations that will enable you to fill in the blanks correctly.

INDEX OF CRIME IN CENTRAL CITY, U.S.A., 2011-2020

	Crime Index Total	Violent Crime[1]	Property Crime[2]	Murder	Forcible Rape	Robbery	Aggra-vated Assault	Burglary	Larceny Theft	Motor Vehicle Theft
2011	8,717	875		19	51	385	420	2,565	4,347	930
2012	10,252	974	9278	20	55	443	456		5,262	977
2013	11,256	1,026	10,230	20		465	485	3,253	5,977	1,000
2014	11,304	986		18	58	420	490	3,089	6,270	959
2015	10,935	1,009	9,926	19	63	405	522	3,053	5,605	968
2016	11,140	1,061	10,079	19	67	417	558	3,104	5,983	992
2017	12,152	1,178	10,974	23	75	466	614	3,299	6,578	1,097
2018	13,294	1,308	11,986	23	83		654	3,759	7,113	1,114
2019	13,289	1,321	11,968	22	82	574	643	3,740	7,154	1,074
2020	12,856	1,285	11,571	22	77	536	650	3,415	7,108	1,048

33. What was the TOTAL number of Property Crimes in 2011? 33.____
A. 9,740 B. 10,252 C. 16,559 D. 7,842

34. What was the TOTAL number of Burglaries for 2012? 34.____
A. 2,062 B. 3,039 C. 3,259 D. 4,001

35. In 2020, the total number of Aggravated Assaults was MOST NEARLY what percent of the total number of Violent Crimes for that year? 35.____
A. 49.1 B. 46.3 C. 50.6 D. 41.7

36. In 2015, Property Crime was MOST NEARLY what percent of the Crime Index Total? 36.____
A. 90.8 B. 9.3 C. 10.1 D. 89.9

37. What was the TOTAL number of Property Crimes for 2014? 37.____
A. 10,318 B. 11,304 C. 98 D. 10,808

38. What was the TOTAL number of Robberies for 2018? 38.____
A. 654 B. 571 C. 548 D. 1,202

39. Robbery made up what percent of the TOTAL number of Violent Crimes for 2020? 39.____
A. 68.8% B. 4.1% C. 21.9% D. 41.7%

40. What was the TOTAL number of Forcible Rapes for 2013? 40.____
A. 47 B. 56 C. 55 D. 101

KEY (CORRECT ANSWERS)

1.	D	11.	D	21.	A	31.	A
2.	B	12.	A	22.	C	32.	A
3.	B	13.	B	23.	C	33.	D
4.	A	14.	A	24.	B	34.	B
5.	D	15.	D	25.	C	35.	C
6.	D	16.	C	26.	D	36.	A
7.	B	17.	C	27.	C	37.	A
8.	C	18.	A	28.	B	38.	C
9.	D	19.	C	29.	C	39.	D
10.	D	20.	D	30.	B	40.	B

TEST 2

DIRECTIONS: Each question or incomplete statement is followed by several suggested answers or completions. Select the one that BEST answers the question or completes the statement. *PRINT THE LETTER OF THE CORRECT ANSWER IN THE SPACE AT THE RIGHT.*

Questions 1-8.

DIRECTIONS: Each of Questions 1 through 8 consists of three lines of code letters and numbers. The numbers on each line should correspond to the code letters on the same line in accordance with the table below.

Code Letter	X	B	L	T	V	M	P	F	J	S
Corresponding Number	0	1	2	3	4	5	6	7	8	9

On some of the lines, an error exists in the coding. Compare the letters and numbers in each question carefully. If you find an error or errors on:
Only one of the lines in the question, mark your answer A;
Any two of the lines in the question, mark your answer B;
All three lines in the question, mark your answer C;
None of the lines in the question, mark your answer D.

SAMPLE QUESTION: MSXVLPT—5904263
SBFJLTP—9178246
XVMBTPF—8451367

In the above sample, the first line is correct since each code letter listed has the correct corresponding number. On the second line, an error exists because code letter T should have number 3 instead of number 4. On the third line, an error exists because the code letter X should have the number 0 instead of the number 8. Since there are errors on two of the three lines, the correct answer is B.

1. VFSTPLM—4793625
SBXFLTP—9017236
BT[JFSV—1358794
1.____

2. TSLFVPJ—3927468
JLFTVXS—8273409
MVSXBFL—5490172
2.____

3. XFTJSVT—0739843
VFMTFLB—4753721
LTFJSFM—2378985
3.____

4. SJMSJVL—9859742
VFBXMPF—3710568
PFPXLBS—7670219
4.____

5. MFPXVFP—5764076 5.____
PTFJBLX—6378120
VXSVSTB—4094931

6. BXFPVJT—1076483 6.____
STFMVLT—9375423
TXPBTTM—3061335

7. VLSBLVP—4290246 7.____
FPSFBMV—7679154
XTMXMLL—0730522

8. JFVPMTJ—8746538 8.____
TFPMXBL—3765012
TJSFMFX—4987570

Questions 9-18.

DIRECTIONS: Questions 9 through 18 each consists of two columns, each containing four lines of names, numbers and/or addresses. For each question, compare the lines in Column I with the lines in Column II to see if they match exactly, and mark your answer (A, B, C, or D) according to the following instructions:

A. all four lines match exactly
B. only three lines match exactly
C. only two lines match exactly
D. only one line matches exactly

9.	(1)	Earl Hodgson	Earl Hodgson	9.____
	(2)	1409870	1408970	
	(3)	Shore Ave.	Schore Ave.	
	(4)	Macon Rd.	Macon Rd.	
10.	(1)	9671485	9671485	10.____
	(2)	470 Astor Court	470 Astor Court	
	(3)	Halprin, Phillip	Halperin, Phillip	
	(4)	Frank D. Poliseo	Frank D. Poliseo	
11.	(1)	Tandem Associates	Tandom Associates	11.____
	(2)	144-17 Northern Blvd.	144-17 Northern Blvd.	
	(3)	Alberta Forchi	Albert Forchi	
	(4)	Kings Park, NY 10751	Kings Point, NY 10751	
12.	(1)	Bertha C. McCormack	Bertha C. McCormack	12.____
	(2)	Clayton, MO	Clayton, MO	
	(3)	976-4242	976-4242	
	(4)	New City, NY 10951	New City, NY 10951	

13.	(1)	George C. Morill	George C. Morrill	13.____
	(2)	Columbia, SC 29201	Columbia, SD 29201	
	(3)	Louis Ingham	Louis Ingham	
	(4)	3406 Forest Ave.	3406 Forest Ave.	
14.	(1)	506 S. Elliott Pl.	506 S. Elliott Pl.	14.____
	(2)	Herbert Hall	Hurbert Hall	
	(3)	4712 Rockaway Pkway	4712 Rockaway Pkway	
	(4)	169 E. 7 St.	169 E. 7 St.	
15.	(1)	345 Park Ave.	345 Park Pl.	15.____
	(2)	Colman Oven Corp.	Coleman Oven Corp.	
	(3)	Robert Conte	Robert Conti	
	(4)	6179846	6179846	
16.	(1)	Grigori Schierber	Grigori Schierber	16.____
	(2)	Des Moines, Iowa	Des Moines, Iowa	
	(3)	Gouverneur Hospital	Gouverneur Hospital	
	(4)	91-35 Cresskill Pl.	91-35 Cresskill Pl.	
17.	(1)	Jeffery Janssen	Jeffrey Janssen	17.____
	(2)	8041071	8041071	
	(3)	40 Rockefeller Plaza	40 Rockafeller Plaza	
	(4)	407 6 St.	406 7 St.	
18.	(1)	5971996	5871996	18.____
	(2)	3113 Knickerbocker Ave.	3113 Knickerbocker Ave.	
	(3)	8434 Boston Post Rd.	8424 Boston Post Rd.	
	(4)	Penn Station	Penn Station	

Questions 19-22.

DIRECTIONS: Questions 19 through 22 are to be answered by looking at the 4 groups of names and addresses listed below (I, II, III, and IV) and then finding out the number of groups that have their corresponding numbered lines exactly the same.

	Group I	Group II
Line 1	Ingersoll Public Library	Ingersoil Public Library
Line 2	Reference and Research Dept.	Reference and Research Dept.
Line 3	95-12 238 St.	95-12 238 St.
Line 4	East Elmhurst, N.Y. 11357	East Elmhurst, N.Y. 11357

	Group III	Group IV
Line 1	Ingersoll Public Library	Ingersoll Poblic Library
Line 2	Reference and Research Dept.	Referance and Research Dept.
Line 3	92-15 283 St.	95-12 283 St.
Line 4	East Elmhurst, N.Y. 11357	East Elmhurst, N.Y. 1357

19. In how many groups is line one exactly the same? 19.____
A. Two B. Three C. Four D. None

20. In how many groups is line two exactly the same? 20.____
A. Two B. Three C. Four D. None

21. In how many groups is line three exactly the same? 20.____
A. Two B. Three C. Four D. None

22. In how many groups is line four exactly the same? 22.____
A. Two B. Three C. Four E. None

Questions 23-26.

DIRECTIONS: Questions 23 through 26 are to be answered by looking at the 4 groups of names and addresses listed below (I, II, III, and IV) and then finding out the number of groups that have their corresponding numbered lines exactly the same.

	Group I	Group II
Line 1	Richmond General Hospital	Richman General Hospital
Line 2	Geriatric Clinic	Geriatric Clinic
Line 3	3975 Paerdegat St.	3975 Peardegat St.
Line 4	Loudonville, New York 11538	Londonville, New York 11538

	Group III	Group IV
Line 1	Richmond General Hospital	Richmend General Hospital
Line 2	Geriatric Clinic	Geriatric Clinic
Line 3	3795 Paerdegat St.	3975 Paerdegat St.
Line 4	Loudonville, New York 11358	Loudonville, New York 11538

23. In how many groups is line one exactly the same? 23.____
A. Two B. Three C. Four D. None

24. In how many groups is line two exactly the same? 24.____
A. Two B. Three C. Four D. None

25. In how many groups is line three exactly the same? 25.____
A. Two B. Three C. Four D. None

26. In how many groups is line four exactly the same? 26.____
A. Two B. Three C. Four D. None

Questions 27-34.

DIRECTIONS: Each of Questions 27 through 34 consists of four or six numbered names. For each question, choose the option (A, B, C, or D) which indicates the order in which the names should be filed in accordance with the following file instructions:

- File alphabetically according to last name, then first name, then middle initial.
- File according to each successive letter within a name.
- When comparing two names where the letters in the longer name are identical with the corresponding letters in the shorter name, the shorter name is filed first.
- When the last names are the same, initials are always filed before names beginning with the same letter.

27. I. Ralph Robinson 27.____
II. Alfred Ross
III. Luis Robles
IV. James Roberts
The CORRECT filing sequence for the above names should be
A. IV, II, I, III B. I, IV, III, II C. III, IV, I, II D. IV, I, III, II

28. I. Irwin Goodwin 28.____
II. Inez Gonzalez
III. Irene Goodman
IV. Ira S. Goodwin
V. Ruth I. Goldstein
VI. M.B. Goodman
The CORRECT filing sequence for the above names should be
A. V, II, I, IV, III, VI B. V, II, VI, III, IV, I
C. V, II, III, VI, IV, I D. V, II, III, VI, I, IV

29. I. George Allan 29.____
II. Gregory Allen
III. Gary Allen
IV. George Allen
The CORRECT filing sequence for the above names should be
A. IV, III, I, II B. I, IV, II, III C. III, IV, I, II D. I, III, IV, II

30. I. Simon Kauffman 30.____
II. Leo Kauffman
III. Robert Kaufmann
IV. Paul Kauffman
The CORRECT filing sequence for the above names should be
A. I, IV, II, III B. II, IV, I, III C. III, II, IV, I D. I, II, III, IV

31. I. Roberta Williams 31.____
II. Robin Wilson
III. Roberta Wilson
IV. Robin Williams
The CORRECT filing sequence for the above names should be
A. III, II, IV, I B. I, IV, III, II C. I, II, III, IV D. III, I, II, IV

32. I. Lawrence Shultz 32.___
II. Albert Schultz
III. Theodore Schwartz
IV. Thomas Schwarz
V. Alvin Schultz
VI. Leonard Shultz
The CORRECT filing sequence for the above names should be
A. II, V, III, IV, I, VI B. IV, III, V, I, II, VI
C. II, V, I, VI, III, IV D. I, VI, II, V, III, IV

33. I. McArdle 33.___
II. Mayer
III. Maletz
IV. McNiff
V. Meyer
VI. MacMahon
The CORRECT filing sequence for the above names should be
A. I, IV, VI, III, II, V B. II, I, IV, VI, III, V
C. VI, III, II, I, IV, V D. VI, III, II, V, I, IV

34. I. Jack E. Johnson 34.___
II. R.H. Jackson
III. Bertha Jackson
IV. J.T. Johnson
V. Ann Johns
VI. John Jacobs
The CORRECT filing sequence for the above names should be
A. II, III, VI, V, IV, I B. III, II, VI, V, IV, I
C. VI, II, III, I, V, IV D. III, II, VI, IV, V, I

Questions 35-40.

DIRECTIONS: Questions 35 through 40 are to be answered SOLELY on the basis of the following passage.

An aide assigned to the Complaint Room must be familiar with the various forms used by that office. Some of these forms and their uses are:

Complaint Report: Used to record information on or information about crimes reported to the Police Department.
Complaint Report Follow-Up: Used to record additional information after the initial complaint report has been filed
Aided Card: Used to record information pertaining to sick and injured persons aided by the police.
Accident Report: Used to record information on or information about injuries and/or property damage involving motorized vehicles.
Property Vouch: Used to record information on or information about property which comes into possession of the Police Department. (Motorized vehicles are not included.)

Auto Voucher: Used to record information on or information about a motorized vehicle which comes into possession of the Police Department.

35. Mr. Brown walks into the police precinct and informs the Administrative Aide that, while he was at work, someone broke into his apartment and removed property belonging to him. He does not know everything that was taken, but he wants to make a report now and will make a list of what was taken and bring it in later. 35.____
According to the above passage, the CORRECT form to use in this situation should be the
   A. Property Voucher
   B. Complaint Report
   C. Complaint Report Follow-Up
   D. Aided Card

36. Mrs. Wilson telephones the precinct and informs the Administrative Aide she wishes to report additional property which was taken from her apartment. The Administrative Aide finds a Complaint Report had been previously filed for Mrs. Wilson. 36.____
According to the above passage, the CORRECT form to use in this situation should be the
   A. Property Voucher
   B. Complaint Report
   C. Complaint Report Follow-Up
   D. Aided Card

37. Police Officer Jones walks into the Complaint Room and informs the Administrative Aide that, while he was on patrol, he observed a woman fall to the sidewalk and remain there, apparently hurt. He comforted the injured woman and called for an ambulance, which came and brought the woman to the hospital. 37.____
According to the above passage, the CORRECT form on which to record this information should be the
   A. Accident Report
   B. Complaint Report
   C. Complaint Report Follow-Up
   D. Aided Card

38. Police Officer Smith informed the Administrative Aide assigned to the Complaint Room that Mr. Green, while crossing the street, was struck by a motorcycle and had to be taken to the hospital. 38.____
According to the above passage, the facts regarding this incident should be recorded on which one of the following forms?
   A. Accident Report
   B. Complaint Report
   C. Complaint Report Follow-Up
   D. Aided Card

39. Police Officer Williams reports to the Administrative Aide assigned to the Complaint Room that he and his partner, Police Officer Murphy, found an auto which was reported stolen and had the auto towed into the police garage. 39.____
Of the following forms listed in the above passage, which is the CORRECT one to use to record this information?
   A. Property Voucher
   B. Auto Voucher
   C. Complaint Report Follow-Up
   D. Complaint Report

40. Administrative Aide Lopez has been assigned to the Complaint Room. During her tour of duty, a person who does not identify herself hands Ms. Lopez a purse. The person states that she found the purse on the street. She then leaves the station house. 40.____
According to the information in the above passage, which is the CORRECT form to fill out to record the incident?
A. Property Voucher
B. Auto Voucher
C. Complaint Report Follow-Up
D. Complaint Report

KEY (CORRECT ANSWERS)

1.	B	11.	D	21.	A	31.	B
2.	D	12.	A	22.	C	32.	A
3.	B	13.	C	23.	A	33.	C
4.	C	14.	B	24.	C	34.	B
5.	A	15.	D	25.	A	35.	B
6.	D	16.	A	26.	A	36.	C
7.	C	17.	D	27.	D	37.	D
8.	A	18.	C	28.	C	38.	A
9.	C	19.	A	29.	D	39.	B
10.	B	20.	B	30.	B	40.	A

EXAMINATION SECTION

TEST 1

DIRECTIONS: Each question or incomplete statement is followed by several suggested answers or completions. Select the one that BEST answers the question or completes the statement. *PRINT THE LETTER OF THE CORRECT ANSWER IN THE SPACE AT THE RIGHT.*

Questions 1-5.

DIRECTIONS: Questions 1 through 5 are to be answered on the basis of the following fact pattern.

Astrid's son, Carlos, attends the local high school. Carlos and another student, Manny, have been bullying another student both on and off school premises. The high school principal has notified the New York Police Department School Safety Unit of the issue. The principal has also been in touch with Astrid and Manny's mother, Mary. Mary believes Carlos is a bad influence to her son, Manny. After obtaining Astrid's phone number, Mary called Astrid and made threats towards her and Carlos. She indicated that if Carlos did not stay away from her son, Manny, she would have them both killed. The next day after school, Carlos is jumped by a group of teenagers and his leg is broken in the brawl. Astrid sues Manny, Mary, and the school district. Mary intends to countersue.

1. Who is the complainant? 1.____
   A. Manny B. Mary C. Astrid D. Carlos

2. Which of the following is NOT a possible cause of action? 2.____
   A. Harassment
   B. Assault
   C. Negligence
   D. Breach of Contract

3. What key information is missing from the complaint? 3.____
   A. The name of the bullied student
   B. The location where Carlos was jumped
   C. The name of the high school principal
   D. The name of the police officer at the NYPD School Safety Unit who was originally notified on the issue

4. Is Mary obligated to countersue because she or her son, Manny, may have been involved in the assault against Carlos? 4.____
   A. Yes; she must answer the suit and countersue as required
   B. Yes; she must countersue to clear her son's name
   C. No; Mary is not obligated to countersue and can simply answer to the claims as alleged
   D. No; Mary is not obligated to countersue but she is obligated to countersue on Manny's behalf

5. Assume that Carlos and Manny are minors. 5.____
What effect, if any, would this fact have on the lawsuit that is filed?
   A. The legal guardians of Carlos and Manny will need to file, and answer, the lawsuit on their behalf.
   B. Carlos and Manny do not need to appear in court.
   C. Minors cannot sue other people.
   D. The lawsuit is unaffected by their age.

6. 6.____

Mary Williams 1 Court Way Smithtown, NY 10170	Mary S. Williams 1 Court Way Smithtown, NY 10170	Mary S. Williams 1 Court Way Smith Town, NY 10170

Which selection below accurately describes the addresses as listed above?
   A. All three addresses are the same.
   B. The first and the third address are the same.
   C. None of the addresses are the same.
   D. The second and third address are the same.

Questions 7-9.

DIRECTIONS: Questions 7 through 9 are to be answered on the basis of the following table.

Schedule – Judge Presser		
Petitioner	**Respondent**	**Status**
Williams	Smith	Dismissed with prejudice
Jones	Johnson	Continued
Adams	Doe	Dismissed with prejudice
Ash	Link	Adjourned
Lam	Garcia	Settled

7. How many cases were adjourned? 7.____
   A. 3 B. 1 C. 4 D. 5

8. In how many cases were money damages awarded by the judge? 8.____
   A. 0 B. 3 C. 4 D. 5

9. How many cases will be heard again? 9.____
   A. 2 B. 1 C. 3 D. 5

10. A warrant for the arrest of Benjamin Lang. Lang lives in Suffolk County, New York. What is recorded on the warrant? 10.____
Lang's
   A. venue
   B. domicile
   C. jurisdiction
   D. subject matter jurisdiction

Questions 11-13.

DIRECTIONS: Questions 11 through 13 are to be answered on the basis of the following table.

455888912	455888812	455888912	455888812
Civil Court	Civil Court	Civil Court	Civil Court
Contract	Contract	Contract	Contract
Pam L. Williams	Pam Williams	Pam Williams	Pam L. Williams

11. Which selection below accurately describes the case captions as listed above? 11.____
    A. All of the captions are the same.
    B. Caption 1 and Caption 3 are the same.
    C. Caption 2 and Caption 4 are the same.
    D. None of the captions are the same.

12. Which digit above is dissimilar in two of the above captions? 12.____
    A. The seventh digit
    B. The fifth digit
    C. The sixth digit
    D. The eighth digit

13. The notation "contract" in each caption above describes the _____ of the case. 13.____
    A. Cause of action
    B. Remedy at issue
    C. Order of the court
    D. Disposition

14. Melinda was seen stealing money from a car on Atlantic Avenue in Brooklyn. Samuel witnessed the crime from his apartment and called the police. Officer Tang recorded the call in the police log. Samuel does not own a car and reported the crime anonymously. Later that same evening, Jeremy returned his car and found the passenger window had been broken and $500 was stolen from the glove compartment. Jeremy called the police to report the crime. In the judge's docket, the petitioner of the case against Melinda is MOST likely 14.____
    A. Jeremy
    B. Samuel
    C. Officer Tang
    D. The petitioner is anonymous

15. Judge Oswald hears cases in the Surrogate Court. Which of the following would NOT be in Judge Oswald's court calendar? 15.____
    A. Adoption
    B. Wills
    C. Estate and Probation
    D. Negligence

Questions 16-19.

DIRECTIONS: Questions 16 through 19 are to be answered on the basis of the following fact pattern.

Judge Laredo, Smith and Ora hear no-fault cases in the 10th Judicial District throughout the week. Judge Laredo hears cases the first Monday of each month. Judge Smith hears cases with amounts in dispute over $10,000 on Tuesday, Wednesday, and Friday. Judge Ora hears cases without amounts in dispute below $25,000 on Tuesdays only.

16. Geico and ABC Chiropractic are parties to a no-fault dispute with an amount in dispute of $8,500. 16.____
If Judge Laredo is unavailable, what day can the case be heard?
A. Wednesday B. Friday C. Monday D. Tuesday

17. Blue Health Medical and Progressive Insurance are parties to a no-fault dispute which is scheduled to be heard February 18th. Blue Health demands Progressive reimburse the provider $5,000 for the primary surgeon fees and $12,000 in assistant surgeon fees. 17.____
Which judge will hear the matter and on which day?
A. Judge Smith on Friday
B. Judge Smith on Tuesday
C. Judge Smith on Wednesday
D. Judge Ora on Tuesday

18. A no-fault dispute is being heard on Monday, June 10th. 18.____
Which statement below must be TRUE?
A. The amount in dispute is above $10,000.
B. The amount in dispute is less than $25,000.
C. The amount in dispute is less than $10,000.
D. Judge Laredo is hearing the case.

19. What information must be obtained in order to properly schedule the court calendar? 19.____
A. The amount in dispute for each case
B. The parties in each case
C. Verification the dispute is "no-fault in nature"
D. All of the above

20. A victim impact statement is an oral or _____ statement that may be read in court. 20.____
A. recorded B. transcribed C. written D. visualized

21. The clerk in the Surrogates Court will need to have access to what information in the preparation of adoption hearings? 21.____
A. Personal information of a child's current or prior legal guardian
B. Emancipation petition documentation
C. Deed or will
D. Probate documentation

Questions 22-25.

DIRECTIONS: Questions 22 through 25 are to be answered on the basis of the following table.

Schedule – Judge Orlando			
Complainant/Plaintiff	**Defendant**	**Case Type**	**Money Awarded**
Williams	Smith	Civil	$5,000
Jones	Johnson	Criminal	No
Adams	Doe	Criminal	$10,000
Ash	Link	Civil	$15,000
Lam	Garcia	Civil	$25,000

22. What is the total amount of money damages from civil disputes? 22.____
    A. $45,000 B. $40,000 C. $5,000 D. 0

23. Which complainant/plaintiff was awarded less than $20,000? 23.____
    A. Williams, Adams, and Ash
    B. Jones, Adams, and Ash
    C. Lam, Williams, and Jones
    D. Jones, Adams, and Lam

24. How many criminal cases were heard by Judge Orlando? 24.____
    A. 4 B. 5 C. 2 D. 3

25. Which defendants are responsible for paying more than $10,000? 25.____
    A. Doe and Link
    B. Link and Garcia
    C. John and Doe
    D. Smith and Garcia

KEY (CORRECT ANSWERS)

1. C
2. D
3. B
4. C
5. A

6. C
7. B
8. A
9. A
10. B

11. D
12. A
13. A
14. A
15. D

16. D
17. D
18. D
19. D
20. C

21. A
22. A
23. A
24. C
25. B

TEST 2

DIRECTIONS: Each question or incomplete statement is followed by several suggested answers or completions. Select the one that BEST answers the question or completes the statement. *PRINT THE LETTER OF THE CORRECT ANSWER IN THE SPACE AT THE RIGHT.*

Questions 1-4.

DIRECTIONS: Questions 1 through 4 are to be answered on the basis of the following text.

After a lengthy trial with multiple ___1___, Jim was acquitted of armed robbery and conspiracy. On the other hand, his alleged partner, Bob, was ___2___ of armed robbery. The conspiracy charge was dropped against Bob since the 12-person ___3___ found he acted alone. Jim's attorney ___4___.

1. Fill in the blank for #1: 1.____
   A. witnesses B. evidence C. discretionary D. turbulent

2. Fill in the blank for #2: 2.____
   A. guilty B. convicted C. indicted D. surmised

3. Fill in the blank for #3: 3.____
   A. judge B. spectator C. jury D. bailiff

4. Fill in the blank for #4: 4.____
   A. appealed B. remanded C. reversed D. rescinded

Questions 5-10.

DIRECTIONS: Questions 5 through 10 are to be answered on the basis of the following table.

Court Schedule - Tuesday			
Judge	**Total Cases**	**Cases Dismissed**	**Cases with Money Awarded**
Presser	10	2	X
O'Dell	5	5	
Williams	6	6	
Sasha	8	7	X

5. How many cases were awarded money damages from Judge Presser's calendar? 5.____
   A. 2 B. 8 C. 6 D. 10

6. How many cases were awarded money damages from Judge Sasha's calendar? 6.____
   A. 8 B. 7 C. 1 D. 0

7. How many cases were dismissed on Tuesday? 7.____
   A. 11 B. 20 C. 7 D. 10

8. How many cases were awarded money damages on Tuesday? 8.____
   A. 9 B. 8 C. 1 D. 10

9. Which judge heard the MOST cases on Tuesday? 9.____
   A. Presser B. O'Dell C. Williams D. Sasha

10. Which judge heard the LEAST cases on Tuesday? 10.____
   A. Presser B. O'Dell C. Willliams D. Sasha

Questions 11-15.

DIRECTIONS: Questions 11 through 15 are to be answered on the basis of the following text.

Judge Smith hears adoption cases on Fridays. Judge Clark hears criminal cases every weekday except Tuesday in the New York City Criminal Court. Judge Clark hears felony criminal cases on Tuesday in Supreme Court. Judge Amy hears felony criminal cases on Thursday in Supreme Court.

11. Daniel is being charged with the murder of his cousin, Jerrell. 11.____
   Which judge can hear the case and on what day?
   A. Judge Smith on Friday
   B. Judge Clark on Monday
   C. Judge Amy on Tuesday
   D. Judge Clark on Tuesday

12. Jamal lives in Staten Island with his sister, Tisha, and Tisha's boyfriend, Hunter. Hunter and Jamal do not get along and one day last January, Hunter and Jamal were involved in a physical altercation. Hunter and Jamal both allege that the other assault and battered the other. 12.____
   Which judge can hear the case and on what day?
   A. Judge Clark on Tuesday
   B. Judge Amy on Thursday
   C. Judge Smith on Friday
   D. Judge Clark on Monday

13. Assuming the crime of assault and battery are not felonies, in which court will Jamal and Hunter's dispute be heard? 13.____
   A. Supreme Court
   B. Surrogates Court
   C. New York City Criminal Court
   D. Small Claims Court

14. Assume that Tisha and Hunter have a six-year-old daughter. 14.____
   If Hunter is incarcerated for his role in the physical altercation with Jamal, which court would have jurisdiction over Hunter's trial?
   A. Surrogates Court
   B. New York City Criminal Court
   C. Bronx Housing Court
   D. Richmond County Civil Court

15. What day of the week are the MOST cases heard between all three judges? 15.____
   A. Monday B. Thursday C. Tuesday D. Friday

Questions 16-19.

DIRECTIONS: Questions 16 through 19 are to be answered on the basis of the following table.

Caption #1	**Caption #2**	**Caption #3**	**Caption #4**
Case 12-908	Case 12-909	Case 12-910	Case 12-911
Bronx Housing Court	Civil Court	Civil Court	Surrogates Court
Landlord/Tenant	Assault	Breach of Contract	Guardianship
ABC Property Mgmt v. Sam Smith	Jim Jones v. Sam Hunt	Terrell Williams v. Daniel Tang	In re: Jane Doe

16. Which caption above contains an INCORRECT cause of action? 16.____
A. 1 B. 2 C. 3 D. 4

17. When were the cases in each of the captions above initiated? 17.____
A. 2015
B. 2016
C. 2012
D. Unable to determine based on the information provided

18. Which case caption above corresponds to a matter that will NOT have monetary damages awarded? 18.____
A. 1 B. 2 C. 3 D. 4

19. Which case caption has a matter involving an institutional, rather than an individual, petitioner? 19.____
A. 1 B. 2 C. 3 D. 4

20. A pro se litigant wants to initiate a lawsuit against his intrusive neighbor. Assuming the pro se litigant prevails, which form should be served against the neighbor after the judgment is entered? 20.____
A. Notice of entry B. Notice of appeal
C. Remand service D. Process discovery

21. A(n) _____ is a hearing for the purpose of determining the amount of damages sue on a claim. The clerk can enter the request on the judge's calendar after the opposing party has defaulted. 21.____
A. imposition B. inquest C. tardy notice D. reversal

22. After a judgment is entered, it becomes enforceable for a period of time. For real property, a transcript of _____ is filed with the County Clerk which makes the judgment enforceable for a period of ten years. 22.____
A. enforcement B. judgment
C. engagement D. affidavit

23. Sensitive information must be _____ before it becomes public record. 23.____
A. retained B. reposed C. redacted D. recanted

24. Service of process can be filed upon the individual or upon the _____. The affidavit of service will state the party that received the service. 24.____
    A. secretary of state
    B. guardian
    C. ad litem
    D. second most suitable person

25. A warrant can be issued to a sheriff or a marshal. The warrant clerk is responsible for reviewing the paperwork and ensuring that all is in order, including 25.____
    A. the names of the parties
    B. address of the premises
    C. the index number
    D. all of the above

KEY (CORRECT ANSWERS)

1.	A	11.	D
2.	B	12.	D
3.	C	13.	C
4.	A	14.	B
5.	B	15.	D
6.	C	16.	B
7.	B	17.	C
8.	A	18.	D
9.	A	19.	A
10.	B	20.	A

21.	B
22.	B
23.	C
24.	A
25.	D

TEST 3

DIRECTIONS: Each question or incomplete statement is followed by several suggested answers or completions. Select the one that BEST answers the question or completes the statement. *PRINT THE LETTER OF THE CORRECT ANSWER IN THE SPACE AT THE RIGHT.*

1. Supreme Court clerks need to be on notice when a(n) _____ is filed as a judge is not assigned until one that parties files this document and pays the filing fee. A case will never go to trial if this document is never filed. 1.____
   A. request for maintenance
   B. request for judicial intervention
   C. remediation
   D. arbitration

Questions 2-4.

DIRECTIONS: Questions 1 through 5 are to be answered on the basis of the following chart.

Row	**Case Type**	**Court**
1	Divorce	Supreme Court
2	Custody/Visitation	Family Court
3	Child Support	Family Court
4	Paternity	Family Court
5	When Someone Dies	Surrogates Court
6	Guardianship	Surrogate's Court
7	Name Change	Supreme Court
8	Housing	New York City Housing Court

2. Assume that you are advising a pro se litigant on the proper forms to file when representing him or herself. Where would John file a small estate affidavit? 2.____
   A. Family Court
   B. Supreme Court
   C. Surrogates Court
   D. New York Civil Court

3. Where would Tom's sister, Emmanuela, file a name change? 3.____
   A. Supreme Court
   B. Family Court
   C. Surrogates Court
   D. New York City Civil Court

4. Tara and her husband, Cassidy, share custody of their twin sons, Drake and Austin. Cassidy would like to petition the court for sole custody. Where would Cassidy file his petition? 4.____
   A. New York City Housing Court
   B. Supreme Court
   C. Family Court
   D. Surrogates Court

5. Richard is representing himself in a lawsuit against his landlord. Richard does not have the financial means to hire an attorney and would like to request a reduction in the court filing fees. Richard must file a request for a _____ which is made by filing a _____ and sworn _____ which explains his finances to the court. 5.____
   A. fee waiver; notice of motion; affirmation
   B. fee waiver, notice of motion, affidavit
   C. affidavit, notice of motion, fee waiver
   D. affidavit, fee waiver, notice of motion

Questions 6-10.

DIRECTIONS: Questions 6 through 10 are to be answered on the basis of the following text.

Daniel walks into this local supermarket after lunch and falls in one of the store aisles. Daniel lies on the floor – which is nearly empty – until one of the store managers finds him, helps him up, and offers to pay for his groceries. Daniel leaves the store bruised, but not seriously injured. Two days later, Daniel falls at another grocery store. This time, Daniel threatens to sue the grocery store. The second grocery store has heard about Daniel and is concerned that he is falsifying his injuries to gain sympathy and money. The second grocery store sues Daniel to get ahead of Daniel suing them.

6. Who is the plaintiff in the case? 6.____
   A. The first grocery store
   B. The second grocery store
   C. The grocery store manager
   D. Daniel

7. Which of the following is the MOST likely cause of action in a suit that Daniel initiates against the grocery store? 7.____
   A. Breach of contract
   B. Discrimination
   C. Negligence
   D. Assault

8. After the lawsuit has commenced, which party would respond or file an answer to the complaint? 8.____
   A. Daniel
   B. The first grocery store
   C. The second grocery store
   D. The grocery store manager

9. Which party is eligible to countersue? 9.____
   A. The first grocery store
   B. The second grocery store
   C. The grocery store manager
   D. Daniel

10. The lawsuit will likely be dismissed. Why? 10.____
   A. Daniel is clearly not exaggerating his injuries.
   B. Daniel has not sued either grocery store.
   C. The store manager did not take a report of Daniel's injuries.
   D. The first grocery store must sue Daniel first.

11. A settlement between parties is not a final and binding legal agreement until the _____ of settlement is signed by both parties. 11.____
   A. amendment
   B. agreement
   C. stipulation
   D. simulation

12. Which of the following are appropriate reasons for filing an Order to Show Cause? 12.____
    A. Changing the terms of a court order
    B. Requesting the court to dismiss a case
    C. Bringing the case back to court for any reason
    D. All of the above

13. Which of the following is NOT an appropriate reason for filing an Order to Show Case? 13.____
    A. Asking for more time to do something previously agreed upon by court order
    B. Explaining why either party missed a court date
    C. Submitting financial information for a landlord/tenant dispute
    D. Fixing errors in a stipulation

Questions 14-17.

DIRECTIONS: Questions 14 through 17 are to be answered on the basis of the following text.

Judge Chin hears child neglect and abuse cases in Family Court on Mondays and Tuesdays. Judge Amy hears divorce cases on Mondays, Wednesdays, and Fridays. Judge Snell hears child support and visitation cases every day of the week except Thursday. Termination of parental rights, foster care placement, and other child support cases are scheduled on Thursdays only with any of the three judges.

14. Tim and Sarah would like to adjust their visitation schedule for their eight-year-old daughter, Samantha. They would like the courts to assist them with this issue as they have been unable to come to an agreement on their own. Which judge will hear the case and on what day? 14.____
    A. Judge Snell on Thursday
    B. Judge Snell on Monday
    C. Judge Chin on Monday
    D. Judge Chin on Friday

15. Amanda would like to file for emancipation from her parents. Which judge is MOST likely to hear her case? 15.____
    A. Judge Chin
    B. Judge Amy
    C. Judge Snell'
    D. Any of the judges can hear Amanda's case

16. Jimmy and Eva are legally separating. Which judge will hear their case and on what day? 16.____
    A. Judge Chin on Monday
    B. Judge Snell on Monday
    C. Judge Amy on Monday
    D. Judge Chin on Tuesday

17. The State of New York intends to file a case against Eric for the abuses and neglect of his daughter, Clare. Eric, however, is not Clare's legal guardian. Clare's legal guardian is her grandmother, Allison. Even though it is not clear that Clare has been neglected, the courts have found that Clare should be placed into foster care until it can be determined who the ultimate caregiver should be. 17.____
Which judge will MOST likely hear this case?
A. Judge Amy
B. Judge Chin
C. Judge Snell
D. Any of the judges can hear this case

Questions 18-25.

DIRECTIONS: Questions 18 through 25 are to be answered on the basis of the following chart.

Item	Fee
Obtaining an index number	$210
RJI	$95
Note of Issue	$30
Motion or Cross-Motion	$45
Demand for Jury Trial	$65
Voluntary Discontinuance	$35
Notice of Appeal	$65

18. What is the final cost to obtain an index number, demand a jury trial, and file a notice of appeal? 18.____
A. $210 B. $35 C. $65 D. $310

19. What is the final cost to obtain an RJI and note of issue? 19.____
A. $125 B. $95 C. $30 D. $65

20. Which of the following is MOST likely to be filed with an RJI? 20.____
A. Demand for jury trial B. Notice of appeal
C. Voluntary discontinuance D. Obtaining an index number

21. Which of the following is the MOST likely outcome of filing a voluntary discontinuance? 21.____
The case
A. is automatically appealed B. is dismissed
C. is rescheduled D. will be remanded

22. What is the final cost of filing a notice of appeal? 22.____
A. $35 B. $65 C. $95 D. $120

23. What is the final cost of all items prior to filing a motion or cross-motion? 23.____
A. $210 B. $95 C. $45 D. $335

24. Jamal would like to petition the court to compel discovery from his adversary and former friend, Bob. He would also like to speed up the date of trial by filing a demand for jury trial and RJI. 24.____
What is the final cost to do so?
A. $160 B. $95 C. $65 D. $205

25. What is the LEAST costly court document filing fee? 25.____
A. Notice of motion B. Demand for jury trial
C. Note of issue D. RJI

KEY (CORRECT ANSWERS)

1. B
2. C
3. A
4. C
5. B

6. B
7. C
8. A
9. D
10. B

11. C
12. D
13. C
14. B
15. D

16. C
17. D
18. D
19. A
20. D

21. B
22. B
23. D
24. D
25. C

TEST 4

DIRECTIONS: Each question or incomplete statement is followed by several suggested answers or completions. Select the one that BEST answers the question or completes the statement. *PRINT THE LETTER OF THE CORRECT ANSWER IN THE SPACE AT THE RIGHT.*

1. A lawsuit for money damages amounting to more than $25,000 can be heard in which court? 1.____
   A. Surrogates Court
   B. Supreme Court
   C. New York City Civil Court
   D. New York City Criminal Court

2. Which of the following will NOT be on a Notice of Entry? 2.____
   A. Name of plaintiff
   B. Name of defendant
   C. Index number
   D. Social Security number

3. Court clerks are prohibited from which of the following? 3.____
   A. Predicting the judgment of the court
   B. Explaining available options for a case or problem
   C. Providing past rulings
   D. Providing citations or copies of the law

4. Court clerks are permitted to do all of the following EXCEPT 4.____
   A. provide forms with instructions
   B. instruct an individual on how to make a complaint
   C. analyze the law based on the specifics of a case
   D. describe court records and their availability

5. Mary would like to sue her neighbor, Jacob, for money damages. Mary claims Jacob ran his car into Mary's garage door while it was down and caused $5,000 in damages. For claims below $1,000, the filing fee is $15, while the filing fee is $5 more for claims above $1,000. 5.____
   How much is Mary's filing fee?
   A. $15 B. $10 C. $20 D. $25

Questions 6-10.

DIRECTIONS: Questions 6 through 10 are to be answered on the basis of the following table.

Schedule – Judge O'Neill		
Wednesday	**Thursday**	**Friday**
Continued	Dismissed with prejudice	Dismissed with prejudice
Continued	Adjourned	Continued
Settled	Dismissed with prejudice	Dismissed without prejudice
Settled	Continued	Settled
Settled	Continued	Settled

6. How many cases were adjourned this week? 6.____
   A. 5 B. 6 C. 1 D. 2

7. How many cases settled this week? 7.____
   A. 5 B. 4 C. 3 D. 8

8. How many cases were dismissed this week? 8.____
   A. 6 B. 4 C. 5 D. 7

9. How many cases will likely be heard again or, in other words, how many cases can be re-filed or are otherwise continued? 9.____
   A. 6 B. 5 C. 7 D. 8

10. Which day was Judge O'Neill the LEAST busy? 10.____
    A. Thursday B. Friday
    C. Wednesday D. Each day was equally busy

Questions 11-15.

DIRECTIONS: Questions 11 through 15 are to be answered on the basis of the following text.

At Alex's arraignment, he pled ___1___ to the charge of driving under the influence and vehicular manslaughter. At trial, the prosecutor presented evidence from several ___2___ that testified Alex had a drinking problem. While Alex's defense attorneys ___3___ to that testimony and argued it was hearsay, the judge overruled those objections and allowed the testimony to be entered in the record as originally spoken. At the conclusion of the trial, Alex was found ___4___ and sentenced to community service.

11. Fill in the blank for #1: 11.____
    A. nolo B. contendere C. not guilty D. guilty

12. Fill in the blank for #2: 12.____
    A. witnesses B. evidence C. testimony D. bearer

13. Fill in the blank for #3: 13.____
    A. disagreed B. objected C. qualified D. disclaimed

14. Fill in the blank for #4: 14.____
    A. arraigned B. protested C. remanded D. guilty

15. An acquittal can also be recorded in court documentation as a finding of 15.____
    A. reversal B. recusal C. not guilty D. remand

16. Evidence must be found _____ before it can be marked and evaluated by the fact finder, either a judge or jury, in civil and criminal cases. 16.____
    A. relevant B. redacted C. qualified D. admissible

17. The party who seeks an appeal from a decision of a court is deemed a(n) _____ and is recorded in court documentation as such. 17.____
    A. petitioner B. respondent C. appellant D. re-respondent

18. How would a condominium be recorded in a bankruptcy proceeding? 18.____
    A. Real property B. Personal property
    C. Intangible asset D. chattel

19. Which of the following is LEAST likely to be recorded as a written statement describing one's legal and factual arguments? 19.____
    A. Attorney's brief B. Motion
    C. Summons D. Complaint

20. A lawsuit where one or more members of a large group of individuals sues on behalf of the other individuals in the large group is recorded as a _____ lawsuit. 20.____
    A. introductory B. class action C. municipality D. winning

21. Jamal has filed for bankruptcy. After the trustee has reviewed Jamal's assets, the trustee proposes a plan to the court where Jamal promises property that he already owns to satisfy the major of his debt. 21.____
    The property Jamal owns that will satisfy the debt is recorded as
    A. demerits B. collateral C. debris D. probate

22. Judge Presser has rendered Emilio's sentence for the charges of armed robbery and kidnapping. Emilio will serve 10 years for armed robbery and 12 years for kidnapping. 22.____
    If Emilio's total time in prison is 12 years, his sentence is recorded as
    A. consecutive B. demonstrative
    C. concurrent D. rebated

23. Assume the same facts as the previous question, but assume Emilio serves 22 years in prison. 23.____
    In this instance, his sentence is recorded as
    A. consecutive B. demonstrative
    C. concurrent D. rebated

24. A conviction can also be recorded in court records as a judgment of _____ against a defendant. 24.____
    A. guilt B. remorse C. retaliation D. acquittal

25. In bankruptcy, Jamal sells his house to his mother for $5 in an effort to hide it from creditors who will require that he sell it to satisfy his debts. 25.____
    This sale is recorded as a
    A. fraudulent transfer B. falsified sale
    C. remarkable trade D. clawback trade

KEY (CORRECT ANSWERS)

1.	B	11.	C
2.	D	12.	A
3.	A	13.	B
4.	C	14.	D
5.	C	15.	C
6.	C	16.	D
7.	A	17.	C
8.	B	18.	A
9.	A	19.	C
10.	C	20.	B

21. B
22. C
23. A
24. A
25. A

OFFICE RECORD KEEPING

EXAMINATION SECTION

TEST 1

DIRECTIONS: Each question or incomplete statement is followed by several suggested answers or completions. Select the one that BEST answers the question or completes the statement. *PRINT THE LETTER OF THE CORRECT ANSWER IN THE SPACE AT THE RIGHT.*

Questions 1-5.

DIRECTIONS: Questions 1 through 5 are to be answered on the basis of the following chart to check for address and zip code errors.

A. No errors
B. Address only
C. Zip code only
D. Both

	Correct List Address	Zip Code	List to be Checked Address	Zip Code	
1.	44-A Western Avenue Bethesda, MD	65564	44-A Western Avenue Bethesda, MD	65654	1.____
2.	567 Opera Lane Jackson, MO	28218	567 Opera Lane Jacksen, MO	28218	2.____
3.	200 W. Jannine Dr. Missoula, MT	30707	200 W. Jannine Dr. Missoula, MT	30307	3.____
4.	28 Champaline Dr. Reno, NV	34101	28 Champaine Way Reno, NV	43101	4.____
5.	65156 Rodojo Parsimony, KY	44590-7326	65156 Rodojo Parsimony, KY	44590-7326	5.____

6. When alphabetized correctly, which of the following would be second? 6.____
   A. flame B. herring C. decadence D. emoticon

7. Which one of the following letters is as far after E as K is before R in the alphabet? 7.____
   A. J B. K C. H D. M

8. How many pairs of the following sets of numbers are exactly alike? 8.____

134232	123456	432512	561343
564643	432123	132439	438318

   A. 0 B. 2 C. 3 D. 4

9. When alphabetized correctly, which of the following would be FOURTH? 9.____
   A. microcosm B. natural C. lithe D. nature

10. When alphabetized correctly, which of the following would be THIRD? 10.____
   A. exoskeleton B. euthanize C. Europe D. eurythmic

11. Which one of the following letters is as far before T as S is after I in the alphabet? 11.____
   A. j B. K C. M D. N

12. How many pairs of the following sets of letters are exactly ALIKE? 12.____

GIHEKE	GIHEKE
KIWNEB	KWINEB
PQMZJI	PMQZJI
OPZIBS	OBZIBS
PONEHE	POENHE

   A. 0 B. 1 C. 2 D. 4

13. When alphabetized correctly, which of the following would be FIRST? 13.____
   A. Catalina B. catcher C. caustic D. curious

14. Which of the following letters is as far after D as U is after B in the alphabet? 14.____
   A. R B. V C. W D. Z

Questions 15-19.

DIRECTIONS: Use the following information and chart to complete Questions 15 through 19.

Every theft reported to an adjuster needs to be assigned a six-letter code containing the following:

First Letter: Type of theft
Second Letter: Witnesses
Third Letter: Value of stolen item
Fourth Letter: Location
Fifth Letter: Time of theft
Sixth Letter: Elapsed between theft and report

<u>Type of Theft:</u>
A. Breaking and Entering
B. Retail Theft
C. Armed robbery
D. Grand Theft Auto

<u>Witnesses</u>
A. None
B. 1 witness
C. Multiple witnesses
D. Security camera

Location
A. Single Family Home
B. Apartment Building
C. Store
D. Office
E. Vehicle
F. Public Space (Parking Garage, Park, etc.)

Time Elapsed Between Theft and Report
A. 0-1 hour
B. 1-4 hours
C. 4-12 hours
D. 12-24 hours
E. 24 Hours

Time of Theft
A. 7 AM – 1 PM
B. 1 PM – 6 PM
C. 6 PM – 11 PM
D. 11 PM – 3 AM
E. 3 AM – 7 AM

Value of Stolen Items
A. $0-$100
B. $101-$250
C. $251-$500
D. $500-$1000
E. $1001-$5000
F. $5000 or more

15. At 9:30 PM, $175 worth of clothing was stolen from a store. The crime was reported right away by a single store associate. Which of the following would be the CORRECT code? 15.____
A. BCCABB B. BBBCCA C. ACCBAB D. CBCABB

16. A Crossover vehicle worth $4,500 was stolen from a park at approximately 6:45 AM this morning. It was reported stolen at 11:00 AM later that morning by the owner. There were no witnesses. What is the CORRECT code? 16.____
A. DEECAF B. CFECAE C. DEFECA D. DAEFEC

17. Although it was just reported, a breaking and entering occurred 5 days ago at 1:30 AM, according to security cameras that recorded the theft at the accounting firm. Although locks and doors were damaged, nothing was stolen. Which of the following would be the CORRECT code? 17.____
A. ADDEEA B. ADDDAE C. ADADDE D. ADEADE

18. Jill Wagner was held at knifepoint this morning at 11:30 AM when she was walking out of her apartment complex. The thief demanded money, and she gave him $54. She was the only witness and reported the crime immediately. Which of the following would be the CORRECT code? 18.____
A. CBABAA B. BBABAA C. CBBABB D. ABBBCA

19. An artifact worth $5,500 was stolen from the home of Chad Judea this early evening while he was out to dinner from 5:30 PM to 6 PM. When he arrived home at 6 PM, he immediately called the police. There were no witnesses. Which of the following would be the CORRECT code? 19.____
A. AABBAF B. AABFAF C. AABABF D. AAFABA

20. Diatribe means MOST NEARLY 20.____
A. argument B. cooperation C. delicate D. arrogance

21. Vitriolic means MOST NEARLY 21.____
A. flammable B. fearful C. spiteful D. asinine

22. Aplomb means MOST NEARLY 22.____
A. self-righteous B. respectable C. dispirited D. self-confidence

23. Pervicacious means MOST NEARLY 23.____
A. rotten B. immoral C. stubborn D. immortal

24. Detrimental means MOST NEARLY 24.____
A. valuable B. selfish C. hopeless D. harmful

25. Heinous means MOST NEARLY 25.____
A. sweating B. glorious C. atrocious D. moderate

KEY (CORRECT ANSWERS)

1.	C	11.	A
2.	B	12.	B
3.	C	13.	A
4.	D	14.	C
5.	A	15.	B
6.	D	16.	D
7.	B	17.	C
8.	A	18.	A
9.	D	19.	D
10.	B	20.	A

21.	C
22.	D
23.	C
24.	D
25.	C

TEST 2

DIRECTIONS: Each question or incomplete statement is followed by several suggested answers or completions. Select the one that BEST answers the question or completes the statement. *PRINT THE LETTER OF THE CORRECT ANSWER IN THE SPACE AT THE RIGHT.*

Questions 1-7.

DIRECTIONS: In answering Questions 1 through 7, you will be presented with analogies (known as word relationships). Select the answer choice that BEST completes the analogy.

1. Coordinated is related to movement as speech is related to 1.____
   A. predictive B. rapid C. prophetic D. articulate

2. Pottery is related to shard as wood is related to 2.____
   A. acorn B. chair C. smoke D. kiln

3. Poverty is related to money as famine is related to 3.____
   A. nourishment B. infirmity C. illness D. care

4. Farmland is related to arable as waterway is related to 4.____
   A. impenetrable B. maneuverable
   C. fertile D. deep

5. 19 is related to 17 as 37 is related to 5.____
   A. 39 B. 36 C. 34 D. 31

6. Cup is related to lip as bird is related to 6.____
   A. beak B. grass C. forest D. bush

7. ZRYQ is related to KCJB as PWOV is related to 7.____
   A. GBHA B. ISJT C. ELDK D. EOFP

Questions 8-12.

DIRECTIONS: In answering Questions 8 through 12, each of the questions has a group. Find out which one of the given alternatives will be another member of that group.

8. Springfield, Sacramento, Tallahassee 8.____
   A. Buffalo B. Bangor C. Pittsburgh D. Providence

9. Lock, Shut, Fasten 9.____
   A. Window B. Iron C. Door D. Block

10. Pathology, Radiology, Ophthalmology 10.____
    A. Zoology B. Hematology C. Geology D. Biology

11. Karate, Jujitsu, Boxing 11.____
    A. Polo B. Pole-vault C. Judo D. Swimming

12. Newspaper, Hoarding, Television 12.____
    A. Press B. Rumor C. Media D. Broadcast

Questions 13-18.

DIRECTIONS: Questions 13 through 18 are to be answered on the basis of the following pie chart.

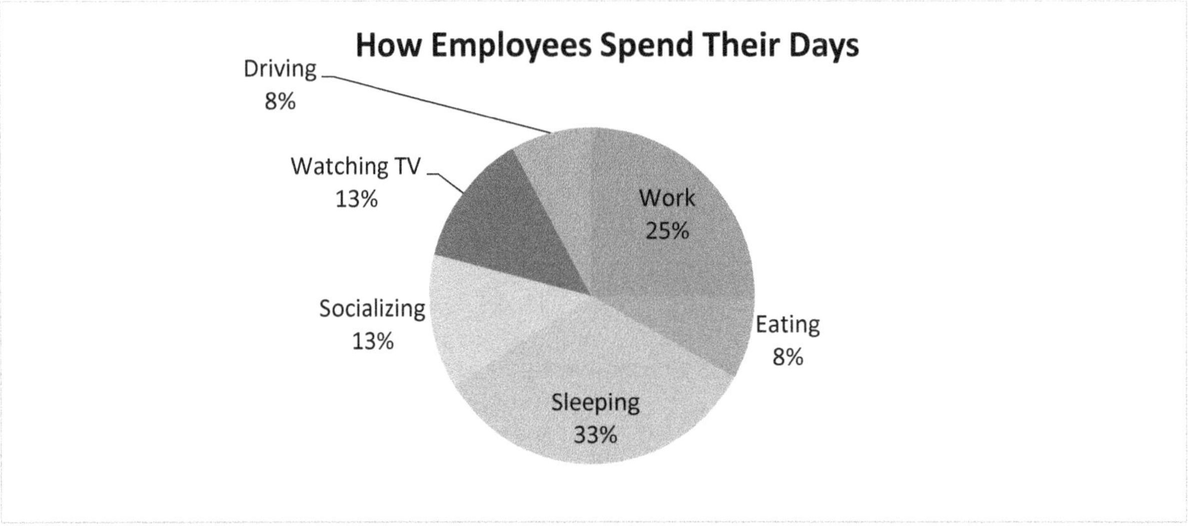

13. Approximately how many hours a day are spent eating? 13.____
    A. 2 hours B. 5 hours C. 1 hour D. 30 minutes

14. According to the graph, for each 48 hour period, about how many hours are spent socializing and watching TV? 14.____
    A. 9 hours B. 6 hours C. 12 hours D. 3 hours

15. If an employee ate two-thirds of their meals at a restaurant, what percentage of the total day is spent eating at home? 15.____
    A. 2.5% B. 5.3% C. 8% D. 1.4%

16. About how many hours a day are spent working and sleeping? 16.____
    A. 7 B. 10 C. 12 D. 14

17. Which of the following equations could be used to figure out how much time an employee spends watching TV during a week? T equals the total amount of time watching TV during the week. 17.____
    A. T = 13% x 24 x 7 B. T = 24 x 13 x 7
    C. T = 24/13% x 7 D. T = 1.3 x 7 x 24

18. How many hours a week does the average employee spend socializing? 18.____
    A. 20 B. 22 C. 23 D. 24

Questions 19-25.

DIRECTIONS: Questions 19 through 25 are to be answered on the basis of the following charts.

DIAL DIRECT	WEEKDAY FULL RATE		EVENING 40% DISCOUNT		WEEKEND 60% DISCOUNT	
SAMPLE RATES FROM SEATTLE TO	FIRST MINUTE	EACH ADDITIONAL MINUTE	FIRST MINUTE	EACH ADDITIONAL MINUTE	FIRST MINUTE	EACH ADDITIONAL MINUTE
Savannah, GA	.52	.23	.31	.14	.21	.08
Providence, RI	.52	.223	.31	.14	.21	.08
Golden, CO	.52	.23	.31	.14	.21	.08
Indianapolis, IN	.48	.19	.29	.11	.19	.07
San Diego, CA	.54	.24	.32	.14	.22	.09
Tallahassee, FL	.54	.24	.32	.14	.22	.09
Milwaukee, WI	.57	.27	.34	.16	.23	.09
Minneapolis, MN	.49	.22	.29	.13	.20	.08
Baton Rouge, LA	.52	.23	.31	.14	.21	.08
Buffalo, NY	.52	.23	.31	.14	.21	.08
Annapolis, MD	.54	.24	.32	.14	.22	.09
Washington, DC	.52	.23	.31	.14	.21	.08

OPERATOR ASSISTED		
STATION-TO-STATION		PERSON-TO-PERSON
1 – 10 MILES	$.75	$3.00 FEE FOR ALL MILEAGES
11 - 22 MILES	$1.10	*NOTE: Add to this base charge – the minute rates from the above chart
23-3000 MILES	$1.55	

19. What is the price of a 6-minute dial direct call to Annapolis, MD when you call on a weekend? 19.____
A. $0.59 B. $0.54 C. $0.67 D. $0.49

20. What is the difference in cost between a 10 minute dial direct to Buffalo, NY and a 10 minute person-to-person call to Buffalo, NY? 20.____
A. $1.55 B. $3.00 C. $0.55 D. $4.55

21. What is the price of a 15-minute operator-assisted Station-to-Station call to Indianapolis, IN on a Monday at noon? 21.____
A. $3.74 B. $7.80 C. $3.45 D. $4.69

22. What is the difference in price between an 11-minute dial direct call to Milwaukee, WI at 11:00 AM on a Wednesday and the same call made at 9 PM that night? 22.____
A. $2.27 B. $3.00 C. $1.55 D. $1.336

23. Which of the following is NOT a type of charge for a dial direct call? 23.____
    A. Holiday B. Evening C. Weekend D. Weekday

24. If a 3.5% tax applied to the total cost of any call, what would be the TOTAL cost of a 13-minute weekday, dial direct call to Golden, CO? 24.____
    A. $3.28 B. $3.39 C. $4.94 D. $6.39

25. What is the amount of discount from a dial direct, weekday call to Tallahassee, FL cost as compared to a dial direct, weekend call to Tallahassee? 25.____
    A. 45% B. 30% C. 60% D. 20%

KEY (CORRECT ANSWERS)

1.	D	11.	C
2.	B	12.	D
3.	A	13.	A
4.	C	14.	C
5.	D	15.	A
6.	A	16.	D
7.	C	17.	A
8.	D	18.	B
9.	D	19.	C
10.	B	20.	B

21.	D
22.	D
23.	A
24.	B
25.	C

TEST 3

DIRECTIONS: Each question or incomplete statement is followed by several suggested answers or completions. Select the one that BEST answers the question or completes the statement. *PRINT THE LETTER OF THE CORRECT ANSWER IN THE SPACE AT THE RIGHT.*

Questions 1-7.

DIRECTIONS: Questions 1 through 7 are to be answered on the basis of the following graph.

Corporate Fundraiser – Candy Sales by the Case

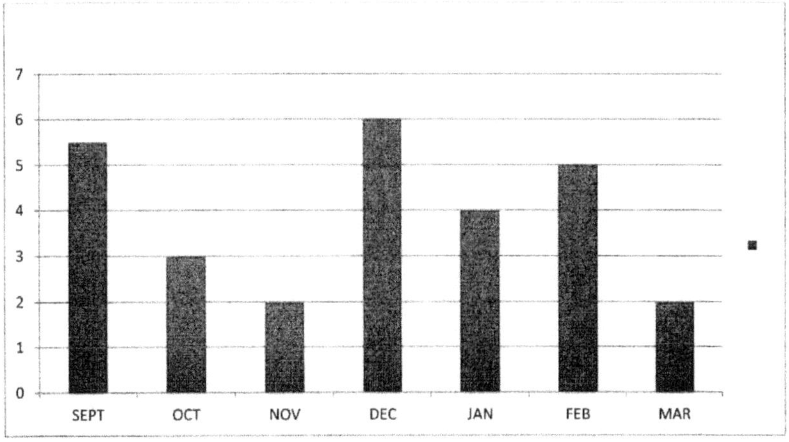

1. The vertical scale ranging from 0 to 7 represents the number of 1.____
   A. students selling candy
   B. candy sold in each case
   C. days each month that candy was sold
   D. cases of candy sold

2. Which two months had approximately the same amount of candy sold? 2.____
   A. November and March B. September and February
   C. November and October D. October and March

3. Which month showed a 100% increase in sales over the month of November? 3.____
   A. March B. January C. April D. December

4. From month-to-month, which month saw an approximate 33% drop in sales from the previous month? 4.____
   A. March B. September C. January D. October

5. The amount of candy sold in December is twice the amount of candy sold in which other month? 5.____
   A. October B. March C. January D. September

6. What was the total amount of candy sold during the months shown on the graph? 6.____
   A. 44 cases B. 35.5 cases C. 23.5 cases D. 27.5 cases

7. If the fundraiser extended the additional five months of the year and added an additional 65% in sales, approximately how many cases would be sold in total for an entire year? 7.____
   A. 40.5 cases B. 37 cases C. 45 cases D. 27.5 cases

Questions 8-11.

DIRECTIONS: Questions 8 through 11 are to be answered on the basis of the following chart.

S = 10 students
s = 5 students

Mr. Hucklebee	S S S S s
Ms. Shopenhauer	S S S
Mr. White	S S S s
Mrs. Mulrooney	S S S

8. The size of Mr. White's class is _____ students. 8.____
   A. 30 B. 35 C. 40 D. 4

9. The total of all students in all four classes is _____ students. 9.____
   A. 150 B. 140 C. 125 D. 14

10. The average class size based on the above chart is _____ students. 10.____
   A. 140 B. 45 C. 35 D. 30

11. In order to ensure each teacher has the same amount of students in each class, how many students would need to transfer out of Mr. Hucklebee's class? 11.____
   A. 10
   B. 5
   C. 0
   d. 15 would need to transfer into his class

12. When alphabetized correctly, which of the following would be THIRD? 12.____
   A. box B. departed C. electrical D. elemental

13. When alphabetized correctly, which of the following would be SECOND? 13.____
   A. polarize B. omnipotent C. polygraph D. omniscient

14. When alphabetized correctly, which of the following would be THIRD? 14.____
   A. Macklemore, Jonathan B. Mackelmore, J.
   C. DiCastro, Darian D. Castro, Darren Henry

15. The group fought through the fog, *shambling* through the night, doing their best to stay upright. 15.____
The word *shambling* means
A. frozen in place
B. running
C. walking awkwardly
D. shivering uncontrollably

16. Many doctors agree that Gen-aspirin is the best for fighting headaches. It comes in different flavors and is easy to swallow. 16.____
Is this a valid or invalid argument?
A. Invalid
B. Valid

Questions 17-21.

DIRECTIONS: Questions 17 through 21 are to be answered on the basis of the following paragraph.

Hospital workers and volunteers often ask Mr. Ansley to educate children who are hospitalized with primary ciliary dyskinesia (PCD). As he goes through the precautionary cleaning process (scrubbing, donning sterilized clothes, etc.) in order to see his students, Mr. Ansley wonders why their parents add the stress and pressure of schooling and trying to play catch-up because of the amount of time spent in the hospital and not in the classroom, which is an unfortunate side effect of patients with PCD. These children go through so many painful treatments on a given day that it seems punishing to subject them to schooling as normal children do, especially with life expectancy being as short as it is.

17. What is meant by *precautionary* in the second sentence? 17.____
A. Careful
B. Protective
C. Sterilizing
D. Medical

18. What is the MAIN idea of this passage? 18.____
A. The preparation to visit a patient with primary ciliary dyskinesia is extensive.
B. Children with PCD are unable to live normal lives.
C. Children with PCD die young.
D. Certain allowances should be made for children with PCD.

19. What is the author's purpose? 19.____
A. To advise
B. To educate
C. To establish credibility
D. To amuse

20. What is the author's tone? 20.____
A. Cruel
B. Sympathetic
C. Disbelieving
D. Cheerful

21. How is Mr. Ansley so familiar with the procedures used when visiting a child with PCD? 21.____
A. He has read about it
B. He works in the hospital.
C. His child has PCD.
D. He tutors them on a regular basis.

Questions 22-25.

DIRECTIONS: One of the underlined words in Questions 22 through 25 should be changed. Select the one that should be changed and print the letter of the word that would change the underlined word.

22. After we washed the fruit that had growing in the garden, we knew there was a store that would buy them. 22.____
A. washing B. grown C. is D. No change

23. When the temperature drops under 32 degrees (F), the water on the lake freezes, which allowed children to skate across it. 23.____
A. dropped B. froze C. allows D. No change

24. My friend's bulldog, while chasing cars in the street, always manages to knock over our garbage bins. 24.____
A. chased B. manage C. knocks D. No change

25. Some of the ice on the driveway has melted. 25.____
A. having melted
B. have melted
C. has melt
D. No change

KEY (CORRECT ANSWERS)

1.	D	11.	A
2.	A	12.	C
3.	B	13.	D
4.	C	14.	B
5.	A	15.	C
6.	D	16.	A
7.	C	17.	C
8.	B	18.	D
9.	B	19.	A
10.	C	20.	B

21.	D
22.	B
23.	C
24.	D
25.	D

TEST 4

DIRECTIONS: Each question or incomplete statement is followed by several suggested answers or completions. Select the one that BEST answers the question or completes the statement. *PRINT THE LETTER OF THE CORRECT ANSWER IN THE SPACE AT THE RIGHT.*

Questions 1-2.

DIRECTIONS: One of the underlined words in Questions 1 and 2 should be changed. Select the one that should be changed and print the letter of the word that would change the underlined word.

1. <u>You</u> can get to Martha's Vineyard by driving from Boston to Woods Hole. Once there, you can travel over on a boat, but <u>you</u> may find traveling by airplane to be more exciting. 1.____
   A. they B. visitors C. it D. No change

2. When John wants to go to the store looking for <u>milk and eggs</u>, <u>you</u> must remember to bring <u>his</u> wallet. 2.____
   A. them B. he C. its D. No change

3. An item that sells for $400 is put on sale at $145. What is the percentage of decrease? 3.____
   A. 25% B. 28% C. 64% D. 36%

4. Two Junior College Mathematics courses have a total of 510 students. The 9:00 AM class has 60 more than the 12:30 PM class. How many students are in the 12:30 class? 4.____
   A. 225 B. 285 C. 255 D. 205

5. If a car gets 26 miles per gallon and it has driven 75,210 miles, approximately what is the number of gallons of gas that it has used? 5.____
   A. 3,000 B. 2,585 C. 165 D. 1,800

6. Which one of the following sentences about proper telephone usage is NOT always correct? When answering a telephone, you should 6.____
   A. know who you are speaking to
   B. give the caller your undivided attention
   C. identify yourself to the caller
   D. obtain the information your caller wishes before you do other work

7. You are part of the "Safety at Work" committee, which is dedicated to ensuring safety of employees. During your regular shift, you notice an employee in violation of one of your committee's rules. Which of the following actions should you take FIRST? 7.____
   A. Speak with the employee about the safety rules and mandate them to stop breaking the rules.
   B. Speak to the employee about safety rules and point out the rule they violated.
   C. Bring up the issue during the next committee meeting.
   D. Report the violation to the employee's superiors.

8. Part of your duties is overseeing employee confidential information. A friend and coworker of yours asks to obtain information concerning another employee. Which is the BEST action to take? 8.____
   A. Ask the coworker if you can share the information.
   B. Ask your supervisor if you can give the information to your friend.
   C. Refuse to give the information to your friend.
   D. Give the information to your friend.

9. Which of the following words means the OPPOSITE of protract? 9.____
   A. Extend B. Hesitant C. Curtail D. Plethora

10. Which of the following words means the OPPOSITE of conserve? 10.____
   A. Relinquish B. Waste C. Proficient D. Rigid

11. Which of the following words means the SAME as dissipate? 11.____
   A. Scatter B. Emancipate
   C. Engage D. Accumulate

12. Your office just purchased 14 fax machines. Each fax machine costs $79.99. How much did the 14 fax machines cost? 12.____
   A. $1,119.86 B. $1,108.77 C. $1,201.44 D. $1,788.22

Questions 13-19.

DIRECTIONS: Questions 13 through 19 are to be answered on the basis of the following chart.

Office City	Sales Rank	Production Materials Produced	Rank for Production	Damaged Materials	Employees	Percent of Profit	Sales Points	Weeks Without Injuries
Springfield	13.6	271	12	1	34	35	36	7
Philadelphia	17	274	4	3	25	41	20	4
Gary	16	260	10	5	34	34	21	3
Boulder	5	10	6	9	38	15	20	8
Miami	81	3	81	77	133	4	2	0
Houston	2	370	2	0	95	66	100	16
Battle Creek	82	290	82	81	91	13	9	2

13. Between Philadelphia and Battle Creek, how many damaged materials were there? 13.____
    A. 84 B. 78 C. 45 D. 86

14. How many offices have had 5 or more weeks without injuries? 14.____
    A. 3 B. 4 C. 2 D. 0

15. What was the TOTAL number of damaged materials for the offices in Boulder, Miami, Houston, and Springfield offices? 15.____
    A. 91 B. 87 C. 80 D. 77

16. What were the TOTAL sales points of Houston, Battle Creek, and Gary? 16.____
    A. 115 B. 145 C. 160 D. 130

17. Which of the offices had the LOWEST number of weeks without an injury? 17.____
    A. Battle Creek B. Miami C. Gary D. Philadelphia

18. If worker efficiency is a percentage based on the number of workers at an office and the amount of materials produced, which office has the GREATEST worker efficiency? 18.____
    A. Philadelphia B. Springfield C. Boulder D. Gary

19. If the company was looking to close a facility, which of the following factors would NOT be a reason to close the Miami office? 19.____
    A. Weeks without injury B. Sales rank
    C. Production materials produced D. Employees

Questions 20-25.

DIRECTIONS: In answering Questions 20 through 25, select the sentence in which the underlined word is used correctly.

20. A. Jon needs to increase his <u>capitol</u> by 30% to invest in my business. 20.____
    B. The organization is reevaluating <u>it's</u> decision to purchase the building.
    C. The office supply store sells computer paper and <u>stationery</u>.
    D. The quarterback and running back left <u>there</u> helmets on the bus.

21. A. The police sergeant <u>sited</u> me for disorderly conduct and driving without a license. 21.____
    B. The votes have <u>already</u> been counted.
    C. The professor's theory contradicts the <u>principals</u> of Einstein and Newton.
    D. <u>Who's</u> glass of water is on the table?

22. A. The board of trustees decided to <u>accept</u> the CEO's resignation. 22.____
    B. <u>Lose</u> hats will help keep your head from hurting.
    C. She <u>complemented</u> me on my exquisite dinner tastes.
    D. Jamaal offered him some sound <u>advise</u>.

23. A. In class today, Maya lead us in the reciting of the pledge. 23.____
    B. Doctors worry about the affects of drinking red wine right before bed.
    C. The workers used sledge hammers to break up the pavement.
    D. The teacher gave her students wise council.

24. A. This building was formerly the site of one of the city's oldest department stores. 24.____
    B. In his position, Albert must be very discrete in handling confidential information.
    C. He was to tired to continue the race.
    D. Each of his mortgage payments as about evenly divided between principle and interest.

25. A. The police spent several hours at the cite of the accident. 25.____
    B. A majority of the public support capitol punishment.
    C. The magician used mirrors to create a convincing illusion.
    D. The heiress flouted her wealth by wearing expensive jewelry.

KEY (CORRECT ANSWERS)

1.	D	11.	A
2.	B	12.	A
3.	C	13.	A
4.	A	14.	A
5.	A	15.	B
6.	D	16.	D
7.	B	17.	B
8.	C	18.	A
9.	C	19.	D
10.	B	20.	C

21.	B
22.	A
23.	C
24.	A
25.	C

CLERICAL ABILITIES TEST

EXAMINATION SECTION

TEST 1

DIRECTIONS: Each question or incomplete statement is followed by several suggested answers or completions. Select the one that BEST answers the question or completes the statement. *PRINT THE LETTER OF THE CORRECT ANSWER IN THE SPACE AT THE RIGHT.*

Questions 1-10.

DIRECTIONS: Questions 1 through 10 consist of lines of names, dates, and numbers. For each question, you are to choose the option (A, B, C, or D) in Column II which EXACTLY matches the information in Column I. *PRINT THE LETTER OF THE CORRECT ANSWER IN THE SPACE AT THE RIGHT.*

SAMPLE QUESTION

Column I	Column II
Schneider 11/16/75 581932	A. Schneider 11/16/75 518932
	B. Schneider 11/16/75 581932
	C. Schnieder 11/16/75 581932
	D. Shnieder 11/16/75 518932

The correct answer is B. Only Option B shows the name, date, and number exactly as they are in Column I. Option A has a mistake in the number. Option C has a mistake in the name. Option D has a mistake in the name and in the number. Now answer Questions 1 through 10 in the same manner.

	Column I	Column II	
1.	Johnston 12/26/74 659251	A. Johnson 12/23/74 659251	1.____
		B. Johston 12/26/74 659251	
		C. Johnston 12/26/74 695251	
		D. Johnston 12/26/74 659251	
2.	Allison 1/26/75 9939256	A. Allison 1/26/75 9939256	2.____
		B. Alisson 1/26/75 9939256	
		C. Allison 1/26/76 9399256	
		D. Allison 1/26/75 9993356	
3.	Farrell 2/12/75 361251	A. Farell 2/21/75 361251	3.____
		B. Farrell 2/12/75 361251	
		C. Farrell 2/21/75 361251	
		D. Farrell 2/12/75 361151	

4. Guerrero 4/28/72 105689
A. Guererro 4/28/72 105689
B. Guererro 4/28/72 105986
C. Guerrero 4/28/72 105869
D. Guerrero 4/28/72 105689
4.____

5. McDonnell 6/05/73 478215
A. McDonnell 6/15/73 478215
B. McDonnell 6/05/73 478215
C. McDonnell 6/05/73 472815
D. MacDonell 6/05/73 478215
5.____

6. Shepard 3/31/71 075421
A. Sheperd 3/31/71 075421
B. Shepard 3/13/71 075421
C. Shepard 3/31/71 075421
D. Shepard 3/13/71 075241
6.____

7. Russell 4/01/69 031429
A. Russell 4/01/69 031429
B. Russell 4/10/69 034129
C. Russell 4/10/69 031429
D. Russell 4/01/69 034129
7.____

8. Phillips 10/16/68 961042
A. Philipps 10/16/68 961042
B. Phillips 10/16/68 960142
C. Phillips 10/16/68 961042
D. Philipps 10/16/68 916042
8.____

9. Campbell 11/21/72 624856
A. Campbell 11/21/72 624856
B. Campbell 11/21/72 624586
C. Campbell 11/21/72 624686
D. Campbel 11/21/72 624856
9.____

10. Patterson 9/18/71 76199176
A. Patterson 9/18/72 76191976
B. Patterson 9/18/71 76199176
C. Patterson 9/18/72 76199176
D. Patterson 9/18/71 76919176
10.____

Questions 11-15.

DIRECTIONS: Questions 11 through 15 consist of groups of numbers and letters which you are to compare. For each question, you are to choose the option (A, B,C, or D) in Column I which EXACTLY matches the group of numbers and letters given in Column I.

SAMPLE QUESTION

<u>Column I</u>
B92466

<u>Column II</u>
A. B92644
B. B94266
C. A92466
D. B92466

The correct answer is D. Only Option D in Column II shows the group of numbers and letters EXACTLY as it appears in Column I. Now answer Questions 11 through 15 in the same manner.

	Column I	Column II	
11.	925AC5	A. 952CA5 B. 925AC5 C. 952AC5 D. 925CA6	11.____
12.	Y006925	A. Y060925 B. Y006295 C. Y006529 D. Y006925	12.____
13.	J236956	A. J236956 B. J326965 C. J239656 D. J932656	13.____
14.	AB6952	A. AB6952 B. AB9625 C. AB9652 D. AB6925	14.____
15.	X259361	A. X529361 B. X259631 C. X523961 D. X259361	15.____

Questions 16-25.

DIRECTIONS: Each of questions 16 through 25 consists of three lines of code letters and three lines of numbers. The numbers on each line should correspond with the code letters on the same line in accordance with the table below.

Code Letter	S	V	W	A	Q	M	X	E	G	K
Corresponding Number	0	1	2	3	4	5	5	7	8	9

On some of the lines, an error exists in the coding. Compare the letters and numbers in each question carefully. If you find an error or errors on:

only one of the lines in the question, mark your answer A;
any two lines in the question, mark your answer B;
all three lines in the question, mark your answer C;
none of the lines in the question, mark your answer D.

SAMPLE QUESTION

WQGKSXG	2489068
XEKVQMA	6591453
KMAESXV	9527061

In the above sample, the first line is correct since each code letter listed has the correct corresponding number. On the second line, an error exists because code letter E should have the number 7 instead of the number 5. On the third line, an error exists because the code letter A should have the number 3 instead of the number 2. Since there are errors in two of the three lines, the correct answer is B. Now answer Questions 16 through 25 in the same manner.

16. SWQEKGA 0247983
KEAVSXM 9731065
SSAXGKQ 0036894
16.____

17. QAMKMVS 4259510
MGGEASX 5897306
KSWMKWS 9125920
17.____

18. WKXQWVE 2964217
QKXXQVA 4966413
AWMXGVS 3253810
18.____

19. GMMKASE 8559307
AWVSKSW 3210902
QAVSVGK 4310189
19.____

20. XGKQSMK 6894049
QSVKEAS 4019730
GSMXKMV 8057951
20.____

21. AEKMWSG 3195208
MKQSVQK 5940149
XGQAEVW 6843712
21.____

22. XGMKAVS 6858310
SKMAWEQ 0953174
GVMEQSA 8167403
22.____

23. VQSKAVE 1489317
WQGKAEM 2489375
MEGKAWQ 5689324
23.____

24. XMQVSKG 6541098
QMEKEWS 4579720
KMEVGKG 9571983
24.____

25. GKVAMEW 88912572 25.____
AXMVKAE 3651937
KWAGMAV 9238531

Questions 26-35.

DIRECTIONS: Each of Questions 26 through 35 consists of a column of figures. For each question, add the column of figures and choose the correct answer from the four choices given.

26. 5,665.43 26.____
2,356.69
6,447.24
7,239.65

A. 20,698.01 B. 21,709.01
C. 21,718.01 D. 22,609.01

27. 817,209.55 27.____
264,354.29
82,368.76
849,964.89

A. 1,893.977.49 B. 1,989,988.39
C. 2,009,077.39 D. 2,013,897.49

28. 156,366.89 28.____
249,973.23
823,229.49
56,869.45

A. 1,286,439.06 B. 1,287,521.06
C. 1,297,539.06 D. 1,296,421.06

29. 23,422.15 29.____
149,696.24
238,377.53
86,289.79
505,533.63

A. 989,229.34 B. 999,879.34
C. 1,003,330.34 D. 1,023,329.34

30. 2,468,926.70
656,842.28
49,723.15
832,369.59 30.____

A. 3,218,062.72 B. 3,808,092.72
C. 4,007,861.72 D. 4,818,192.72

31. 524,201.52
7,775,678.51
8,345,299.63
40,628,898.08
31,374,670.07 31.____

A. 88,646,647.81 B. 88,646,747.91
C. 88,648,647.91 D. 88,648,747.81

32. 6,824,829.40
682,482.94
5,542,015.27
775,678.51
7,732,507.25 32.____

A. 21,557,513.37 B. 21,567,513.37
C. 22,567,503.37 D. 22,567,513.37

33. 22,109,405.58
6,097,093.43
5,050,073.99
8,118,050.05
4,313,980.82 33.____

A. 45,688,593.87 B. 45,688,603.87
C. 45,689,593.87 D. 45,689,603.87

34. 79,324,114.19
99,848,129.74
43,331,653.31
41,610,207.14 34.____

A. 264,114,104.38 B. 264,114,114.38
C. 265,114,114.38 D. 265,214,104.38

35. 33,729,653.94   35.____
5,959,342.58
26,052,715.47
4,452,669.52
7,079,953.59

A. 76,374,334.10   B. 76,375,334.10
C. 77,274,335.10   D. 77,275,335.10

Questions 36-40.

DIRECTIONS: Each of Questions 36 through 40 consists of a single number in Column I and four options in Column II. For each question, you are to choose the option (A, B, C, or D) in Column II which EXACTLY matches the number in Column I.

SAMPLE QUESTION

Column I	Column II
5965121	A. 5956121
	B. 5965121
	C. 5966121
	D. 5965211

The correct answer is B. Only Option B shows the number EXACTLY as it appears in Column I. Now answer Questions 36 through 40 in the same manner.

	Column I	Column II	
36.	9643242	A. 9643242	36.____
		B. 9462342	
		C. 9642442	
		D. 9463242	
37.	3572477	A. 3752477	37.____
		B. 3725477	
		C. 3572477	
		D. 3574277	
38.	5276101	A. 5267101	38.____
		B. 5726011	
		C. 5271601	
		D. 5276101	
39.	4469329	A. 4496329	39.____
		B. 4469329	
		C. 4496239	
		D. 4469239	

40. 2326308

A. 2236308
B. 2233608
C. 2326308
D. 2323608

40.____

KEY (CORRECT ANSWERS)

1.	D	11.	B	21.	A	31.	D
2.	A	12.	D	22.	C	32.	A
3.	B	13.	A	23.	B	33.	B
4.	D	14.	A	24.	D	34.	A
5.	B	15.	D	25.	A	35.	C
6.	C	16.	D	26.	B	36.	A
7.	A	17.	C	27.	D	37.	C
8.	C	18.	A	28.	A	38.	D
9.	A	19.	D	29.	C	39.	B
10.	B	20.	B	30.	C	40.	C

TEST 2

DIRECTIONS: Each question or incomplete statement is followed by several suggested answers or completions. Select the one that BEST answers the question or completes the statement. *PRINT THE LETTER OF THE CORRECT ANSWER IN THE SPACE AT THE RIGHT.*

Questions 1-5.

DIRECTIONS: Each of Questions 1 through 5 consists of a name and a dollar amount. In each question, the name and dollar amount in Column II should be an EXACT copy of the name and dollar amount in Column I. If there is:
a mistake only in the name, mark your answer A;
a mistake only in the dollar amount, mark your answer B;
a mistake in both the name and the dollar amount, mark your answer C;
no mistake in either the name or the dollar amount, mark your answer D.

SAMPLE QUESTION

Column I	Column II
George Peterson $125.50	George Petersson $125.50

Compare the name and dollar amount in Column II with the name and dollar amount in Column I. The name *Petersson* in Column II is spelled *Peterson* in Column I. The amount is the same in both columns. Since there is a mistake only in the name, the answer to the sample question is A. Now answer Questions 1 through 5 in the same manner.

	Column I	Column II	
1.	Susanne Shultz $3440	Susanne Schultz $3440	1.____
2.	Anibal P. Contrucci $2121.61	Anibel P. Contrucci $2112.61	2.____
3.	Eugenio Mendoza $12.45	Eugenio Mendozza $12.45	3.____
4.	Maurice Gluckstadt $4297	Maurice Gluckstadt $4297	4.____
5.	John Pampellonne $4656.94	John Pammpellonne $4566.94	5.____

Questions 6-11.

DIRECTIONS: Each of Questions 6 through 11 consist of a set of names and addresses, which you are to compare. In each question, the name and addresses in Column II should be an EXACT copy of the name and address in Column I. If there is:
a mistake only in the name, mark your answer A;
a mistake only in the address, mark your answer B;
a mistake in both the name and address, mark your answer C;
no mistake in either the name or address, mark your answer D.

SAMPLE QUESTION

Column I	Column II
Michael Filbert 456 Reade Street New York, N.Y. 10013	Michael Filbert 645 Reade Street New York, N.Y. 10013

Since there is a mistake only in the address (the street number should be 456 instead of 645), the answer to the sample question is B. Now answer Questions 6 through 11 in the same manner.

	Column I	Column II	
6.	Hilda Goettelmann 55 Lenox Rd. Brooklyn, N.Y. 11226	Hilda Goettelman 55 Lenox Ave. Brooklyn, N.Y. 11226	6.____
7.	Arthur Sherman 2522 Batchelder St. Brooklyn, N.Y. 11235	Arthur Sharman 2522 Batcheder St. Brooklyn, N.Y. 11253	7.____
8.	Ralph Barnett 300 West 28 Street New York, New York 10001	Ralph Barnett 300 West 28 Street New York, New York 10001	8.____
9.	George Goodwin 135 Palmer Avenue Staten Island, New York 10302	George Godwin 135 Palmer Avenue Staten Island, New York 10302	9.____
10.	Alonso Ramirez 232 West 79 Street New York, N.Y. 10024	Alonso Ramirez 223 West 79 Street New York, N.Y. 10024	10.____
11.	Cynthia Graham 149-34 83 Street Howard Beach, N.Y. 11414	Cynthia Graham 149-35 83 Street Howard Beach, N.Y. 11414	11.____

Questions 12-20.

DIRECTIONS: Questions 12 through 20 are problems in subtraction. For each question do the subtraction and select your answer from the four choices given.

12. 232,921.85
-179,587.68 12.____

A. 52,433.17
B. 52,434.17
C. 53,334.17
D. 53,343,17

13. 5,531,876.29
-3,897,158.36 13.____

A. 1,634,717.93
B. 1,644,718.93
C. 1,734,717.93
D. 1,7234,718.93

14. 1,482,658.22
-937,925.76 14.____

A. 544,633.46
B. 544,732.46
C. 545,632.46
D. 545,732.46

15. 937,828.17
-259,673.88 15.____

A. 678,154.29
B. 679,154.29
C. 688,155.39
D. 699,155.39

16. 760,412.38
-263,465.95 16.____

A. 496,046.43
B. 496,946.43
C. 496,956.43
D. 497,046.43

17. 3,203,902.26
-2,933,087.96 17.____

A. 260,814.30
B. 269,824.30
C. 270,814.30
D. 270,824.30

18. 1,023,468.71
-934,678.88 18.____

A. 88,780.83
B. 88,789.83
C. 88,880.83
D. 88,889.83

19. 831,549.47
-772,814.78 19.____

A. 58,734.69 B. 58,834.69
C. 59,735.69 D. 59,834.69

20. 6,306,181.74
-3,617,376.99 20.____

A. 2,687,904.99 B. 2,688,904.99
C. 2,689,804.99 D. 2,799,905.99

Questions 21-30.

DIRECTIONS: Each of Questions 21 through 30 consists of three lines of code letters and three lines of numbers. The numbers on each line should correspond with the code letters on the same line in accordance with the table below.

Code Letter	J	U	B	T	Y	D	K	R	L	P
Corresponding Number	0	1	2	3	4	5	5	7	8	9

On some of the lines, an error exists in the coding. Compare the letters and numbers in each question carefully. If you find an error or errors on:
only *one* of the lines in the question, mark your answer A;
any *two* lines in the question, mark your answer B;
all *three* lines in the question, mark your answer C;
none of the lines in the question, mark your answer D.

SAMPLE QUESTION

BJRPYUR 2079417
DTBPYKJ 5328460
YKLDBLT 4685283

In the above sample, the first line is correct since each code letter listed has the correct corresponding number. On the second line, an error exists because code letter P should have the number 9 instead of the number 8. The third line is correct since each code letter listed has the correct corresponding number. Since there is an error in *one* of the three lines, the correct answer is A. Now answer Questions 21 through 30 in the same manner.

21. BYPDTJL 2495308 21.____
PLRDTJU 9815301
DTJRYLK 5207486

22. RPBYRJK 7934706 22.____
PKTYLBU 9624821
KDLPJYR 6489047

23.	TPYBUJR	3942107	23.____
	BYRKPTU	2476931	
	DUKPYDL	5169458	
24.	KBYDLPL	6345898	24.____
	BLRKBRU	2876261	
	JTULDYB	0318542	
25.	LDPYDKR	8594567	25.____
	BDKDRJL	2565708	
	BDRPLUJ	2679810	
26.	PLRLBPU	9858291	26.____
	LPYKRDJ	88936750	
	TDKPDTR	3569527	
27.	RKURPBY	7617924	27.____
	RYUKPTJ	7426930	
	RTKPTJD	7369305	
28.	DYKPBJT	5469203	28.____
	KLPJBTL	6890238	
	TKPLBJP	3698209	
29.	BTPRJYL	2397148	29.____
	LDKUTYR	8561347	
	YDBLRPJ	4528190	
30.	ULPBKYT	1892643	30.____
	KPDTRBJ	6953720	
	YLKJPTB	4860932	

KEY (CORRECT ANSWERS)

1.	A	11.	D	21.	B
2.	C	12.	C	22.	C
3.	A	13.	A	23.	D
4.	D	14.	B	24.	B
5.	C	15.	A	25.	A
6.	C	16.	B	26.	C
7.	C	17.	C	27.	A
8.	D	18.	B	28.	D
9.	A	19.	A	29.	B
10.	B	20.	B	30.	D

NAME AND NUMBER COMPARISONS

COMMENTARY

This test seeks to measure your ability and disposition to do a job carefully and accurately, your attention to exactness and preciseness of detail, your alertness and versatility in discerning similarities and differences between things, and your power in systematically handling written language symbols.

It is actually a test of your ability to do academic and/or clerical work, using the basic elements of verbal (qualitative) and mathematical (quantitative) learning—words and numbers.

EXAMINATION SECTION

TEST 1

DIRECTIONS: In each line across the page there are three names or numbers that are much alike. Compare the three names or numbers and decide which ones are exactly alike. *PRINT IN THE SPACE AT THE RIGHT THE LETTER:*

A. if all THREE names or numbers are exactly alike
B. if only the FIRST and SECOND names or numbers are ALIKE
C. if only the FIRST and THIRD names or numbers are alike
D. if only the SECOND or THIRD names or numbers are alike
E. if ALL THREE names or numbers are DIFFERENT

1.	Davis Hazen	David Hozen	David Hazen	1.____
2.	Lois Appel	Lois Appel	Lois Apfel	2.____
3.	June Allan	Jane Allan	Jane Allan	3.____
4.	10235	10235	10235	4.____
5.	32614	32164	32614	5.____

TEST 2

1.	2395890	2395890	2395890	1.____
2.	1926341	1926347	1926314	2.____
3.	E. Owens McVey	E. Owen McVey	E. Owen McVay	3.____
4.	Emily Neal Rouse	Emily Neal Rowse	Emily Neal Rowse	4.____
5.	H. Merritt Audubon	H. Merriott Audubon	H. Merritt Audubon	5.____

TEST 3

1.	6219354	6219354	6219354	1.____
2.	231793	2312793	2312793	2.____
3.	1065407	1065407	1065047	3.____
4.	Francis Ransdell	Frances Ramsdell	Francis Ramsdell	4.____
5.	Cornelius Detwiler	Cornelius Detwiler	Cornelius Detwiler	5.____

TEST 4

1.	6452054	6452564	6542054	1.____
2.	8501268	8501268	8501286	2.____
3.	Ella Burk Newham	Ella Burk Newnham	Elena Burk Newnham	3.____
4.	Jno. K. Ravencroft	Jno. H. Ravencroft	Jno. H. Ravencoft	4.____
5.	Martin Wills Pullen	Martin Wills Pulen	Martin Wills Pullen	5.____

TEST 5

1.	3457988	3457986	3457986	1.____
2.	4695682	4695862	4695682	2.____
3.	Stricklund Kaneydy	Sticklund Kanedy	Stricklund Kanedy	3.____
4.	Joy Harlor Witner	Joy Harloe Witner	Joy Harloe Witner	4.____
5.	R.M.O. Uberroth	R.M.O. Uberroth	R.N.O. Uberroth	5.____

3

TEST 6

1.	1592514	1592574	1592574	1.____
2.	2010202	2010202	2010220	2.____
3.	6177396	6177936	6177396	3.____
4.	Drusilla S. Ridgeley	Drusilla S. Ridgeley	Drusilla S. Ridgeley	4.____
5.	Andrei I. Tooumantzev	Andrei I. Tourmantzev	Andrei I. Toumantzov	5.____

TEST 7

1.	5261383	5261383	5261338	1.____
2.	8125690	8126690	8125609	2.____
3.	W.E. Johnston	W.E. Johnson	W.E. Johnson	3.____
4.	Vergil L. Muller	Vergil L. Muller	Vergil L. Muller	4.____
5.	Atherton R. Warde	Asheton R. Warde	Atherton P. Warde	5.____

TEST 8

1.	013469.5	023469.5	02346.95	1.____
2.	33376	333766	333766	2.____
3.	Ling-Temco-Vought	Ling-Tenco-Vought	Ling-Temco Vought	3.____
4.	Lorilard Corp.	Lorillard Corp.	Lorrilard Corp.	4.____
5.	American Agronomics Corporation	American Agronomics Corporation	American Agronomic Corporation	5.____

TEST 9

1.	436592864	436592864	436592864	1.____
2.	197765123	197755123	197755123	2.____
3.	Dewaay Cortvriendt International S.A.	Deway Cortvriendt International S.A.	Deway Corturiendt International S.A.	3.____
4.	Crédit Lyonnais	Crèdit Lyonnais	Crèdit Lyonais	4.____
5.	Algemene Bank Nederland N.V.	Algamene Bank Nederland N.V.	Algemene Bank Naderland N.V.	5.____

TEST 10

1.	00032572	0.0032572	00032522	1.____
2.	399745	399745	398745	2.____
3.	Banca Privata Finanziaria S.p.A.	Banca Privata Finanzaria S.P.A.	Banca Privata Finanziaria S.P.A.	3.____
4.	Eastman Dillon, Union Securities & Co.	Eastman Dillon, Union Securities Co.	Eastman Dillon, Union Securities & Co.	4.____
5.	Arnhold and S. Bleichroeder, Inc.	Arnhold & S. Bleichroeder, Inc.	Arnold and S. Bleichroeder, Inc.	5.____

TEST 11

DIRECTIONS: Answer the questions below on the basis of the following instructions: For each such numbered set of names, addresses, and numbers listed in Columns I and II, select your answer from the following options:
A. The names in Columns I and II are different
B. The addresses in Columns I and II are different
C. The numbers in Columns I and II are different
D. The names, addresses and numbers are identical

1.	Francis Jones 62 Stately Avenue 96-12446	Francis Jones 62 Stately Avenue 96-21446	1.____
2.	Julio Montez 19 Ponderosa Road 56-73161	Julio Montez 19 Ponderosa Road 56-71361	2.____
3.	Mary Mitchell 2314 Melbourne Drive 68-92172	Mary Mitchell 2314 Melbourne Drive 68-92172	3.____
4.	Harry Patterson 25 Dunne Street 14-33430	Harry Patterson 25 Dunne Street 14-34330	4.____
5.	Patrick Murphy 171 West Hosmer Street 93-81214	Patrick Murphy 171 West Hosmer Street 93-18214	5.____

TEST 12

1.	August Schultz 816 St. Clair Avenue 53-40149	August Schultz 816 St. Claire Avenue 53-40149	1.____
2.	George Taft 72 Runnymede Street 47-04033	George Taft 72 Runnymede Street 47-04023	2.____
3.	Angus Henderson 1418 Madison Street 81-76375	Angus Henderson 1418 Madison Street 81-76375	3.____
4.	Carolyn Mazur 12 Rivenlew Road 38-99615	Carolyn Mazur 12 Rivervane Road 38-99615	4.____
5.	Adele Russell 1725 Lansing Lane 72-91962	Adela Russell 1725 Lansing Lane 72-91962	5.____

TEST 13

DIRECTIONS: The following questions are based on the instructions given below. In each of the following questions, the 3-line name and address in Column I is the master-list entry, and the 3-line entry in Column II is the information to be checked against the master list.
If there is one line that is NOT exactly alike, mark your answer A.
If there are two lines NOT exactly alike, mark your answer B.
If there are three lines NOT exactly alike, mark your answer C.
If the lines ALL are exactly alike, mark your answer D.

	Column I	Column II	
1.	Jerome A. Jackson 1243 14th Avenue New York, N.Y. 10023	Jerome A. Johnson 1234 14th Avenue New York, N.Y. 10023	1.____
2.	Sophie Strachtheim 33-28 Connecticut Ave. Far Rockaway, N.Y. 11697	Sophie Strachtheim 33-28 Connecticut Ave. Far Rockaway, N.Y. 11697	2.____
3.	Elisabeth NT. Gorrell 256 Exchange St New York, N.Y. 10013	Elizabeth NT. Correll 256 Exchange St. New York, N.Y. 10013	3.____
4.	Maria J. Gonzalez 7516 E. Sheepshead Rd. Brooklyn, N.Y. 11240	Maria J. Gonzalez 7516 N. Shepshead Rd. Brooklyn, N.Y. 11240	4.____
5.	Leslie B. Brautenweiler 21-57A Seller Terr. Flushing, N.Y. 11367	Leslie B. Brautenwieler 21-75ASeiler Terr. Flushing, N.J. 11367	5.____

KEY (CORRECT ANSWERS)

TEST 1	TEST 2	TEST 3	TEST 4	TEST 5	TEST 6	TEST 7
1. E	1. A	1. A	1. E	1. D	1. D	1. B
2. B	2. E	2. A	2. B	2. C	2. B	2. E
3. D	3. E	3. B	3. E	3. E	3. C	3. D
4. A	4. D	4. E	4. E	4. D	4. A	4. A
5. C	5. C	5. A	5. C	5. B	5. E	5. E

TEST 8	TEST 9	TEST 10	TEST 11	TEST 12	TEST 13
1. E	1. A	1. E	1. C	1. B	1. B
2. D	2. D	2. B	2. C	2. C	2. D
3. E	3. E	3. E	3. D	3. D	3. A
4. E	4. E	4. C	4. C	4. B	4. A
5. B	5. E	5. E	5. C	5. A	5. C

ABILITY TO APPLY STATED LAWS, RULES AND REGULATIONS

EXAMINATION SECTION

TEST 1

DIRECTIONS: Each question or incomplete statement is followed by several suggested answers or completions. Select the one that BEST answers the question or completes the statement. *PRINT THE LETTER OF THE CORRECT ANSWER IN THE SPACE AT THE RIGHT.*

Questions 1-2.

DIRECTIONS: Questions 1 and 2 are to be answered on the basis of the following passage.

Effective January 1, 2022, employees who are entitled to be paid at an overtime minimum wage rate according to the terms of a state minimum wage order must be paid for overtime at a rate at least time and one-half of the appropriate regular minimum wage rate for non-overtime work. For the purpose of this policy statement, the term *appropriate regular minimum* wage rate means $10.05 per hour or a lower minimum wage rate established in accordance with the provisions of a state minimum wage order. OVERTIME MINIMUM WAGES MAY NOT BE OFFSET BY PAYMENTS IN EXCESS OF THE REGULAR MINIMUM RATE OR NON-OVERTIME WORK.

1. A worker who ordinarily works forty hours a week at an agreed wage of $12.00 an hour is required to work ten hours in excess of forty during a payroll week and is paid for the extra ten hours at his $12.00 per hour rate. 1.____
Using the information contained in the above passage, it is BEST to conclude
   A. this was a correct application of the regulation
   B. this was an incorrect application of the regulation
   C. the employee was not underpaid because he or she agreed upon the wage rate
   D. the employee did not perform his job well

2. According to the information in the above passage, the employee in Question 1 was MOST likely underpaid at least 2.____
   A. $180.00 B. $30.75
   C. $60.00 D. not underpaid at all

Question 3.

DIRECTIONS: Question 3 is to be answered on the basis of the following passage.

The following guidelines establish a range of monetary assessments for various types of child labor violations. They are general in nature and may not cover every specific situation. In determining the appropriate monetary amount within the range shown, consideration will be given to the criteria enumerated in the statute, namely *the size of the employer's business, the good faith of the employer, the gravity of the violation, the history of previous violations, and the failure to comply with record keeping or other requirements.* For example, the penalty for a larger firm (25 or more employees) would tend to be in the higher range since such firms should have knowledge of the laws. The gravity of the violation would depend on such factors as the age of the minor, whether required to be in school, and the degree of exposure to the hazards of prohibited occupations. Failure to keep records of the hours of work of the minors would also have a bearing on the size of the penalty.

1. a. No employment certificate—child of employer (Sec. 131 or 132) b. No posted hours of work (Sect. 178)	1st Violation - $0-$100 2nd Violation - $100-$250 3rd Violation - $250-$500
2. a. Invalid employment certificate, e.g., student non-factory rather than general for a 16 year old in non-factory work (Sec. 132) b. Maximum or prohibited hours—less than one half hour beyond limit on any day, occasional, no pattern. (Sec. 130. 2e, 131.3f, 170.1, 171.1, 170l2, 172.1, 173.1; Ed. L. 3227, 3228)	1st Violation - $0-$100 2nd Violation - $150-$250 3rd Violation - $250-$500
3. a. No employment certificate. (Sec. 130.2e, 131.3f, 131, 132, 138; Ed. L. 3227, 3228; ACAL 35.01, 35.05) b. Maximum of prohibited hours – (1) less than one half hour beyond limit on regular basis, (2) more than one half hour beyond limit either occasional or on a regular basis (Sec. 130.2e, 131.3f, 170.1, 170.2, 172.1, 173.1;Ed. L. 3227, 3228)	1st Violation - $100-$250 2nd Violation - $250-$500 3rd Violation - $400-$500
4. Prohibited Occupations—Hazardous Employment (Sec. 130.1, 131.3f, 131.2, 133)	1st Violation - $300-$500 2nd Violation - $400-$500 3rd Violation - $400-$500

COMPLIANCE CONFERENCE PRIOR TO ASSESSMENT OF PENALTY

After a child labor violation is reported, a compliance conference will be scheduled affording the employer the opportunity to be heard on the reported violation. A determination regarding the assessment of a civil penalty will be made following the conference.

RIGHT TO APPEAL

If the employer is aggrieved by the determination following such conference, the employer has the right to appeal such determination within 60 days of the date of issuance to the Industrial Board of Appeals, 194 Washington Avenue, Albany, New York 12210 as prescribed by its Rules of Procedure.

3. According to the above passage, a firm with its third violation of child labor laws regarding no posted hours of work (Sec. 178) and prohibited occupations-hazardous employment would be fined 3.____
   A. $600$1,000
   B. $650
   C. $1,000
   D. cannot be determined from the information given

Question 4.

DIRECTIONS: Question 4 is to be answered on the basis of the following passage.

Section 198c. Benefits or Wage Supplements

1. In addition to any other penalty or punishment otherwise prescribed by law, any employer who is party to an agreement to pay or provide benefits or wage supplements to employees or to a third party or fund for the benefit of employees and who fails, neglects, or refuses to pay the amount or amounts necessary to provide such benefits or furnish such supplements within thirty days after such payments are required to be made, shall be guilty of a misdemeanor, and upon conviction shall be punished as provided in Section One Hundred Ninety-Eight-a of this article. Where such employer is a corporation, the president, secretary treasurer, or officers exercising corresponding functions shall each be guilty of a misdemeanor.

2. As used in this section, the term *benefits* or *wage supplements* includes, but is not limited to, reimbursement for expenses; health, welfare, and retirement benefits; and vacation, separation or holiday pay.

4. According to the above passage, an employer who had agreed to furnish an employee with a car and then failed to provide a car is 4.____
   A. not guilty of a misdemeanor
   B. most likely guilty of a misdemeanor
   C. not affected by the above regulation
   D. guilty of a felony

Question 5.

DIRECTIONS: Question 5 is to be answered on the basis of the following passage.

Manual workers must be paid weekly and not later than seven calendar days after the end of the week in which the wages are earned. However, a manual worker employed by a non-profitmaking organization must be paid in accordance with the agreed terms of employment, but not less frequently than semi-monthly. A manual worker means a mechanic, workingman, or laborer. Railroad workers, other than executives, must be paid on or before Thursday of each week the wages earned during the seven day period ending on Tuesday of the preceding week. Commission sales personnel must be paid in accordance with the agreed terms of employment but not less frequently than once in each month and not later than the last day of the month following the month in which the money is earned. If the monthly payment of wages, salary, drawing account or commissions is substantial, then additional compensation such as incentive earnings may be paid less frequently than once in each month, but in no event later than the time provided in the employment agreement.

5. A non-executive railroad worker has not been paid for the previous week's work. It is Wednesday. 5.____
According to the above passage, which of the following is TRUE?
The above regulation
   A. was not violated since the ending period is the following Tuesday
   B. was violated
   C. was not violated since the employee could be paid on Thursday
   D. does not apply in this case

Questions 6.

DIRECTIONS: Question 6 is to be answered on the basis of the following passage.

No deductions may be made from wages except deductions authorized by law, or which are authorized in writing by the employee and are for the employee's benefit. Authorized deductions include payments for insurance premiums, pensions, U.S. bonds, and union dues, as well as similar payments for the benefit of the employee. An employer may not make any payment by separate transaction unless such charge or payment is permitted as a deduction from wages. Examples of illegal deductions or charges include payments by the employee for spoilage, breakage, cash shortages or losses, and cost and maintenance of required uniforms.

6. An employee working on a cash register is short $40 at the end of his shift. The $40 is deducted from his wages. 6.____
According to the above passage, the deduction is
   A. legal because it is legal to deduct cash losses
   B. legal because the employee is at fault
   C. illegal because the employee was not told of the deduction in advance
   D. illegal

Questions 7-8.

DIRECTIONS: Questions 7 and 8 are to be answered on the basis of the following passage.

No employee shall be paid a wage at a rate less than the rate at which an employee of the opposite sex in the same establishment is paid for equal work on a job, the performance of which requires equal skill, effort, and responsibility, and which is performed under similar working conditions, except where payment is made pursuant to a differential based on:

a. A system which measures earnings by quantity or quality of production
b. A merit system
c. A seniority system; or
d. Any other factor other than sex.

Any violation of the above is illegal.

7. A woman working in a factory on a piece-rate system as a sewing machine operator received less pay than a male sewing machine operator who finished more items. 7.____
According to the above regulation, this is
   A. legal
   B. illegal
   C. legal, but not ethical
   D. no conclusion can be made from the information given

8. A male worker is in the same job title as a female worker. The male worker has been employed by the firm for three years, the female for two. 8.____
Using the regulation stated above, if the male worker is paid more than the female worker, the action is
   A. legal
   B. illegal
   C. legal, but not ethical
   D. no conclusion can be made from the information given

Question 9.

DIRECTIONS: Question 9 is to be answered on the basis of the following passage.

Section 162. <u>Time Allowed for Meals</u>

1. Every person employed in or in connection with a factory shall be allowed at least sixty minutes for the noon day meal.

2. Every person employed in or in connection with a mercantile or other establishment or occupation coming under the provisions of this chapter shall be allowed at least forty-five minutes for the noon day meal, except as in this chapter otherwise provided.

3. Every person employed for a period or shift starting before noon and continuing later than seven o'clock in the evening shall be allowed an additional meal period of at least twenty minutes between five and seven o'clock in the evening.

4. Every person employed for a period or shift of more than six hours starting between the hours of one o'clock in the afternoon and six o'clock in the morning, shall be allowed at least sixty minutes for a meal period when employed in or in connection with a factory, and forty-five minutes for a meal period when employed in or in connection with a mercantile or other establishment or occupation coming under the provision of this chapter, at a time midway between the beginning and end of such employment.

5. The commissioner may permit a shorter time to be fixed for meal periods than hereinbefore provided. The permit therefore shall be in writing and shall be kept conspicuously posted in the main entrance of the establishment. Such permit may be revoked at any time.

In administering this statute, the Department applies the following interpretations and guidelines:

Employee Coverage: Section 162 applies to every person in any establishment or occupation covered by the Labor Law. Accordingly, all categories of workers are covered, including white collar management staff.

Shorter Meal Periods: The Department will permit a shorter meal period of not less than 30 minutes as a matter of course, without application by the employer, so long as there is no indication of hardship to employees. A meal period of not less than 20 minutes will be permitted only in special or unusual cases after investigation and issuance of a special permit.

9. An employee is given twenty minutes for lunch 9.____
According to the information given in the above passage, the employer
A. is in violation
B. is not in violation
C. should be fined $250
D. no conclusion can be made from the information given

Question 10.

DIRECTIONS: Question 10 is to be answered on the basis of the following passage.

An employee shall not be obliged to incur expenses in the arrangement whereby the employee's wages or salary are directly deposited in a bank or financial institution or in the withdrawal of such wages or salary from the bank or financial institution. Some examples of expenses are as follows:

1. A service charge, per check charge, or administrative or processing charge.
2. Carfare in order to get to the bank or financial institution to withdraw wages.

An employee shall not be obliged to lose a substantial amount of uncompensated time in order to withdraw wages from a bank or financial institution. Although the employer is not required to provide employees with paid time in which to withdraw such monies, the Department has held that the employer should provide for the loss of time when the employee requires more than 15 minutes to withdraw wages. Such time includes travel time to and from, as well as actual time spent at the bank or financial institution in withdrawing such monies. The loss of such time without compensation constitutes a difficulty.

The withdrawal of wages may not interfere with an employee's meal period to the extent that it decreases the meal period to less than 30 minutes. Thus, although the time required for withdrawal of wages may be 15 minutes or less, the loss of even 8 or 9 minutes from a thirty minute meal period creates a difficulty.

10. An employee is unable to withdraw wages at any time other than her lunch break. She needs twenty minutes to withdraw wages and has a forty-five minute lunch break. 10.____
According to the information contained in the above passage, the employer
   A. is in violation
   B. is not in violation
   C. should be fined $250
   D. no conclusion can be made from the information given

KEY (CORRECT ANSWERS)

1.	B	6.	D
2.	B	7.	A
3.	D	8.	A
4.	B	9.	D
5.	C	10.	A

SOLUTIONS

1. The answer is choice B. According to the passage, the employee should have been paid "at a rate at least time and one half of the appropriate regular minimum wage rate for non-overtime work." Remember, it's important to consider only what has been given in the reading passage. Choice C is incorrect because it is illegal in this case to agree on something other than the law. Minimum standards are set by law so that employers cannot coerce, or otherwise persuade, employees to work at less than what is deemed fair. It could be argued that this is outside knowledge, but if you think about it, it's only common sense. Why bother having a minimum wage law, or minimum rates for overtime, or child labor laws if someone can just sign away his or her rights when an employer asks him or her to? If you didn't know this, you could still have eliminated this choice because the passage says, "ordinarily works 40 hours at an agreed wage of $12.00 per hour." The wording implies that this was agreed on for the normal work week.

2. The answer is choice B. The employee needs to be paid at a rate of time and a half. The employee has worked an extra ten hours at the hourly rate of $12.00 an hour. The passage states that the employee must be paid "at least time and one half of the appropriate regular minimum wage rate for non-overtime work." Minimum wage is given as $10.05 per hour. Time and a half of that would be $10.05 times 1.5, or $15.075 per hour. This employee is paid only $12.00 per hour for each hour of overtime. That's $3.075 less for each of the ten hours over forty hours, or a total of $30.75 less than he should have been paid. (10 × $3.075 = $30.75) You may have read the passage incorrectly, and thought the employee should have been paid time and a half on the $12.00 wage, but the passage does not state this. It states that the minimum payment is time and a half on minimum hourly wage, not on the employee's current wage rate. If you assumed the employee should have been paid $18.00 an hour, you probably would have picked choice C. Very tricky question. NOTE: The employee could have been paid less than half the minimum wage under special circumstances. Since there is nothing to indicate that the special circumstances apply, and since the question stem says "most likely," choice B is still considered the best choice.

3. The answer is choice D. This is another tricky question. The passage states, "The following guidelines establish a range of monetary assessments for various types of violations. They are general in nature and may not cover every specific situation. In determining the appropriate monetary amount within the range shown, considered will be given to the criteria enumerated in the statute...." The passage then goes on to list all of, the various possibilities. We don't know the circumstances, so choice D is the safest choice. If the question stem had been phrased "would most likely be fined," a case might possibly have been made for a different answer. The way it stands, choice D is the best choice because we can't say what, the fine definitely would be.

4. The answer is choice B. The last sentence states that "the term benefits or wage supplements includes but is not limited to...." This, coupled with the wording of the first paragraph, would mean that there is a good possibility the broken agreement would be judged a misdemeanor.

5. The answer is choice C. This is directly supported by the fourth sentence.

6. The answer is choice D. The last sentence states that "examples of illegal deductions or charges include payments by the employee for spoilage, breakage, cash shortages or losses...."

7. The answer is choice A. The key here is the phrase piece-rate system. The passage states that one of the exceptions is "a system which measures earnings by quantity or quality of production." That's piecework where extra pay may be given for extra production or effort. It's logical—and not too much—to assume that the man was paid more because he finished more items.

8. The answer is choice A. The passage states that one of the exceptions is a seniority system. The question stem says that the man had worked there for three years while the woman had only worked there for two years.

9. The answer is choice D. The last sentence of the passage states that "a meal period of not less than twenty minutes will be permitted only in special or unusual cases after investigation and issuance of the special permit." Since we don't know the circumstances, we can't definitely say the employer is or is not in violation.

10. The answer is choice A. The next to last sentence of the passage states that "the withdrawal of wages may not interfere with an employee's meal period to the extent that it decreases the meal period to less than twenty minutes." The employee can only withdraw wages during her meal period. If the employee has a forty-five minute lunch break, and needs twenty minutes to withdraw funds, then she only has twenty-five minutes for lunch, which the passage states is not sufficient.

MEMORY FOR FACTS AND INFORMATION

These questions test for the ability to remember facts and information presented in written form after you have been given a period to read and study the information.

TEST TASK: You will be given a Memory Booklet containing a story. The story will be considerably longer than the one presented here. You will have 5 minutes to read and study the information in the Memory Booklet. You will NOT be allowed to take notes. At the end of the study period, the monitor will collect the Memory Booklets containing the story and then will hand out the test booklets containing the test questions. The first group of questions in this test booklet will ask you to recall the facts and information presented in the Memory Booklet.

> **SAMPLE MEMORY STORY**: Officer Gary Hanson of the Burke Police Department was questioning Mathew Meyers, the owner of Meyers Sporting Goods located at 321 Payne Avenue, about a burglary that occurred the previous evening. Meyers said that when he arrived at the store at 8:50 A.M., he noticed that the rear door had been broken into. Meyers said that, after he had checked his inventory, he was missing 20 rifles, 16 pellet guns, 12 shotguns, and 8 pistols.
>
> SAMPLE QUESTION: How many shotguns did Meyers tell the Officer were missing from his store?
>
> A. 8
> B. 12
> C. 16
> D. 20

The answer is B.

SOLUTION: This question asks how many <u>shotguns</u> did Meyers tell the Officer were missing from his store. The last sentence in the Memory Story states, "...Meyers said that ... he was missing 20 rifles, 16 pellet guns, 12 shotguns, and 8 pistols."

Choice A: This is the number of missing <u>pistols</u>. Choice A is incorrect.

Choice B: This is the number of missing <u>shotguns</u>. Choice B is correct.

Choice C: This is the number of missing <u>pellet guns</u>. Choice C is incorrect.

Choice D: This is the number of <u>missing rifles</u>. Choice D is incorrect.

EXAMINATION SECTION
TEST 1

DIRECTIONS: Each question or incomplete statement is followed by several suggested answers or completions. Select the one that BEST answers the question or completes the statement. *PRINT THE LETTER OF THE CORRECT ANSWER IN THE SPACE AT THE RIGHT.*

Questions 1-10. MEMORY

DIRECTIONS: Questions 1 through 10 are to be answered SOLELY on the basis of the following passage, which contains a story about an incident involving police officers. You will have ten minutes to read and study the story. You may not write or make any notes while studying it. After ten minutes, close the memory booklet and do not look at it again. Then, answer the questions that follow.

You are one of a number of police officers who have been assigned to help control a demonstration inside Baldwin Square, a major square in the city. The demonstration is to protest the U.S. involvement in Iraq. As was expected, the demonstration has become nasty. You and nine other officers have been assigned to keep the demonstrators from going up Bell Street which enters the Square from the northwest. During the time you have been assigned to Bell Street, you have observed a number of things.

Before the demonstration began, three vans and a wagon entered the Square from the North on Howard Avenue. The first van was a 1989 blue Ford, plate number 897-JLK. The second van was a 1995 red Ford, plate number 899-LKK. The third van was a 1997 green Dodge step-van, plate number 997-KJL. The wagon was a blue 1998 Volvo with a luggage rack on the roof, plate number 989-LKK. The Dodge had a large dent in the left-hand rear door and was missing its radiator grill. The Ford that was painted red had markings under the paint which made you believe that it had once been a telephone company truck. Equipment for the speakers' platform was unloaded from the van, along with a number of demonstration signs. As soon as the vans and wagon were unloaded, a number of demonstrators picked up the signs and started marching around the square. A sign reading *U.S. Out Now* was carried by a woman wearing red jeans, a black tee shirt, and blue sneakers. A man with a beard, a blue shirt, and Army pants began carrying a poster reading *To Hell With Davis.* A tall, Black male and a Hispanic male had been carrying a large sign with *This Is How Vietnam Started* in big black letters with red dripping off the bottom of each letter.

A number of the demonstrators are wearing black armbands and green tee shirts with the peace symbol on the front. A woman with very short hair who was dressed in green and yellow fatigues is carrying a triangular-shaped blue sign with white letters. The sign says *Out Of Iraq.*

A group of 12 demonstrators have been carrying six fake coffins back and forth across the Square between Apple Street on the West and Webb Street on the East. They are shouting *Death to Hollis and his Henchmen.* Over where Victor Avenue enters the Square from the South, a small group of demonstrators (two men and three women) just started painting slogans on the walls surrounding the construction of the First National Union Bank and Trust.

1. Which street is on the opposite side of the Square from Victor Avenue? 1.____
   A. Bell B. Howard C. Apple D. Webb

2. How many officers are assigned with you? 2.____
   A. 8 B. 6 C. 9 D. 5

3. Howard Avenue enters the Square from which direction? 3.____
   A. Northwest B. North C. East D. Southwest

4. The van that had PROBABLY been a telephone truck had plate number 4.____
   A. 899-LKK B. 989-LKK C. 897-JKL D. 997-KJL

5. What is the color of the sign carried by the woman with very short hair? 5.____
   A. Blue B. White C. Black D. Red

6. The man wearing the army pants has a(n) 6.____
   A. Afro B. beard
   C. triangular-shaped sign D. black armband

7. Which vehicle had plate number 989-LKK? The 7.____
   A. red Ford B. blue Ford C. Volvo D. Dodge

8. The bank under construction is located ______ of the Square. 8.____
   A. north B. south C. east D. west

9. How many people are painting slogans on the walls surrounding the construction site? 9.____
   A. 4 B. 5 C. 6 D. 7

10. What is the name of the bank under construction? 10.____
   A. National Union Bank and Trust
   B. First National Bank and Trust
   C. First Union National Bank and Trust
   D. First National Union Bank and Trust

KEY (CORRECT ANSWERS)

1.	B	6.	B
2.	C	7.	C
3.	B	8.	B
4.	A	9.	B
5.	A	10.	D

TEST 2

DIRECTIONS: Each question or incomplete statement is followed by several suggested answers or completions. Select the one that BEST answers the question or completes the statement. *PRINT THE LETTER OF THE CORRECT ANSWER IN THE SPACE AT THE RIGHT.*

Questions 1-15.

DIRECTIONS: Questions 1 through 15 are to be answered SOLELY on the basis of the Memory Booklet given below.

MEMORY BOOKLET

The following passage contains a story about an incident involving police officers. You will have ten minutes to read and study the story. You may not write or make any notes while studying it. The first questions in the examination will be based on the passage. After ten minutes, close the memory booklet, and do not look at it again. Then, answer the questions that follow.

Police Officers Boggs and Thomas are patrolling in a radio squad car on a late Saturday afternoon in the spring. They are told by radio that a burglary is taking place on the top floor of a six-story building on the corner of 5th Street and Essex and that they should deal with the incident.

The police officers know the location and know that the Gold Jewelry Company occupies the entire sixth floor. They also know that, over the weekends, the owner has gold bricks in his office safe worth $500,000.

When the officers arrive at the location, they lock their radio car. They then find the superintendent of the building who opens the front door for them. He indicates he has neither seen nor heard anything suspicious in the building. However, he had just returned from a long lunch hour. The officers take the elevator to the sixth floor. As the door of the elevator with the officers opens on the sixth floor, the officers hear the door of the freight elevator in the rear of the building closing and the freight elevator beginning to move. They leave the elevator and proceed quickly through the open door of the office of the Gold Jewelry Company. They see that the office safe is open and empty. The officers quickly proceed to the rear staircase. They run down six flights of stairs, and they see four suspects leaving through the rear entrance of the building.

They run through the rear door and out of the building after the suspects. The four suspects are running quickly through the parking lot at the back of the building. The suspects then make a right-hand turn onto 5th Street and are clearly seen by the officers. The officers see one white male, one Hispanic male, one Black male, and one white female.

The white male has a beard and sunglasses. He is wearing blue jeans, a dark red and blue jacket, and white jogging shoes. He is carrying a large green duffel bag over his shoulder.

The Hispanic male limps slightly and has a dark moustache. He is wearing dark brown slacks, a dark green sweat shirt, and brown shoes. He is carrying a large blue duffel bag.

The Black male is clean-shaven, wearing black corduroy pants, a multi-colored shirt, a green beret, and black boots. He is carrying a tool box.

The white female has long dark hair and is wear-ing light-colored blue jeans, a white blouse, sneakers, and a red kerchief around her neck. She is carrying a shotgun.

The officers chase the suspects for three long blocks without getting any closer to them. At the intersection of 5th Street and Pennsylvania Avenue, the suspects separate. The white male and the Black male rapidly get into a 1992 brown Ford stationwagon. The stationwagon has a roof rack on top and a Connecticut license plate with the letters *JEAN* on it. The stationwagon departs even before the occupants close the door completely.

The Hispanic male and the white female get into an old blue Dodge van. The van has a CB antenna on top, a picture of a cougar on the back doors, a dented right rear fender, and a New Jersey license plate. The officers are not able to read the plate numbers on the van.

The officers then observe the stationwagon turn left and enter an expressway going to Connecticut. The van turns right onto Illinois Avenue and proceeds toward the tunnel to New Jersey.

The officers immediately run back to their radio car to radio in what happened.

1. Which one of the following suspects had sunglasses on? 1.____

   A. White male
   B. Hispanic male
   C. Black male
   D. White female

2. Which one of the following suspects was carrying a shotgun? 2.____

   A. White male
   B. Hispanic male
   C. Black male
   D. White female

3. Which one of the following suspects was wearing a green beret? 3.____

   A. White male
   B. Hispanic male
   C. Black male
   D. White femal

4. Which one of the following suspects limped slightly? 4.____

   A. White male
   B. Hispanic male
   C. Black male
   D. White female

5. Which one of the following BEST describes the stationwagon used? 5.____
   A

   A. 1992 brown Ford
   B. 1992 blue Dodge
   C. 1979 brown Ford
   D. 1979 blue Dodge

6. Which one of the following BEST describes the suspect or suspects who used the stationwagon? 6.____
A

A. Black male and a Hispanic male
B. white male and a Hispanic male
C. Black male and a white male
D. Black male and a white female

7. The van had a license plate from which of the following states? 7.____

A. Connecticut
B. New Jersey
C. New York
D. Pennsylvania

8. The license plate on the stationwagon read as follows: 8.____

A. JANE
B. JOAN
C. JEAN
D. JUNE

9. The van used had a dented ______ fender. 9.____

A. left rear
B. right rear
C. right front
D. left front

10. When last seen by the officers, the van was headed toward 10.____

A. Connecticut
B. New Jersey
C. Pennsylvania
D. Long Island

11. The female suspect's hair can BEST be described as 11.____

A. long and dark-colored
B. short and dark-colored
C. long and light-colored
D. short and light-colored

12. Which one of the following suspects was wearing a multicolored shirt? 12.____

A. White male
B. Hispanic male
C. Black male
D. White female

13. Blue jeans were worn by the ______ male suspect and the suspect. 13.____

A. Hispanic; white female
B. Black; Hispanic male
C. white; white female
D. Black; white male

14. The color of the duffel bag carried by the Hispanic male suspect was 14.____

A. blue
B. green
C. brown
D. red

15. The Hispanic male suspect was wearing 15.____

A. brown shoes
B. black shoes
C. black boots
D. jogging shoes

KEY (CORRECT ANSWERS)

1. A
2. D
3. C
4. B
5. A
6. C
7. B
8. C
9. B
10. B
11. A
12. C
13. C
14. A
15. A

READING COMPREHENSION
UNDERSTANDING AND INTERPRETING WRITTEN MATERIAL

COMMENTARY

The ability to read, understand, and interpret written materials texts, publications, newspapers, orders, directions, expositions, legal passages is a skill basic to a functioning democracy and to an efficient business or viable government.

That is why almost all examinations—for beginning, middle, and senior levels—test reading comprehension, directly or indirectly.

The reading test measures how well you understand what you read. This is how it is done: You read a paragraph and several statements based on a question. From the statements, you choose the one statement, or answer, that is BEST supported by, or BEST matches, what is said in the paragraph.

SAMPLE QUESTIONS

DIRECTIONS: Each question has five suggested answers, lettered A, B, C, D, and E. Decide which one is the BEST answer. *PRINT THE LETTER OF THE CORRECT ANSWER IN THE SPACE AT THE RIGHT.*

1. The prevention of accidents makes it necessary not only that safety devices be used to guard exposed machinery but also that mechanics be instructed in safety rules which they must follow for their own protection and that the light in the plant be adequate. 1.____
   The paragraph BEST supports the statement that industrial accidents
   A. are always avoidable
   B. may be due to ignorance
   C. usually result from inadequate machinery
   D. cannot be entirely overcome
   E. result in damage to machinery

ANALYSIS

Remember what you have to do:

First: Read the paragraph.
Second: Decide what the paragraph means.
Third: Read the five suggested answers.
Fourth: Select the one answer which BEST matches what the paragraph says or is BEST supported by something in the paragraph. (Sometimes you may have to read the paragraph again in order to be sure which suggested answer is best.)

This paragraph is talking about three steps that should be taken to prevent industrial accidents:

1. Use safety devices on machines
2. Instruct mechanics in safety rules
3. Provide adequate lighting

SELECTION

With this in mind, let's look at each suggested answer. Each one starts with "industrial accidents..."

SUGGESTED ANSWER A

Industrial accidents (A) are always avoidable

(The paragraph talks about how to avoid accidents but does not say that accidents are always avoidable.)

SUGGESTED ANSWER B

Industrial accidents (B) may be due to ignorance.

(One of the steps given in the paragraph to prevent accidents is to instruct mechanics on safety rules. This suggests that lack of knowledge or ignorance of safety rules causes accidents. This suggested answer sounds like a good possibility for being the right answer.)

SUGGESTED ANSWER C

Industrial accidents (C) usually result from inadequate machinery.

(The paragraph does suggest that exposed machines cause accidents, but it doesn't say that it is the usual cause of accidents. The word *usually* makes this a wrong answer.)

SUGGESTED ANSWER D

Industrial accidents (D) cannot be entirely overcome.

(You may know from your own experience that this is a true statement. But that is not what the paragraph is talking about. Therefore, it is NOT the correct answer.)

SUGGESTED ANSWER E

Industrial accidents (E) result in damage to machinery.

(This is a statement that may or may not be true, but, in any case, it is NOT covered by the paragraph.)

Looking back, you see that the one suggested answer of the five given that BEST matches what the paragraph says is:

Industrial accidents (B) may be due to ignorance.

The CORRECT answer then is B.

Be sure you read ALL the possible answers before you make your choice. You may think that none of the five answers is really good, but choose the BEST one of the five.

---

2. Probably few people realize, as they drive on a concrete road, that steel is used to keep the surface flat in spite of the weight of the busses and trucks. Steel bars, deeply embedded in the concrete, provide sinews to take the stresses so that the stresses cannot crack the slab or make it wavy. 2.____
The paragraph BEST supports the statement that a concrete road
   A. is expensive to build
   B. usually cracks under heavy weights
   C. looks like any other road
   D. is used only for heavy traffic
   E. is reinforced with other material

<u>ANALYSIS</u>

This paragraph is commenting on the fact that

1. few people realize, as they drive on a concrete road, that steel is deeply embedded
2. steel keeps the surface flat
3. steel bars enable the road to take the stresses without cracking or becoming wavy

<u>SELECTION</u>

Now read and think about the possible answers:

A. A concrete road is expensive to build.
(Maybe so, but that is not what the paragraph is about.)

B. A concrete road usually cracks under heavy weights.
(The paragraph talks about using steel bars to prevent heavy weights from cracking concrete roads. It says nothing about how usual it is for the roads to crack. The word *usually* makes this suggested answer wrong.)

C. A concrete road looks like any other road.
(This may or may not be true. The important thing to note is that it has nothing to do with what the paragraph is about.)

D. A concrete road is used only for heavy traffic.
(This answer at least has something to do with the paragraph—concrete roads are used with heavy traffic but it does not say "used only.")

E. A concrete road is reinforced with other material.
This choice seems to be the correct one on two counts. First, the paragraph does suggest that concrete roads are made stronger by embedding steel bars in them. This is another way of saying "concrete roads are reinforced with steel bars." Second, by the process of elimination, the other four choices are ruled out as correct answers simply because they do not apply.

You can be sure that not all the reading question will be so easy as these.

4

SUGGESTIONS FOR ANSWERING READING QUESTIONS

1. Read the paragraph carefully. Then read each suggested answer carefully. Read every word, because often one word can make the difference between a right or wrong answer.
2. Choose that answer which is supported in the paragraph itself. Do not choose an answer which is a correct statement unless it is based on information in the paragraph.
3. Even though a suggested answer has many of the words used in the paragraph, it may still be wrong.
4. Look out for words—such as *always*, *never*, *entirely*, or *only*—which tend to make a suggested answer wrong.
5. Answer first those questions which you can answer most easily. Then, work on the other questions.
6. If you can't figure out the answer to the question, guess.

READING COMPREHENSION

UNDERSTANDING AND INTERPRETING WRITTEN MATERIAL

STRATEGIES

SURVEYING PASSAGES, SENTENCES AS CUES

While individual readers develop unique reading styles and skills, there are some known strategies which can assist any reader in improving his or her reading comprehension and performance on the reading subtest. These strategies include understanding how single paragraphs and entire passages are structured, how the ideas in them are ordered, and how the author of the passage has connected these ideas in a logical and sequential way for the reader.

The section that follows highlights the importance of reading a passage through once for meaning, and provides instruction on careful reading for context cues within the sentences before and after the missing word.

SURVEY THE ENTIRE PASSAGE

To get a sense of the topic and the organization of ideas in a passage, it is important to survey each passage initially in its entirety and to identify the main idea. (The first sentence of a paragraph usually states the main idea.) Do not try to fill in the blanks initially. The purpose or surveying a passage is to prepare for the more careful reading which will follow. You need a sense of the big picture before you start to fill in the details; for example, a quick survey of the passage on page 11 indicate that the topic is the early history of universities. The paragraphs are organized to provide information on the origin of the first universities, the associations formed by teachers and students, the early curriculum, and graduation requirements.

READ PRECEDING SENTENCES CAREFULLY

The missing words in a passage cannot be determined by reading and understanding only the sentences in which the deletions occur. Information from the sentences which precede or follow can provide important cues to determine the correct choice. For example, if you read the first sentence from the passage about universities which contains a blank, you will notice that all the alternatives make sense if this one sentence is read in isolation:

Nobody actually _____ them.

A. started	B. guarded	C. blamed
D. compared	E. remembered	

The only way that you can make the correct word choice is to read the preceding sentences. In the excerpt below, notice that the first sentence tells the reader what the passage will be about: how universities developed. A key word in the first sentence is *emerged*, which is closely related in meaning to one of the five choices for the first blank. The second sentence explains the key word *emerged*, by pointing out that we have no historical record of a decree or a date indicating when the first university was established. Understanding the ideas in the first two sentences makes it possible to select the correct word for the blank. Look at the sentence with the deleted word in the context of the preceding sentences and think about why you are now able to make the correct choice.

> The first universities emerged at the end of the 11th century and beginning of the 12th. These institutions were not founded on any particular date or created by any formal action. Nobody actually _____ them.
>
> A. started B. guarded C. blamed
> D. compared E. remembered

Started is the best choice because it fits the main idea of the passage and is closely related to the key word *emerged.*

READ THE SENTENCE WHICH FOLLOWS TO VERIFY YOUR CHOICE

The sentences which follow the one from which a word has been deleted may also provide cues to the correct choice. For example, look at an excerpt from the passage about universities again, and consider how the sentence which follows the one with the blank helps to reinforce the choice of the word *started.*

> The first universities emerged at the end of the 11th century and the beginning of the 12th. These institutions were not founded on any particular date or created by any formal action. Nobody actually _____ them. Instead, they developed gradually in places like Paris, Oxford, and Bologna, where scholars had long been teaching students.
>
> A. started B. guarded C. blamed
> D. compared E. remembered

The words *developed gradually* mean the same as the key word *emerged.* The signal word *instead* helps to distinguish the difference between starting on a specific date as a result of some particular act or event and emerging over a period of time as a result of various factors.

Here is another example of how the sentence which follows the one from which a word is deleted might help you decide which of two good alternatives is the correct choice. This excerpt is from the practice passage about bridges (page 10).

> Bridges are built to allow a continuous flow of highway and railway traffic across water lying in their paths. But engineers cannot forget that river traffic, too, is essential to our economy. The role of _____ is important. To keep these vessels moving freely, bridges are built big enough, when possible, to let them pass underneath.
>
> A. wind B. boats C. weight
> D. wires E. experience

After the first two sentences, the reader may be uncertain about the direction the writer intended to take in the rest of the paragraph. If the writer intended to continue the paragraph with information concerning how engineers make choices about the relative importance and requirements of land traffic and rive traffic, *experience* might be the appropriate choice for the missing word. However, the sentence following the one in which the deletion occurs makes it clear that *boats* is the correct choice. It provides the synonym *vessels*, which in the noun phrase *these vessels* must refer back to the previous sentence or sentences. The phrase *to let them pass underneath* also helps make it clear that *boats* is the appropriate choice. *Them* refers back to *these vessels* which, in turn, refers back to *boats* when the word *boats* is placed in the previous sentence. Thus, the reader may use these cohesive ties (the pronoun referents) to verify the final choice.

Even when the text following a sentence with a deletion is not necessary to choose the best alternative, it may be helpful in other ways. Specifically, complete sentences provide important transitions into a related topic which is developed in the rest of the paragraph or in the next paragraph of the same passage. For example, the first paragraph in the passage about universities ends with a sentence which introduces the term *guilds*: *But, over time, they joined together to form guilds.* Prior to this sentence, information about the slow emergence of universities and about how independently scholars had acted was introduced. The next paragraph begins with two sentences about guilds in general. Someone who had not read the last sentence in the first paragraph might have missed the link between guilds and scholars and universities and, thus, might have been unnecessarily confused.

COHESIVE TIES AS CUES

Sentences in a paragraph may be linked together by several devices called cohesive ties. Attention to these ties may provide further cues about missing words. This section will describe the different types of cohesive ties and show how attention to them can help you to select the correct word.

PERSONAL PRONOUNS

Personal pronouns (e.g., he, she, they, it, its) are often used in adjoining sentences to refer back to an already mentioned person, place, thing, or idea. The word to which the pronoun refers is called the antecedent.

> Tools used in farm work changed very slowly from ancient times to the eighteenth century, and the changes were minor. Since the eighteenth century *they* have changed quickly and dramatically.

The word *they* refers back to *tools* in the example above.

In the examination reading subtest, a deleted word sometimes occurs in a sentence in which the sentence subject is a pronoun that refers back to a previously mentioned noun. You must correctly identify the referent for the particular pronoun in order to interpret the sentence and select the correct answer. Here is an example from the passage about bridges.

> An ingenious engineer designed the bridge so that it did not have to be raised above traffic. Instead it was _____.
>
> A. burned B. emptied C. secured
> D. shared E. lowered

Q. What is the antecedent of *it* in both cases in the example?
A. The antecedent, of course, is *bridge.*

DEMONSTRATIVE PRONOUNS

Demonstrative pronouns (e.g., this, that, these) are also used to refer to a specific, previously mentioned noun. They may occur alone as noun replacements, or they may accompany and modify nouns.

I like jogging, swimming, and tennis. *These* are the only sports I enjoy.

In the sentence above, the word *these* is a replacement noun. However, demonstrative pronouns may also occur as adjectives modifying nouns.

I like jogging, swimming, and tennis. *These* sports are the only ones I enjoy.

The word *these* in the example above is an adjective modifier. The word *these* in each of the two previous examples refers to *jogging, swimming,* and *tennis.*

Here is an example from the passage about universities on page 11.

Undergraduates took classes in Greek philosophy, Latin grammar, arithmetic, music, and astronomy. These were the only _____ available.

A. rooms
B. subjects
C. clothes
D. pens
E. company

Q. Which word is a noun replacement?
A. The word *these* is the replacement for *Greek philosophy, Latin grammar, arithmetic, music,* and *astronomy.*

Here is another example from the same passage.

The concept of a fixed program of study leading to a degree first evolved in Medieval Europe. This _____ had not appeared before.

A. idea
B. desk
C. library
D. capital

Q. What is the antecedent of *this*?
A. The antecedent is *the concept of a fixed program of study leading to a degree.*

COMPARATIVE ADJECTIVES AND ADVERBS

When comparative adjectives and adverbs (e.g., so, such, better, more) occur, they refer to something else in the passage, otherwise a comparison could not be made.

The hotels in the city were all full; so were the motels and boarding houses.

Q. To what in the first sentence does the word *so* refer?
A. So tells us to compare the *motels* and *boarding houses* to the *hotels in the city.*

Q. In what way are the *hotels, motels,* and *boarding houses* similar to each other?
A. The *hotels, motels,* and *boarding houses* are similar in that they were all *full.*

Look at an example from the passage about universities.

Guilds were groups of tradespeople, somewhat akin to modern trade unions. In the Middle Ages, all the crafts had such

A. taxes B. secrets C. products
D. problems E. organizations

Q. To what in the first sentence does the word *such* refer?
A. *Such* refers to *groups of tradespeople*.

SUBSTITUTIONS

Substitution is another form of cohesive tie. A substitution occurs when one linguistic item (e.g., a noun) is replaced by another. Sometimes the substitution provides new or contrasting information. The substitution is not identical to the original, or antecedent, idea. A frequently occurring substitution involves the use of *one*. A noun substitution may involve another member of the same class as the original one.

My car is falling apart. I need a new one.

Q. What in the first sentence is replaced in the second sentence with *one*?
A. *One* is a substitute for the specific car mentioned in the first sentence. The contrast comes from the fact that the *new one* isn't the writer's current car.

The substitution may also pinpoint a specific member of a general class.

1. There are many unusual courses available at the university this summer. The *one* I am taking is called *Death and Dying.*
2. There are many unusual courses available at the university this summer. *Some* have never been offered before.

Q. In these examples, what is the general class in the first sentence that is replaced by *one* and by *some*?
A. In both cases the words *one* and *some* replace *many unusual* courses.

SYNONYMS

Synonyms are words that have similar meaning. In the examination reading subtest, a synonym of a deleted word is sometimes found in one of the sentences before and/or after the sentence with the deletion. Examine the following excerpt from the passage about bridges again.

But engineers cannot forget that river traffic, too, is essential to our economy. The role of _____ is important. To keep these vessels moving freely, bridges are built high enough, when possible, to let them pass underneath.

A. wind B. boats C. weight
D. wires E. experience

Q. Can you identify synonyms in the sentences, before and after the sentence containing the deletion, which are cues to the correct deleted word?

A. If you identified the correct words, you probably noticed that *river traffic* is not exactly a synonym since it is a slightly more general term than the word *boats* (the correct choice). But the word *vessels* is a direct synonym. Demonstrative pronouns (this, that, these, those) are sometimes used as modifiers for synonymous nouns in sentences which follow those containing deletions. The word *these* in *these vessels* is the demonstrative pronoun (modifier) for the synonymous noun *vessels*.

ANTONYMS

Antonyms are words of opposite meaning. In the examination reading subtest passages, antonyms may be cues for missing words. A contrasting relationship, which calls for the use of an antonym, is often signaled by the connective words *instead*, *however*, *but*, etc. Look at an excerpt from the passage about bridges.

An ingenious engineer designed the bridges so that it did not have to be raised above traffic. Instead it was

A. burned B. emptied C. secured
D. shared E. lowered

Q: Can you identify an antonym in the first sentence for one of the five alternatives?

A. The word *raised* is an antonym for the word *lowered.*

SUBORDINATE-SUBORDINATE WORDS

In the examination reading subtest, a passage sometimes contains a general term which provides a cue that a more specific term is the appropriate alternative. At other times, the passage may contain a specific term which provides cues that a general term is the appropriate alternative for a particular deletion. The general and more specific words are said to have superordinate-subordinate relationships.

Look at Example 1 below. The more specific word *boy* in the first sentence serves as the antecedent for the more general word *child* in the second sentence. In Example 2, the relationship is reversed. In both examples, the words *child* and *boy* reflect a superordinate-subordinate relationship.

1. The *boy* climbed the tree. Then the *child* fell.
2. The *child* climbed the tree. Then the *boy* fell.

In the practice passage about bridges on Page 11, the phrase *river traffic* is a general term that is superordinate to the alternative *boats* (Item 1). Later in the passage about bridges the following sentences also contain superordinate-subordinate words:

A lift bridge was desired, but there were wartime shortages of steel and machinery needed for the towers. It was hard to find enough _____.

A. work B. material C. time
D. power E. space

Q. Can you identify two words in the first sentence that are specific examples for the correct response in the second sentence?
A. Of course, the words *steel* and *machinery* are the specific examples for the more general term *material*.

WORDS ASSOCIATED BY ENTAILMENT

Sometimes the concept described by one word within the context of the passage entails, or implies, the concept described by another word. For example, consider again Item 7 in the practice passage about bridges. Notice how the follow-up sentence to Item 7 provides a cue to the correct response.

An ingenious engineer designed the bridge so that it did not have to be raised above traffic. Instead it was _____. It could be submerged seven meters below the surface of the river.
A. burned B. emptied C. secured
D. shared E. lowered

Q. What word in the sentence after the blank implies the concept of an alternative?
A. *Submerged* implies *lowered*. The concept of submerging something implies the idea of lowering the object beneath the surface of the water.

WORDS ASSOCIATED BY PART-WHOLE RELATIONSHIPS

Words may be related because they involve part of a whole and the whole itself; for example, *nose* and *face*. Words may also be related because they involve two parts of the same whole; for example, *radiator* and *muffler* both refer to parts of a car.

The captain of the ship was nervous. The storm was becoming worse and worse. The hardened man paced the _____.
A. floor B. hall C. deck D. court

Q. Which choice has a part-whole relationship with a word in the sentences above?
A. A *deck* is a part of a *ship*. Therefore, *deck* has a part-whole relationship with *ship*.

CONJUNCTIVE AND CONNECTIVE WORDS AND PHRASES

Conjunctions or connectives are words or phrases that connect parts of sentences or parts of a passage to each other. Their purpose is to help the reader understand the logical and conceptual relationships between ideas and events within a passage. Examples of these words and phrases include coordinate conjunctions (e.g., and, but, yet), subordinate conjunctions (e.g., because, although, since, after), and other connective words and phrases (e.g., too, also, on the other hand, as a result).

Listed below are types of logical relationships expressed by conjunctive, or connective words. Also listed are examples of words used to cue relationships to the reader.

Additive and comparative words and phrases: and, in addition to, too, also, furthermore, similarly.

Adversative and contrastive words and phrases: yet, though, only, but, however, instead, rather, on the other hand, conversely.

Causal words or phrases: so, therefore, because, as a result, if...then, unless, except, in that case, under the circumstances.

Temporal words and phrases: before, after, when, while, initially, lastly, finally, until.

Examples

1. I enjoy fast-paced sports like tennis and volleyball, but my brother prefers _____ sports.
   A. running B. slower C. team D. active

   Q. What is the connective word that tells you to look for a contrast relationship between the two parts of the sentence?
   A. The connective word *but* signals that a contrast relationship exists between the two parts of the sentence.

   Q. Of the four options, what is the best choice for the blank?
   A. The word *slower* is the best response here.

2. The child stepped to close to the edge of the brook. As a result, he _____ in.
   A. fell B. waded C. ran D. jumped

   Q. What is the connective phrase that links the two sentences?
   A. The connective phrase *as a result* links the two sentences.

   Q. Of the four relationships of words and phrases listed previously, what kind of relationship between the two sentences does the connective phrase in the example signal to the reader?
   A. The phrase *as a result* signals that a cause and effect relationship exists between the two sentences.

   Q. Identify the correct response which makes the second sentence reflect and cause and effect relationship.
   A. The correct response is *fell*.

Understanding connectives is very important to success on the examination reading subtest. Sentences with deletions are often very closely related to adjacent sentences in meaning, and the relationships often signaled by connective words or phrases. Here is an example from the practice passage about universities.

At first, these tutors had not been associated with one another. Rather, they had been _____. But, over time, they joined together to form guilds.
A. curious B. poor C. religious
D. ready E. independent

Q. Identify the connective and contrastive words and phrases in the example.

A. *At first* and *over time* are connective phrases that set up temporal progression. *Rather* and *but* are contrastive items. The use of *rather* in the sentence with the deletion tells the reader that the missing word has to convey a meaning in contrast to *associated with one another.* (Notice also that *rather* occurs after a negative statement.) The use of *but* in the sentence after the one with the deletion indicates that the deleted word in the previous sentence has to reflect a meaning that contrasts with *joined together.* Thus, the reader is given two substantial cues to the meaning of the missing word. *Independent* is the only choice that meets the requirement for contrastive meaning.

SAMPLE QUESTIOINS

DIRECTIONS: There are two passages on the following pages. In each passage some words are missing. Wherever a word is missing, there is a blank line with a number on it. Below the passage you will find the same number and five words. Choose the word that makes the best sense in the blank. You may not be sure of the answer to a question until you read the sentences that come after the blank, so be sure to read enough to answer the questions. As you work on these passages, you will find that the second passage is harder to read than the first. Answer as many questions as you can.

Bridges are built to allow a continuous flow of highway and railway traffic across water lying in their paths. But engineers cannot forget that river traffic, too, is essential to our economy. The role of __1__ is important. To keep these vessels moving freely, bridges are built high enough, when possible, to let them pass underneath. Sometimes, however, channels must accommodate very tall ships. It may be uneconomical to build a tall enough bridge. The __2__ would be too high. To save money, engineers build movable bridges.

In the swing bridge, the middle part pivots or swings open. When the bridge is closed, this section joins the two ends of the bridge, blocking tall vessels. But this section __3__. When swung open, it is perpendicular to the ends of the bridge, creating two free channels for river traffic. With swing bridges channel width is limited by the bridge's piers. The largest swing bridge provides only a 75-meter channel. Such channels are sometimes __4__. In such cases, a bascule bridge may be built.

Bascule bridges are drawbridges with two arms that swing upward. They provide an opening as wide as the span. They are also versatile. These bridges are not limited to being fully opened or fully closed. They can be __5__ in many ways. They can be fixed at different angles to accommodate different vessels.

In vertical lift bridges, the center remains horizontal. Towers at both ends allow the center to be lifted like an elevator. One interesting variation of this kind of bridge was built during World War II. A lift bridge was desired, but there were wartime shortages of the steel and machinery needed for the towers. It was hard enough to find enough __6__. An ingenious engineer designed the bridge so that it did not have to be raised above traffic. Instead it was __7__. It could be submerged seven meters below the surface of the river. Ships sailed over it.

1. A. wind B. boats C. experience D. wires E. experience 1.____

2. A. levels B. cost C. standards D. waves E. deck 2.____

3. A. stands B. floods C. wears D. turns E. supports 3.____

4. A. narrow B. rough C. long D. deep E. straight 4.____

5. A. crossed B. approached C. lighted D. planned E. positioned 5.____

6. A. work B. material C. time 6.____
D. power E. space

7. A. burned B. emptied C. secured 7.____
D. shared E. lowered

The first universities emerged at the end of the 11th century and beginning of the 12th. These institutions were not founded on any particular date or created by any formal action. Nobody actually __8__ them. Instead, they developed gradually in places like Paris, Oxford, and Bologna, where scholars had long been teaching students. At first, these tutors had not been associated with one another. Rather, they had been __9__. But, over time, they joined together to form guilds.

Guilds were groups of tradespeople, somewhat akin to modern unions. In the Middle Ages, all the crafts had such __10__. The scholars' guilds built school buildings and evolved an administration which charged fees and set standards for the curriculum. It set prices for members' services and fixed requirements for entering the profession.

Professors were not the only schoolpeople forming associations. In Italy, students joined guilds to which teachers had to swear obedience. The students set strict rules, fining professors for beginning class a minute late. Teachers had to seek their students' permission to marry, and such permission was not always granted. Sometimes the students __11__. Even if they said yes, the teacher got only one day's honeymoon.

Undergraduates took classes in Greek philosophy, Latin grammar, arithmetic, music, and astronomy. These were the only __12__ available. More advanced study was possible in law, medicine, and theology, but one could not earn such postgraduate degrees quickly. It took a long time to __13__. Completing the requirements in theology, for example, took at least 13 years.

The concept of a fixed program of study leading to a degree first evolved in medieval Europe. This __14__ had not appeared before, in earlier academic settings, notions about *meeting requirements meeting requirements* and *graduating* had been absent. Since the middle ages, though, we have continued to view education as a set curriculum culminating in a degree.

8. A. started B. guarded C. blamed 8.____
D. compared E. remembered

9. A. curious B. poor C. religious 9.____
D. ready E. independent

10. A. taxes B. secrets C. products 10.____
D. problems E. organizations

11. A. left B. copied C. refused 11.____
D. paid E. prepared

12. A. rooms B. subjects C. clothes 12.____
D. pens E. markets

13. A. add B. answer C. forget 13.____
D. finish E. travel

14. A. idea B. desk C. library 14.____
D. capital E. company

KEY (CORRECT ANSWERS)

1.	B	6.	B	11.	C
2.	B	7.	E	12.	B
3.	D	8.	A	13.	D
4.	A	9.	E	14.	A
5.	E	10.	E		

READING COMPREHENSION
UNDERSTANDING AND INTERPRETING WRITTEN MATERIAL

EXAMINATION SECTION

TEST 1

DIRECTIONS: Read the following passages, and select the MOST appropriate word from the five alternatives provided for each deleted word. *PRINT THE LETTER OF THE CORRECT ANSWER IN THE SPACE AT THE RIGHT.*

PASSAGE I

Bridges are built to allow a continuous flow of highway and railway traffic across water lying in their paths. But engineers cannot forget the fact that river traffic, too, is essential to or economy. The role of 1 is important. To keep these vessels moving freely, bridges are built high enough, when possible, to let them pass underneath. Sometimes, however, channels must accommodate very tall ships. It may be uneconomical to build a tall enough bridge. The 2 would be too high. To save money, engineers build movable bridges.

1. A. wind B. boats C. weight D. wires E. experience 1.____

2. A. levels B. cost C. standards D. waves E. deck 2.____

In the swing bridge, the middle part pivots or swings open. When the bridge is closed, this section joins the two ends of the bridge, blocking tall vessels. But this section 3. When swung open, it is perpendicular to the ends of the bridge, creating two free channels for river traffic. With swing bridges, channel width is limited by the bridge's piers. The largest swing bridge provides only a 75-meter channel. Such channels are sometimes too 4. In such cases, a bascule bridge may be built.

3. A. stands B. floods C. wears D. turns E. supports 3.____

4. A. narrow B. rough C. long D. deep E. straight 4.____

Bascule bridges are drawbridges with two arms that swing upward. They provide an opening as wide as the span. They are also versatile. These bridges are not limited to being fully opened or fully closed. They can be 5 in many ways. They can be fixed at different angles to accommodate different vessels.

5. A. approached B. crossed C. lighted D. planned E. positioned 5.____

In vertical lift bridges, the center remains horizontal. Towers at both ends allow the center to be lifted like an elevator. One interesting variation of this kind of bridge was built during World War II. A lift bridge was desired, but there were wartime shortages of the steel and machinery needed for the towers. It was hard to find enough 6. An ingenious engineer designed the bridge so that it did not have to be raised above traffic. Instead it was 7. It could be submerged seven meters below the river surface. Ships sailed over it.

6. A. work B. material C. time D. power E. space 6.____

7. A. burned B. emptied C. secured D. shared E. lowered 7.____

PASSAGE II

Before anesthetics were discovered, surgery was carried out under very severe time restrictions. Patients were awake, tossing and screaming in terrible pain. Surgeons were forced to hurry in order to constrain suffering and minimize shock. 8 was essential. Haste, however, did not make for good outcomes in surgery. No surprise then, that the 9 were often poor.

8. A. Blood B. Silence C. Speed D. Water E. Money 8.____

9. A. quarters B. teeth C. results D. materials E. families 9.____

The discovery of anesthetics happened, in part, by accident. During the early 1800's, nitrous oxide and ether were used for entertainment. At "either frolics" in theaters, volunteers would breathe these gases, become lightheaded, and run around the stage laughing and dancing. By chance, a Connecticut dentist saw such a 10. One volunteer banged his leg against a sharp edge. But he did not 11. He paid no attention to his wound, as though he felt nothing. This gave the dentist the idea of using gas to kill pain,

10. A. show B. machine C. face D. source E. growth 10.____

11. A. dream B. recover C. succeed D. agree E. notice 11.____

At first, using the "open drip method," ether and chloroform were filtered through a cotton pad placed over the mouth and nose. This direct dose was difficult to regulate and irritating to the nose and throat. Patients would hold their breath, cough, or gag. This made it impossible for them to relax, let alone sleep. Consequently, surgery was often 12. It couldn't begin until the patient had quieted and the anesthesia had taken hold.

12. A. delayed B. required C. blamed D. observed E. repeated 12.____

Today's procedures are safer and more accurate. In the "closed method," a fixed amount of gas is released from sealed bottles into an inhalator bag when the patient exhales. He inhales this gas through tubes with his next breath. In this way, the gas is 13. The system carefully regulates how much gas reached the patient.

13. A. heated B. controlled C. cleaned D. selected E. wasted 13.____

For dentistry and minor operations, patients need not be asleep. Newer anesthetics can be used which deaden nerves only in the affected part of the body. These 14 anesthetics offer several advantages. For instance, since the anesthesia is fairly light and patients remain awake, they can cooperate with their doctors.

14. A. local B. natural C. ancient D. heavy E. three

PASSAGE III

An indispensable element in the development of telephony was the continual improvement of telephone station instruments, those operating units located at the clients premises. Modern units normally consist of a transmitter, receiver, and transformer. They also contain a bell or equivalent summoning device, a mechanism for controlling the unit's connection to the client's line, and various associated items, like dials. All of these 15 have changed over the years. The transmitter, especially, has undergone enormous refinement during the last century.

15. A. parts B. costs C. services D. models E. routes 15.____

Bell's original electromagnetic transmitter functioned likewise as receiver, the same instrument being held alternately to mouth and ear. But having to 16 the instrument this way was inconvenient. Suggestions understandably emerged for mounting the transmitter and receiver onto a common handle, thereby creating what are now known as handsets. Transmitter and receiver were, in fact, later 17 his way. Combination handsets were produced for commercial utilization late in the nineteenth century, but prospects for their acceptance were uncertain as the initial quality of transmissions with the handsets was disappointing. But 18 transmissions followed. With adequately high transmission standards attained, acceptance of handsets was virtually assured.

16. A. store B. use C. test D. strip E. clean 16.____

17. A. grounded B. marked C. covered D. priced E. coupled 17.____

18. A. shorter B. fewer C. better D. faster E. cheaper 18.____

Among the most significant improvements in transmitters has been the enormous amplification (up to a thousandfold) of speech sounds. This increased 19 has benefited telecommunications enormously. Nineteenth century telephone conversations frequently were only marginally audible whereas nowadays even murmured conversations can be transmitted successfully, barring unusual atmospheric or electronic disturbances.

19. A. distance B. speed C. market D. volume E number 19.____

Vocal quality over nineteenth century instruments was distorted, the speaker not readily identifiable. By comparison, current sound is characterized by considerably greater naturalism. Modern telephony produces speech sounds more nearly resembling an individual's actual voice. Thus, it is easier to 20 the speaker. A considerable portion of this improvement is attributable to practical applications of laboratory investigations concerning the mechanisms of human speech and audition. These 21 have exerted a profound influence. Their results prompted technical innovations in modern transmitter design which contributed appreciably to the excellent communication available nowadays.

20. A. time B. help C. bill D. stop E. recognize 20.____

21. A. studies B. rates C. materials D. machines E. companies 21.____

PASSAGE IV

The dramatic events of December 7, 1941, plunged this nation into war. The full 22 of the war we cannot even now comprehend, but one of the effects stands out in sharp relief —the coming of the air age. The airplane, which played a relatively 23 part in World War I, has already soared to heights undreamed of save by the few with mighty vision.

In wartime the airplane is the 24 on wings and the battleship that flies. To man in his need it symbolizes deadly extremes; friend or foe; deliverance or 25.

It is a powerful instrument of war revolutionizing military strategy, but its peacetime role is just as 26. This new master of time and space, fruit of man's inventive genius, has come to stay, smalling the earth and smoothing its surface.

To all of us, then, to youth, and to 27 alike comes the winged challenge to get ourselves ready—to 28 ourselves for living in an age which the airplane seems destined to mold.

22. A. destruction B. character C. history D. import E. picture 22.____

23. A. important B. dull C. vast D. unknown E. minor 23.____

24. A. giant B. ant C. monster D. artillery E. robot 24.____

25. A. ecstasy B. bombardment C. death D. denial E. survival 25.____

26. A. revolting B. revolutionary C. residual D. reliable E. regressive 26.____

27. A. animals B. nations C. women D. men E. adult 27.____

28. A. distract B. engage C. determine D. deter E. orient 28.____

PASSAGE V

Let us consider how voice training may contribute to 29 development and an improved social 30.

In the first place, it has been fairly well established that individuals tend to become what they believe 31 people think them to be.

When people react more favorably toward us because our voices 32 the impression that we are friendly, competent, and interesting, there is a strong tendency for us to develop those 33 in our personality.

If we are treated with respect by others, we soon come to have more respect for 34.

Then, too, one's own consciousness of having a pleasant, effective voice of which he does not need to be ashamed contributes materially to a feeling of poise, self-confidence, and a just pride in himself.

A good voice, like good clothes, can do much for an 35 that otherwise might be inclined to droop.

29. A. facial B. material C. community D. personality E. physical 29.____

30. A. adjustment B. upheaval C. development D. bias E. theories 30.____

31. A. some B. hostile C. jealous D. inferior E. destroy 31.____

32. A. betray B. imply C. destroy D. transfigure E. convey 32.____

33. A. detects B. qualities C. techniques D. idiosyncrasies E. quirks 33.____

34. A. others B. their children C. their teachers D. ourselves E. each other 34.____

35. A. mind B. heart C. brain D. feeling E. ego 35.____

PASSAGE VI

How are symphony orchestras launched, kept going, and built up in smaller communities? Recent reports from five of them suggest that, though the 36 changes, certain elements are fairly common. One thing shines out; 37 is essential.

Also, aside from the indispensable, instrumentalists who play, the following personalities, either singly, or preferably in 38 seem to be the chief needs; a conductor who wants to conduct so badly he will organize his own orchestra if it is the only way he can get one; a manager with plenty of resourcefulness in rounding up audiences and finding financial support; an energetic community leader, generally a woman, who will take up locating the orchestra as a 39; and generous visiting soloists who will help draw those who are 40 that anything local can be used.

36. A. world B. pattern C. reason D. scene E. cast 36.____

37. A. hatred B. love C. enthusiasm D. participation E. criticism 37.____

38. A. combination B. particular C. isolation D. sympathy E. solitary 38.____

39. A. chore B. duty C. hobby D. delight E. career 39.____

40. A. convinced B. skeptical C. happy D. unhappy E. unsure 40.____

KEY (CORRECT ANSWERS)

1.	B	11.	E	21.	A	31.	E
2.	B	12.	A	22.	D	32.	E
3.	D	13.	B	23.	E	33.	B
4.	A	14.	A	24.	D	34.	D
5.	E	15.	A	25.	C	35.	E
6.	B	16.	B	26.	B	36.	B
7.	E	17.	E	27.	E	37.	C
8.	C	18.	C	28.	E	38.	A
9.	C	19.	D	29.	D	39.	C
10.	A	20.	E	30.	A	40.	B

READING COMPREHENSION
UNDERSTANDING AND INTERPRETING WRITTEN MATERIAL

EXAMINATION SECTION
TEST 1

DIRECTIONS: Each question or incomplete statement is followed by several suggested answers or completions. Select the one that BEST answers the question or completes the statement. *PRINT THE LETTER OF THE CORRECT ANSWER IN THE SPACE AT THE RIGHT.*

Questions 1-5.

DIRECTIONS: Questions 1 through 5 are to be answered on the basis of the following passage.

The laws with which criminal courts are concerned contain threats of punishment for infraction of specified rules. Consequently, the courts are organized primarily for implementation of the punitive societal reaction of crime. While the informal organization of most courts allows the judge to use discretion as to which guilty persons actually are to be punished, the threat of punishment for all guilty persons always is present. Also, in recent years a number of formal provisions for the use of non-punitive and treatment methods by the criminal courts have been made, but the threat of punishment remains, even for the recipients of the treatment and non-punitive measures. For example, it has become possible for courts to grant probation, which can be non-punitive, to some offenders, but the probationer is constantly under the threat of punishment, for, if he does not maintain the conditions of his probation, he may be imprisoned. As the treatment reaction to crime becomes more popular, the criminal courts may have as their sole function the determination of the guilt or innocence of the accused persons, leaving the problem of correcting criminals entirely to outsiders. Under such conditions, the organization of the court system, the duties and activities of court personnel, and the nature of the trial all would be decidedly different.

1. Which one of the following is the BEST description of the subject matter of the above passage? The 1.____

   A. value of non-punitive measures for criminals
   B. effect of punishment on guilty individuals
   C. punitive functions of the criminal courts
   D. success of probation as a deterrent of crime

2. It may be INFERRED from the above passage that the present traditional organization of the criminal court system is a result of 2.____

   A. the nature of the laws with which these courts are concerned
   B. a shift from non-punitive to punitive measures for correctional purposes
   C. an informal arrangement between court personnel and the government
   D. a formal decision made by court personnel to increase efficiency

3. All persons guilty of breaking certain specified rules, according to the above passage, are subject to the threat of 3.____

A. treatment
B. punishment
C. probation
D. retrial

4. According to the above passage, the decision whether or not to punish a guilty person is a function USUALLY performed by 4.____

A. the jury
B. the criminal code
C. the judge
D. corrections personnel

5. According to the above passage, which one of the following is a possible effect of an increase in the *treatment reactions to crime?* 5.____

A. A decrease in the number of court personnel
B. An increase in the number of criminal trials
C. Less reliance on probation as a non-punitive treatment measure
D. A decrease in the functions of the court following determination of guilt

Questions 6-8.

DIRECTIONS: Questions 6 through 8 are to be answered on the basis of the following passage.

A glaring exception to the usual practice of the judicial trial as a means of conflict resolution is the utilization of administrative hearings. The growing tendency to create administrative bodies with rule-making and quasi-judicial powers has shattered many standard concepts. A comprehensive examination of the legal process cannot neglect these newer patterns.

In the administrative process, the legislative, executive, and judicial functions are mixed together, and many functions, such as investigating, advocating, negotiating, testifying, rule making, and adjudicating, are carried out by the same agency. The reason for the breakdown of the separation-of-powers formula is not hard to find. It was felt by Congress, and state and municipal legislatures, that certain regulatory tasks could not be performed efficiently, rapidly, expertly, and with due concern for the public interest by the traditional branches of government. Accordingly, regulatory agencies were delegated powers to consider disputes from the earliest stage of investigation to the final stages of adjudication entirely within each agency itself, subject only to limited review in the regular courts.

6. The above passage states that the usual means for conflict resolution is through the use of 6.____

A. judicial trial
B. administrative hearing
C. legislation
D. regulatory agencies

7. The above passage IMPLIES that the use of administrative hearing in resolving conflict is a(n) ______ approach. 7.____

A. traditional
B. new
C. dangerous
D. experimental

8. The above passage states that the reason for the breakdown of the separation-of-powers formula in the administrative process is that 8.____

A. Congress believed that certain regulatory tasks could be better performed by separate agencies
B. legislative and executive functions are incompatible in the same agency
C. investigative and regulatory functions are not normally reviewed by the courts
D. state and municipal legislatures are more concerned with efficiency than with legality

Questions 9-10.

DIRECTIONS: Questions 9 and 10 are to be answered SOLELY on the basis of the information given in the following paragraph.

An assumption commonly made in regard to the reliability of testimony is that when a number of persons report upon the same matter, those details upon which there is an agreement may, in general, be considered as substantiated. Experiments have shown, however, that there is a tendency for the same errors to appear in the testimony of different individuals, and that, quite apart from any collusion, agreement of testimony is no proof of dependability.

9. According to the above paragraph, it is commonly assumed that details of an event are substantiated when 9.____

A. a number of persons report upon them
B. a reliable person testifies to them
C. no errors are apparent in the testimony of different individuals
D. several witnesses are in agreement about them

10. According to the above paragraph, agreement in the testimony of different witnesses to the same event is 10.____

A. evaluated more reliably when considered apart from collusion
B. not the result of chance
C. not a guarantee of the accuracy of the facts
D. the result of a mass reaction of the witnesses

Questions 11-12.

DIRECTIONS: Questions 11 and 12 are to be answered SOLELY on the basis of the information given in the following paragraph.

The accuracy of the information about past occurrence obtainable in an interview is so low that one must take the stand that the best use to be made of the interview in this connection is a means of finding clues and avenues of access to more reliable sources of information. On the other hand, feelings and attitudes have been found to be clearly and correctly revealed in a properly conducted personal interview.

11. According to the above paragraph, information obtained in a personal interview 11.____

A. can be corroborated by other clues and more reliable sources of information revealed at the interview
B. can be used to develop leads to other sources of information about past events
C. is not reliable
D. is reliable if it relates to recent occurrences

12. According to the above paragraph, the personal interview is suitable for obtaining 12.____

A. emotional reactions to a given situation
B. fresh information on factors which may be forgotten
C. revived recollection of previous events for later use as testimony
D. specific information on material already reduced to writing

Questions 13-15.

DIRECTIONS: Questions 13 through 15 are to be answered on the basis of the following paragraph.

Admissibility of handwriting standards (samples of handwriting for the purpose of comparison) as a basis for expert testimony is frequently necessary when the authenticity of disputed documents may be at issue. Under the older rules of common law, only that writing relating to the issues in the case could be used as a basis for handwriting testimony by an expert. Today, most jurisdictions admit irrelevant writings as standards for comparison. However, their genuineness, in all instances, must be established to the satisfaction of the court. There are a number of types of documents, however, not ordinarily relevant to the issues which are seldom acceptable to the court as handwriting standards, such as bail bonds, signatures on affidavits, depositions, etc. These are usually already before the court as part of the record in a case. Exhibits written in the presence of a witness or prepared voluntarily for a law enforcement officer are readily admissible in most jurisdictions. Testimony of a witness who is considered familiar with the writing is admissible in some jurisdictions. In criminal cases, it is possible that the signature on the fingerprint card obtained in connection with the arrest of the defendant for the crime currently charged may be admitted as a handwriting standard. In order to give the defendant the fairest possible treatment, most jurisdictions do not admit the signatures on fingerprint cards pertaining to prior arrests. However, they are admitted sometimes. In such instances, the court usually requires that the signature be photographed or removed from the card and no reference be made to the origin of the signature.

13. Of the following, the types of handwriting standards MOST likely to be admitted in evidence by most jurisdictions are those 13.____

A. appearing on depositions and bail bonds
B. which were written in the presence of a witness or voluntarily given to a law enforcement officer
C. identified by witnesses who claim to be familiar with the handwriting
D. which are in conformity with the rules of common law only

14. The PRINCIPAL factor which generally determines the acceptance of handwriting standards by the courts is 14.____

A. the relevance of the submitted documents to the issues of the case
B. the number of witnesses who have knowledge of the submitted documents
C. testimony that the writing has been examined by a handwriting expert
D. acknowledgment by the court of the authenticity of the submitted documents

15. The MOST logical reason for requiring the removal of the signature of a defendant from fingerprint cards pertaining to prior arrests, before admitting the signature in court as a handwriting standard, is that 15.____

A. it simplifies the process of identification of the signature as a standard for comparison
B. the need for identifying the fingerprints is eliminated
C. mention of prior arrests may be prejudicial to the defendant
D. a handwriting expert does not need information pertaining to prior arrests in order to make his identification

Questions 16-20.

DIRECTIONS: Questions 16 through 20 are to be answered SOLELY on the basis of the information contained in the following paragraph.

A statement which is offered in an attempt to prove the truth of the matters therein stated, but which is not made by the author as a witness before the court at the particular trial in which it is so offered, is hearsay. This is so whether the statement consists of words (oral or written), of symbols used as a substitute for words, or of signs or other conduct offered as the equivalent of a statement. Subject to some well-established exceptions, hearsay is not generally acceptable as evidence, and it does not become competent evidence just because it is received by the court without objection. One basis for this rule is simply that a fact cannot be proved by showing that somebody stated it was a fact. Another basis for the rule is the fundamental principle that in a criminal prosecution the testimony of the witness shall be taken before the court, so that at the time he gives the testimony offered in evidence he will be sworn and subject to cross-examination, the scrutiny of the court, and confrontation by the accused.

16. Which of the following is hearsay? 16.____
A(n)

A. written statement by a person not present at the court hearing where the statement is submitted as proof of an occurrence
B. oral statement in court by a witness of what he saw
C. written statement of what he saw by a witness present in court
D. re-enactment by a witness in court of what he saw

17. In a criminal case, a statement by a person not present in court is 17.____

A. *acceptable* evidence if not objected to by the prosecutor
B. *acceptable* evidence if not objected to by the defense lawyer
C. *not acceptable* evidence except in certain well-settled circumstances
D. *not acceptable* evidence under any circumstances

18. The rule on hearsay is founded on the belief that 18.____

A. proving someone said an act occurred is not proof that the act did occur
B. a person who has knowledge about a case should be willing to appear in court
C. persons not present in court are likely to be unreliable witnesses
D. permitting persons to testify without appearing in court will lead to a disrespect for law

19. One reason for the general rule that a witness in a criminal case must give his testimony in court is that 19.____

    A. a witness may be influenced by threats to make untrue statements
    B. the opposite side is then permitted to question him
    C. the court provides protection for a witness against unfair questioning
    D. the adversary system is designed to prevent a miscarriage of justice

20. Of the following, the MOST appropriate title for the above passage would be 20.____

    A. WHAT IS HEARSAY?
    B. RIGHTS OF DEFENDANTS
    C. TRIAL PROCEDURES
    D. TESTIMONY OF WITNESSES

21. A person's statements are independent of who he is or what he is. Statements made by a person are not proved true or false by questioning his character or his position. A statement should stand or fall on its merits, regardless of who makes the statement. Truth is determined by evidence only. A person's character or personality should not be the determining factor in logic. Discussions should not become incidents of name calling. According to the above, whether or not a statement is true depends on the 21.____

    A. recipient's conception of validity
    B. maker's reliability
    C. extent of support by facts
    D. degree of merit the discussion has

Question 22-25.

DIRECTIONS: Questions 22 through 25 are to be answered on the basis of the following passage.

The question, whether an act, repugnant to the Constitution, can become the law of the land, is a question deeply interesting to the United States; but, happily, not of an intricacy proportioned to its interest. It seems only necessary to recognize certain principles, supposed to have been long and well-established, to decide it. That the people have an original right to establish, for their future government, such principles as, in their opinion, shall most conduce to their own happiness, is the basis on which the whole American fabric has been erected. The exercise of this original right is a very great exertion; nor can it, nor ought it, to be frequently repeated. The principles, therefore, so established are deemed fundamental; and as the authority from which they proceed is supreme, and can seldom act, they are designed to be permanent.

22. The BEST title for the above passage would be 22.____

    A. PRINCIPLES OF THE CONSTITUTION
    B. THE ROOT OF CONSTITUTIONAL CHANGE
    C. ONLY PEOPLE CAN CHANGE THE CONSTITUTION
    D. METHODS OF CONSTITUTIONAL CHANGE

23. According to the above passage, original right is 23.____

    A. fundamental to the principle that the people may choose their own form of government
    B. established by the Constitution

C. the result of a very great exertion and should not often be repeated
D. supreme, can seldom act, and is designed to be permanent

24. Whether an act not in keeping with Constitutional principles can become law is, according to the above passage, 24.____

A. an intricate problem requiring great thought and concentration
B. determined by the proportionate interests of legislators
C. determined by certain long established principles, fundamental to Constitutional Law
D. an intricate problem, but less intricate than it would seem from the interest shown in it

25. According to the above passage, the phrase *and can seldom act* refers to the 25.____

A. principle enacted early into law by Americans when they chose their future form of government
B. original rights of the people as vested in the Constitution
C. original framers of the Constitution
D. established, fundamental principles of government

KEY (CORRECT ANSWERS)

1.	C	11.	B
2.	A	12.	A
3.	B	13.	B
4.	C	14.	D
5.	D	15.	C
6.	A	16.	A
7.	B	17.	C
8.	A	18.	A
9.	D	19.	B
10.	C	20.	A

21.	C
22.	B
23.	A
24.	D
25.	A

TEST 2

DIRECTIONS: Each question or incomplete statement is followed by several suggested answers or completions. Select the one that BEST answers the question or completes the statement. *PRINT THE LETTER OF THE CORRECT ANSWER IN THE SPACE AT THE RIGHT.*

Questions 1-3.

DIRECTIONS: Questions 1 through 3 are to be answered SOLELY on the basis of the following paragraph.

The police laboratory performs a valuable service in crime investigation by assisting in the reconstruction of criminal action and by aiding in the identification of persons and things. When studied by a technician, physical things found at crime scenes often reveal facts useful in identifying the criminal and in determining what has occurred. The nature of substances to be examined and the character of the examination to be made vary so widely that the services of a large variety of skilled scientific persons are needed in crime investigations. To employ such a complete staff and to provide them with equipment and standards needed for all possible analysis and comparisons is beyond the means and the needs of any but the largest police departments. The search of crime scenes for physical evidence also calls for the services of specialists supplied with essential equipment and assigned to each tour of duty so as to provide service at any hour.

1. If a police department employs a large staff of technicians of various types in its laboratory, it will affect crime investigations to the extent that 1.____

   A. most crimes will be speedily solved
   B. identification of criminals will be aided
   C. search of crime scenes for physical evidence will become of less importance
   D. investigation by police officers will not usually be required

2. According to the above paragraph, the MOST complete study of objects found at the scenes of crimes is 2.____

   A. always done in all large police departments
   B. based on assigning one technician to each tour of duty
   C. probably done only in large police departments
   D. probably done in police departments of communities with low crime rates

3. According to the above paragraph, a large variety of skilled technicians is useful in criminal investigations because 3.____

   A. crimes cannot be solved without their assistance as part of the police team
   B. large police departments need large staffs
   C. many different kinds of tests on various substances can be made
   D. the police cannot predict what methods may be tried by wily criminals

Questions 4-6.

DIRECTIONS: Questions 4 through 6 are to be answered SOLELY on the basis of the following passage.

Probably the most important single mechanism for bringing the resources of science and technology to bear on the problems of crime would be the establishment of a major prestigious science and technology research program within a research institute. The program would create interdisciplinary teams of mathematicians, computer scientists, electronics engineers, physicists, biologists, and other natural scientists, psychologists, sociologists, economists, and lawyers. The institute and the program must be significant enough to attract the best scientists available, and, to this end, the director of this institute must himself have a background in science and technology and have the respect of scientists. Because it would be difficult to attract such a staff into the Federal government, the institute should be established by a university, a group of universities, or an independent nonprofit organization, and should be within a major metropolitan area. The institute would have to establish close ties with neighboring criminal justice agencies that would receive the benefit of serving as experimental laboratories for such an institute. In fact, the proposal for the institute might be jointly submitted with the criminal justice agencies. The research program would require, in order to bring together the necessary *critical mass* of competent staff, an annual budget which might reach 5 million dollars, funded with at least three years of lead time to assure continuity. Such a major scientific and technological research institute should be supported by the Federal government.

4. Of the following, the MOST appropriate title for the foregoing passage is 4.____

   A. RESEARCH - AN INTERDISCIPLINARY APPROACH TO FIGHTING CRIME
   B. A CURRICULUM FOR FIGHTING CRIME
   C. THE ROLE OF THE UNIVERSITY IN THE FIGHT AGAINST CRIME
   D. GOVERNMENTAL SUPPORT OF CRIMINAL RESEARCH PROGRAMS

5. According to the above passage, in order to attract the best scientists available, the research institute should 5.____

   A. provide psychologists and sociologists to counsel individual members of interdisciplinary teams
   B. encourage close ties with neighboring criminal justice agencies
   C. be led by a person who is respected in the scientific community
   D. be directly operated and funded by the Federal government

6. The term *critical mass,* as used in the above passage, refers MAINLY to 6.____

   A. a staff which would remain for three years of continuous service to the institute
   B. staff members necessary to carry out the research program of the institute successfully
   C. the staff necessary to establish relations with criminal justice agencies which will serve as experimental laboratories for the institute
   D. a staff which would be able to assist the institute in raising adequate funds

Questions 7-9.

DIRECTIONS: Questions 7 through 9 are to be answered SOLELY on the basis of the following paragraph.

The use of modern scientific methods in the examination of physical evidence often provides information to the investigator which he could not otherwise obtain. This applies particularly to small objects and materials present in minute quantities or trace evidence because the quantities here are such that they may be overlooked without methodical searching, and often special means of detection are needed. Whenever two objects come in contact with one another, there is a transfer of material, however slight. Usually, the softer object will transfer to the harder, but the transfer may be mutual. The quantity of material transferred differs with the type of material involved and the more violent the contact the greater the degree of transference. Through scientific methods of determining physical properties and chemical composition, we can add to the facts observable by the investigator's unaided senses, and thereby increase the chances of identification.

7. According to the above paragraph, the amount of material transferred whenever two objects come in contact with one another 7.____

   A. varies directly with the softness of the objects involved
   B. varies directly with the violence of the contact of the objects
   C. is greater when two soft, rather than hard, objects come into violent contact with each other
   D. is greater when coarse-grained, rather than smooth-grained, materials are involved

8. According to the above paragraph, the PRINCIPAL reason for employing scientific methods in obtaining trace evidence is that 8.____

   A. other methods do not involve a methodical search of the crime scene
   B. scientific methods of examination frequently reveal physical evidence which did not previously exist
   C. the amount of trace evidence may be so sparse that other methods are useless
   D. trace evidence cannot be properly identified unless special means of detection are employed

9. According to the above paragraph, the one of the following statements which BEST describes the manner in which scientific methods of analyzing physical evidence assists the investigator is that such methods 9.____

   A. add additional valuable information to the investigator's own knowledge of complex and rarely occurring materials found as evidence
   B. compensate for the lack of important evidential material through the use of physical and chemical analyses
   C. make possible an analysis of evidence which goes beyond the ordinary capacity of the investigator's senses
   D. identify precisely those physical characteristics of the individual which the untrained senses of the investigator are unable to discern

Questions 10-13.

DIRECTIONS: Questions 10 through 13 are to be answered SOLELY on the basis of the information contained in the following paragraph.

Under the provisions of the Bank Protection Act of 1968, enacted July 8, 1968, each Federal banking supervisory agency, as of January 7, 1969, had to issue rules establishing minimum standards with which financial institutions under their control must comply with respect to the installation, maintenance, and operation of security devices and procedures, reasonable in cost, to discourage robberies, burglaries, and larcenies, and to assist in the identification and apprehension of persons who commit such acts. The rules set the time limits within which the affected banks and savings and loan associations must comply with the standards, and the rules require the submission of periodic reports on the steps taken. A violator of a rule under this Act is subject to a civil penalty not to exceed $100 for each day of the violation. The enforcement of these regulations rests with the responsible banking supervisory agencies.

10. The Bank Protection Act of 1968 was designed to 10.____

    A. provide Federal police protection for banks covered by the Act
    B. have organizations covered by the Act take precautions against criminals
    C. set up a system for reporting all bank robberies to the FBI
    D. insure institutions covered by the Act from financial loss due to robberies, burglaries, and larcenies

11. Under the provisions of the Bank Protection Act of 1968, each Federal banking supervisory agency was required to set up rules for financial institutions covered by the Act governing the 11.____

    A. hiring of personnel
    B. punishment of burglars
    C. taking of protective measures
    D. penalties for violations

12. Financial institutions covered by the Bank Protection Act of 1968 were required to 12.____

    A. file reports at regular intervals on what they had done to prevent theft
    B. identify and apprehend persons who commit robberies, burglaries, and larcenies
    C. draw up a code of ethics for their employees
    D. have fingerprints of their employees filed with the FBI

13. Under the provisions of the Bank Protection Act of 1968, a bank which is subject to the rules established under the Act and which violates a rule is liable to a penalty of NOT ______ than $100 for each ______. 13.____

    A. more; violation
    B. less; day of violation
    C. less; violation
    D. more; day of violation

Questions 14-17.

DIRECTIONS: Questions 14 through 17 are to be answered SOLELY on the basis of the following passage.

Specific measures for prevention of pilferage will be based on careful analysis of the conditions at each agency. The most practical and effective method to control casual pilferage is the establishment of psychological deterrents.

One of the most common means of discouraging casual pilferage is to search individuals leaving the agency at unannounced times and places. These spot searches may occasionally detect attempts at theft, but greater value is realized by bringing to the attention of individuals the fact that they may be apprehended if they do attempt the illegal removal of property.

An aggressive security education program is an effective means of convincing employees that they have much more to lose than they do to gain by engaging in acts of theft. It is important for all employees to realize that pilferage is morally wrong no matter how insignificant the value of the item which is taken. In establishing any deterrent to casual pilferage, security officers must not lose sight of the fact that most employees are honest and disapprove of thievery. Mutual respect between security personnel and other employees of the agency must be maintained if the facility is to be protected from other more dangerous forms of human hazards. Any security measure which infringes on the human rights or dignity of others will jeopardize, rather than enhance, the overall protection of the agency.

14. The $100,000 yearly inventory of an agency revealed that $50 worth of goods had been stolen; the only individuals with access to the stolen materials were the employees. Of the following measures, which would the author of the above passage MOST likely recommend to a security officer? 14.____

    A. Conduct an intensive investigation of all employees to find the culprit.
    B. Make a record of the theft, but take no investigative or disciplinary action against any employee.
    C. Place a tight security check on all future movements of personnel.
    D. Remove the remainder of the material to an area with much greater security.

15. What does the passage imply is the percentage of employees whom a security officer should expect to be honest? 15.____

    A. No employee can be expected to be honest all of the time
    B. Just 50%
    C. Less than 50%
    D. More than 50%

16. According to the above passage, the security officer would use which of the following methods to minimize theft in buildings with many exits when his staff is very small? 16.____

    A. Conduct an inventory of all material and place a guard near that which is most likely to be pilfered
    B. Inform employees of the consequences of legal prosecution for pilfering
    C. Close off the unimportant exits and have all his men concentrate on a few exits
    D. Place a guard at each exit and conduct a casual search of individuals leaving the premises

17. Of the following, the title BEST suited for this passage is 17.____

    A. CONTROL MEASURES FOR CASUAL PILFERING
    B. DETECTING THE POTENTIAL PILFERER
    C. FINANCIAL LOSSES RESULTING FROM PILFERING
    D. THE USE OF MORAL PERSUASION IN PHYSICAL SECURITY

Questions 18-24.

DIRECTIONS: Questions 18 through 24 are to be answered SOLELY on the basis of the following passage.

Burglar alarms are designed to detect intrusion automatically. Robbery alarms enable a victim of a robbery or an attack to signal for help. Such devices can be located in elevators, hallways, homes and apartments, businesses and factories, and subways, as well as on the street in high-crime areas. Alarms could deter some potential criminals from attacking targets so protected. If alarms were prevalent and not visible, then they might serve to suppress crime generally. In addition, of course, the alarms can summon the police when they are needed.

All alarms must perform three functions: sensing or initiation of the signal, transmission of the signal and annunciation of the alarm. A burglar alarm needs a sensor to detect human presence or activity in an unoccupied enclosed area like a building or a room. A robbery victim would initiate the alarm by closing a foot or wall switch, or by triggering a portable transmitter which would send the alarm signal to a remote receiver. The signal can sound locally as a loud noise to frighten away a criminal, or it can be sent silently by wire to a central agency. A centralized annunciator requires either private lines from each alarmed point, or the transmission of some information on the location of the signal.

18. A conclusion which follows LOGICALLY from the above passage is that 18.____

A. burglar alarms employ sensor devices; robbery alarms make use of initiation devices
B. robbery alarms signal intrusion without the help of the victim; burglar alarms require the victim to trigger a switch
C. robbery alarms sound locally; burglar alarms are transmitted to a central agency
D. the mechanisms for a burglar alarm and a robbery alarm are alike

19. According to the above passage, alarms can be located 19.____

A. in a wide variety of settings
B. only in enclosed areas
C. at low cost in high-crime areas
D. only in places where potential criminals will be deterred

20. According to the above passage, which of the following is ESSENTIAL if a signal is to be received in a central office? 20.____

A. A foot or wall switch
B. A noise-producing mechanism
C. A portable reception device
D. Information regarding the location of the source

21. According to the above passage, an alarm system can function WITHOUT a 21.____

A. centralized annunciating device
B. device to stop the alarm
C. sensing or initiating device
D. transmission device

22. According to the above passage, the purpose of robbery alarms is to 22.____

A. find out automatically whether a robbery has taken place
B. lower the crime rate in high-crime areas
C. make a loud noise to frighten away the criminal
D. provide a victim with the means to signal for help

23. According to the above passage, alarms might aid in lessening crime if they were 23.____

    A. answered promptly by police
    B. completely automatic
    C. easily accessible to victims
    D. hidden and widespread

24. Of the following, the BEST title for the above passage is 24.____

    A. DETECTION OF CRIME BY ALARMS
    B. LOWERING THE CRIME RATE
    C. SUPPRESSION OF CRIME
    D. THE PREVENTION OF ROBBERY

25. Although the rural crime reporting area is much less developed than that for cities and towns, current data are collected in sufficient volume to justify the generalization that rural crime rates are lower than those or urban communities. 25.____
    According to this statement,

    A. better reporting of crime occurs in rural areas than in cities
    B. there appears to be a lower proportion of crime in rural areas than in cities
    C. cities have more crime than towns
    D. crime depends on the amount of reporting

KEY (CORRECT ANSWERS)

1. B
2. C
3. C
4. A
5. C

6. B
7. B
8. C
9. C
10. B

11. C
12. A
13. D
14. B
15. D

16. B
17. A
18. A
19. A
20. D

21. A
22. D
23. D
24. A
25. B

COURTROOM TERMS

A/K/A: Acronym that stands for "also known as" and introduces any alternative or assumed names or aliases of an individual. A term to indicate another name by which a person is known.

Arraignment: The bringing of a defendant before the court to answer the matters charged against him in an indictment or information. The defendant is read the charges and must respond with his plea.

Arrest: Deprivation of one's liberty by legal authority.

Bail: An amount of money set by the court to procure the release of a person from legal custody; this money is to be forfeited if the defendant fails to appear for trial.

Beyond a Reasonable Doubt: The standard of proof required for a finding of guilty in a criminal matter. Satisfied to a moral certainty. This is a higher standard of proof than that required in a civil matter (preponderance of the evidence).

Co-Defendant: Any additional defendant or respondent in the same case.

Confession: A voluntary statement made by a person charged with a crime wherein said person acknowledges his/her guilt of the offense charged and discloses participation in the act.

Controlled Dangerous Substance: That group of legally designated drugs, which, by statute, it is illegal to possess or distribute.

Criminal complaint: The initial written notice to a defendant that he/she is being charged with a public offense.

Due Process of Law: The exercise of the powers of the government with the safeguards for the protection of individual rights as set forth in the constitution, statutes, and common case law.

Felony: A crime of a more serious nature than a misdemeanor, the exact nature of which is defined by state statute and which is punishable by a term of imprisonment exceeding one year or by death.

Grand Jury: A jury of inquiry whose duty is to receive complaints and accusations in criminal cases, hear the evidence presented on the part of the state, and determine whether to indict (see "indictment" below).

Impeach: As used in the Law of Evidence, to call into question the truthfulness of a witness, by means of introducing evidence to discredit him or her.

Indictment: A written accusation presented by a grand jury after having been presented with evidence, charging that a person named therein has done some act, or has been guilty of some omission that by law is a public offense.

Miranda Warnings: The compulsory advisement of a person's rights prior to any custodial interrogation; these include: a) the right to remain silent; b) that any statement made may be used against him/her; c) the right to an attorney; d) the appointment of counsel if the accused cannot afford his or her own attorney. Unless these rights are given, any evidence obtained in an interrogation cannot be used in the individual's trial against him/her.

Misdemeanor: Offense lower than felony and generally punishable by a fine or imprisonment other than in a penitentiary.

Motion to Quash: Application to the court to set aside the complaint, indictment or subpoena due to a lack of probable cause to arrest the defendant, or in matters heard by a grand jury, due to evidence not properly presented to the grand jury.

Motion to Sever: Application to the court made when there are two defendants charged with the same crimes or who acted jointly in the commission of a crime, when their attorneys feel it would be in their best interest if they had separate trials.

Motion to Suppress Evidence: Application to the court to prevent evidence from being presented at trial when said evidence has been obtained by illegal means. It applies to physical evidence, statements made by defendant when not advised by counsel or through wiretapping, prior convictions, etc..

Parole: A conditional release from custody at the discretion of the paroling authority prior to his or her completing the prison sentence imposed. During said release the offender is required to observe conditions of this status under the supervision of a parole agency.

Plea: A defendant's formal answer in court to the charges contained in a charging document.

Guilty: A plea by the defendant in which he acknowledges guilt either of the offense charged or of a less serious offense pursuant to an agreement with the prosecuting attorney. It should be understood, however, that the court may not be obliged to recognize this.

Nolo Contendere: A plea that is admissible in some jurisdictions, in which the defendant states that he does not contest the charges against him. Also called "no contest", this plea has the same effect as a guilty plea, except that it cannot be used against the defendant in civil actions arising out of the same incident which gave rise to the criminal charges.

Not Guilty: A plea of innocence by the defendant.

Not Guilty by Reason of Insanity: A plea that is sometimes entered in conjunction with the "not guilty" plea.

Double Jeopardy: A plea entered by a defendant who has been tried for an offense wherein he asserts that he cannot be tried a second time for said offense, unless he successfully secured a new trial after an appeal, or after a motion for a new trial was granted by the trial court.

Police Report: The official report made by any police officer involved with the incident or appearing after the incident, setting forth the officer's observations and statements of parties and witnesses. It can be used as evidence in a trial.

Pre-Trial Intervention: Utilized in some states when a defendant is accused of a first offense, to divert the defendant from the criminal justice system.

Probation: To allow a person convicted of a minor offense to go at large, under a suspension of sentence, during good behavior, and generally under the supervision of a probation officer.

Prosecutor: The attorney who prosecutes defendants for crimes, in the name of the government.

Search Warrant: A written order, issued by the court, directing the police to search a specified location for particular personal property (stolen or illegally possessed).

Speedy Trial: Mandate by the government that all criminal trials must take place within a specified time after arrest.

Writ of Habeas Corpus: A mandate issued from a court requiring that an individual be brought before the court.

www.ingramcontent.com/pod-product-compliance
Lightning Source LLC
Chambersburg PA
CBHW081802300426
44116CB00014B/2209
* 9 7 8 1 7 9 9 3 0 9 6 6 6 *